"It is a true story. You will learn both from the successes and disappointments Bob Knowling experienced. Gritty detail and candid."

—Ram Charan, coauthor of the bestseller
Execution: The Discipline of Getting Things Done

"Inspiring and practical guidance from an accomplished, self-made leader."

—Stratford Sherman, coauthor of *Control Your Destiny or Someone Else Will*

"A tour de force through a leader's well-experienced life. Extraordinary in its breadth, candor, and wisdom, it would be valuable reading for aspiring and practicing leaders at any stage of their careers."

—Modesto A. Maidique, president emeritus, Center for Leadership

"Bob Knowling delivers foolproof advice on how to make a substantial difference in both your organization and yourself. He convinces you that there is no substitute for playing to win, learning from everybody around you, sharing the credit in good times, and taking the accountability when the times get rough. A real grand slam."

—Lawrence Babbio, former vice chairman, Verizon Communications

"This is an important story of how to build strength of character and purpose out of challenging beginnings. The depth of the learning and how Bob has applied the lessons to make such a difference to so many people are a model for so many of us. I know the challenges he faced and how he turned all that opportunity into *excellence and success*."

—Bob Johnson, former CEO, Honeywell Aerospace

"Bob's story is pure inspiration and a treasure trove of lessons in how a tenacious learner, coupled with sterling character and a passion for developing talented teams, can rise to the top. This is a story of a humble man who loves nothing more than sharing hard-learned lessons and helping others achieve their own potential."

—Mary Tolan, founder and CEO, Accretive Health

"You do not read this book, you live it. It is a powerful journey that will take you to new places in your thinking and in your heart, because you *can* get there from here, and it starts with this book."

—Roseanna DeMaria, adjunct associate professor and chief learning officer, Leadership and Human Capital Management Department, NYU SCPS

"Bob Knowling's remarkable career is a classic American story of business success achieved against great odds and will serve as an inspiration to all young people facing their future. This book is unforgettable."

—Dr. Henry Kressel, managing director, Warburg Pincus; coauthor (with T. V. Lento) of *Investing in Dynamic Markets: Venture Capital in the Digital Age*

"Bob Knowling provides a fascinating and uplifting story of the struggle to overcome obstacles in pursuit of personal and professional success. This book is a reinforcement for those engaged in similar life struggles and a challenge to those who feel stuck in their journey to their own ambitions."

—Michael Brimm, emeritus professor of organizational behavior and management, INSEAD

You *Can* Get There from Here

You *Can* Get There from Here

My Journey from Struggle to Success

Bob Knowling

Portfolio / Penguin

To my children, Jenni, Aimi, Audrey, and Jason.
You inspire me to play like a champion every day.
I'm so proud to be your dad.

PORTFOLIO / PENGUIN
Published by the Penguin Group
Penguin Group (USA) Inc., 375 Hudson Street, New York, New York 10014, U.S.A.; Penguin Group (Canada), 90 Eglinton Avenue East, Suite 700, Toronto, Ontario, Canada M4P 2Y3 (a division of Pearson Penguin Canada Inc.); Penguin Books Ltd, 80 Strand, London WC2R 0RL, England; Penguin Ireland, 25 St. Stephen's Green, Dublin 2, Ireland (a division of Penguin Books Ltd); Penguin Books Australia Ltd, 250 Camberwell Road, Camberwell, Victoria 3124, Australia (a division of Pearson Australia Group Pty Ltd); Penguin Books India Pvt Ltd, 11 Community Centre, Panchsheel Park, New Delhi—110 017, India; Penguin Group (NZ), 67 Apollo Drive, Rosedale, Auckland 0632, New Zealand (a division of Pearson New Zealand Ltd); Penguin Books (South Africa) (Pty) Ltd, 24 Sturdee Avenue, Rosebank, Johannesburg 2196, South Africa

Penguin Books Ltd, Registered Offices: 80 Strand, London WC2R 0RL, England

First published in 2011 by Portfolio / Penguin, a member of Penguin Group (USA) Inc.

10 9 8 7 6 5 4 3 2 1

Photograph credits
Insert page 1 (top and bottom), 2 (middle): Courtesy of Geneva Reynolds; 2 (top): *Kokomo Tribune;* 7 (bottom): The White House; 8 (top): Courtesy of Wabash College; 8 (bottom): Photograph by Buck Miller, courtesy of Wabash College; other photographs courtesy of the author.

LIBRARY OF CONGRESS CATALOGING-IN-PUBLICATION DATA
Knowling, Bob.
    You can get there from here : my journey from struggle to success / Bob Knowling.
        p. cm.
    Includes index.
    ISBN 978-1-59184-422-8
    1. Knowling, Bob. 2. African American Businesspeople—Biography. 3. Success in business. I. Title.
    HC102.5.K64A3 2011
    338.092—dc23
    [B]   2011019059

Printed in the United States of America

Contents

PART ONE

Foundation

Ospreys

I have an unusually revealing story to tell that is not set in the office or a classroom. In fact, it's not inside at all. To understand it, you have to put yourself by the water and recognize that in business and in life, there is a lot to be learned just by watching.

Watching has been the cornerstone of my personal leadership journey. So give me a moment to share with you an amazing example of a creature that perhaps embodies everything I'm trying to articulate in the early pages of this book.

I want to take you outside to observe the osprey.

I want to tell you some things about this magnificent bird.

This sea hawk drifts on the breeze. All the time, it gazes at the surface of the water, perhaps fifty yards below, looking for a hint, a sign.

As though it were suspended on an invisible wire, the bird stops for just a second in the air. It cocks its wings and unleashes a dive that is both fierce and fearless. Breaking the surface talons first—no other diving bird does this—it creates a big, loud splash.

At first submerged, the osprey pops its head from the water and then seems to rise as though it had been flying all along, shaking off a spray of droplets as it climbs. Sometimes it tosses its catch in the air and realigns it so that the fish is parallel to its body, which makes the osprey more aerodynamic. If the osprey misses the target, which happens about half the time, it goes back into the sky and continues searching.

But like all birds of prey, it persists. It is unyielding. It never gives up. It must always win.

Is there a better lesson?

In your job, in your school, on your team, in your family, the hunting osprey presents the perfect image and, I would argue, the perfect metaphor for how to live. Alone in the sky and hunting to provide for its family, the raptor is the living model, the definition, of diligence. People can create endless volumes of words to describe this idea, but the actions of the bird of prey alone, its determination, define this.

I believe this is how we need to be: aggressive, diligent, determined. Persisting, never giving up, embracing the idea that even though you will not always succeed, you must never stop trying to win. I hold a lasting image of legendary North Carolina State coach Jim Valvano in his emotional closing remarks at a televised ESPN awards ceremony. Dying of cancer and knowing that the end was near, he told the world, "Never give up. Don't ever give up!"

That message is at the heart of this book.

You must work hard. You must treat your coworkers decently. You must be honest in whatever you do.

The United States is a nation of phenomenal opportunity. I have been touched by that, moved by that, all my professional life. Countless stories of men and women who achieved greatness by taking advantage of the opportunity to "try" and "never give up" fill our public libraries and our bookshelves at home. It is easy to lose sight of that potential amid endless accounts of economic turmoil, joblessness, and confusion. None of those conditions is permanent, and more important, none of them excuses us from making an effort to be the best at whatever we try to do.

Being the best has to be our objective, even if that goal seems impossibly hard to reach. With excellence as the objective, you will never have to apologize for the effort. Without that objective, a career, a life, can seem aimless.

This is not solely a book about business, because you will need to know more than business practice if you want to succeed. But it is full of stories about *my* experiences. They lifted me from poverty, then into school, and then into the workplace. I think of it more as a book about life: what I have learned and how those experiences might help you.

I know that it will be of great value in the workplace, but I also know it will be of value in school, too, or at home, or on the playing field.

There are a million business books with "leadership" in the title. To me, leadership is an approach to work and life that embraces the drive at the heart of that osprey's dive. And the image of that osprey is an amazing one to hold as you pursue your objectives.

There is no apparent reason the osprey should be able to do what it does. Strip it down to its physical essence and you have just a few ounces of feathers and a few pounds of meat and bone. Spirit and purpose are the two elements that make those parts come together to achieve what that creature is able to achieve.

The drive to win flows from that combination.

I am going to tell you stories of how that drive to win played out in my life.

It hasn't always been there. I very well could have embraced failure instead of success. I might have fallen into the despair and bitterness that often plague black men struggling to escape lives mired in poverty. You might have looked at my childhood and concluded that I had every reason to fail. I could have written a book about nothing but excuses. All the usual excuses were there at one point or another, and I had only examples of failure in front of me on a daily basis. I just never turned to them. The audacity that I could have a different path and outcome is just that: audacity. The mere thought that I could escape my environment and have a different outcome is astounding.

Still, there were also powerful experiences in that childhood spent in poverty that opened pathways where other people might have seen only obstacles. I know the value of people, and of how they intervened in my life.

As a child, I was blessed not only with athletic grace and speed, but also with opportunities in which those physical assets would lift me beyond expectations and put me on higher ground. Basketball, football, track—that is where the competitor was born in me. What I learned about drive and winning on the playing field still informs what I do today.

It doesn't surprise me that I am so drawn to the image of the osprey.

I found inspiration in these birds since I first learned about them in the Bible as a child. There are dozens of specific references to birds of prey in there, almost all of them metaphors for speed, strength, intelligence, and persistence.

If you dig into the science of these birds—their life spans, how they mate, their habitat, how they raise their young—you will find so many characteristics you could easily apply to the challenges of leadership. Birds of prey change their location every year, so they must always learn about their surroundings. These birds almost always build their annual nest a little higher up than the year before, so their range of vision is extended. They mate for life. They ferociously protect their young. There is even a verse in Isaiah that pays tribute to the power of the eagle, another bird of prey I am inspired by: "But they that wait upon the Lord shall renew their strength; they shall mount up with wings as eagles; they shall run, and not be weary; they shall walk and not faint" (Isaiah 40:31).

What is most fascinating to me about birds of prey is that they use everything they have to great intensity and effect. Each feather, each muscle, is a masterwork of purpose and design: light, efficient, and strong. You can find assets like these in people, too, or in yourself, but they may not be apparent at first glance.

A lot of business books offer the promise of guaranteed success if only you do "exactly what I did the way I did it." I am not naïve. I don't believe that. My success has been a function of hard work, skill, timing, experience, and execution. There may be other externals that define your potential for success. It depends on who you are, where you are, and how you have prepared yourself. The question is whether you will recognize these opportunities and understand how to get the most from them.

Winning, then, is in your hands, no matter the challenge. Most likely you already have what you need, depending on the goal. As persistence is the great strength of the osprey, attitude is the great strength you carry into business.

The will to win must be at the heart of your career.

Everyone can't be an osprey, but everyone does have assets. I found them in my own life, with a great deal of help and mentoring over time, and they became the tools I have used consistently in a very successful career. I have drive. I have persistence. I love the company of people I respect. I have a need to find effective ways to reach my goals and to help people find their stride to reach their goals.

This approach lifted me from the kind of poverty that has crushed people for generations. It carried me into the intense competition of high school sports, where I learned invaluable lessons about paying attention to my coaches, the voices of experience and wisdom. It gave me choices when it came time to pick a college. When I went to work, that drive planted the seeds of leadership in me from my first day on the job.

Most important of all, the belief that I must always strive to win has fueled everything I've done in my business life, from the day I walked into Indiana Bell many years ago and decided I needed to know everyone's job to be a good boss, to my latest assignments as the principal at Eagles Landing Partners, with clients in Thailand, Brunei, Mexico, Japan, and the United States.

The most important person in defining how you are perceived is you, no one else. The choices you make and the way you pursue them build the image you present. If you are not honest and fair in your relationships with your coworkers, people will easily and quickly know that about you, and you will pay a price. It may not be comfortable speaking truth to power, but dishonesty is at the heart of so much business wreckage that the value of ethical behavior and honesty should be apparent to everyone.

Honesty enhances everything about a career. One of the achievements I am most proud of after decades on the job at many levels, bottom to top, is that there is an army of people who will always be eager to work with me if I have a job to offer. Time and again I have seen this play out: I shift positions, and it doesn't take long for the phone to ring with requests from people who want to come along.

This is so because I have been able to touch these people in their careers, to help them focus on what had to be done, to help them lead and win. You turn around organizations, in most cases, by turning around individuals. At many points in your career, that process starts with you and your decision to lead and to win.

Have I always succeeded? No. Have I ever stopped trying? No.

There are no mysteries here. That may well be the beauty of it. I have lived an honest and ethical life. That doesn't mean I have lived an easy life. But like the osprey, once I commit, I won't stop until I've won. I have refused to be defined by my limitations: my youth, my race, my background, my humble beginnings.

I made a different choice.

Like the osprey, I chose to win.

CHAPTER ONE

Building a Bridge

All was right with the world on this warm September afternoon in 1960 in Kokomo, Indiana. My older brothers and sisters were bounding down the street from school, and soon we would be consumed by our daily ritual of playing baseball in the backyard. I loved baseball. It was the one thing we all did together on a regular basis in this big family.

Those games were spirited. Fights occurred, but no one ever got hurt because the older kids knew not to hurt the younger ones. One year shy of starting first grade, I would listen spellbound to my siblings' stories about what went on at school. I wanted to be bigger and older just like them.

That particular day, the game was fairly close, and I had a chance to help my team win if I could drive my sister Trudy home from second base. My older brother Aaron stopped me before I got to the plate and whispered in my ear to hit the ball to the right side of the yard; that, he said, would score the run. At five years old, I was a pretty good little hitter, because every one of my older brothers had spent time showing me how to hit, catch, and throw the ball. Even then, I was always looking for lessons.

My older brother Bobby Cecil was the catcher that afternoon. I prepared to hit the ball to the right side, knowing that I had to wait for the pitch. As I got ready to swing, out of the corner of my eye I saw Bobby Cecil move to the right, but I was unsure of what he was doing. I took a full swing . . . and hit him in the head with the bat.

I've never been able to forget that moment. Bobby Cecil did not cry; he simply fell to the ground, his head bleeding profusely. I tried to stop the bleeding with my hands and my shirt. I don't recall how or why I knew to do this. My older sister Ruby was the first to reach us. She told me to keep the shirt on the wound and she helped me hold him.

I don't remember how long it took for the paramedics to reach us. They had to struggle to take Bobby Cecil away from me. It was a total mystery to me where they took him.

At only five years old I didn't have a lot of perspective on life, but I thought I would never see my brother again. The tears I shed lasted for what seemed like hours. There was an eerie silence in the house after they took our brother away. My sister Trudy, who is one year younger than I, never left my side that evening. I remember her hugging me at least a hundred times. She is closer to me today than any of the others.

I could not understand any of the emotions that were flooding my little brain, but I was certain that I would never see Bobby Cecil again. My mom had no money to pay for treatment. (I didn't know how the ambulance had even been summoned, because we didn't own a phone.)

Several hours later my mother came home and I was shocked when Bobby Cecil walked in the door right behind her wearing a bandage on his head. When I think about the special joys in my life, the moment I saw him walk in behind my mom ranks right up at the top for me. My mother came over to me, hugged me, and whispered, "It was an accident, and thank you for holding his head until the paramedics came." I felt so much better after that.

That baseball incident is etched in my memory as a moment in my young life when I knew that I wanted to help my family. My mother and Bobby Cecil were right at the top of that list, even though my mother didn't need my help to take care of herself.

Bobby Cecil was mentally disabled, but I didn't know what that meant. I just knew that he was different and that sometimes other kids teased him, and that made me angry. I remember resolving to help whenever I saw someone in my family being talked down to, mistreated, ridiculed, or disrespected. We were told repeatedly never to throw a first punch in a fight, but I wanted to jump on the boys who made fun of my brother. I carried that attitude with me for a long time.

I never had the influence of television, so my childhood was devoid of TV heroes such as Batman, Superman, and the Lone Ranger. But I saw enough tough characters in my neighborhood to know the difference between big bad Leroy Brown and Mr. Rogers. When it came to my family, I was quick to anger, but I would characterize myself as a nonaggressive, quiet child with a tremendous amount of respect for adults. I had none of the toughness that defined two older brothers.

From There to Here

My life experiences have carried me from the grinding poverty that defined so much of black America in the 1960s all the way to a status that, as a child, I could never have imagined for myself. Writing a book seems surreal to me. My friend Dr. Noel Tichy at the University of Michigan has been encouraging me to write this book for years.

I've always been rather flip in my response to the question "So, Bob, how did you become so successful?" I typically say, "I've been lucky." So I've resisted every overture that has been made to me to do this project. I've always hated rags-to-riches stories. They're painful and, to me, unhelpful. And my attitude has been to let the guys who have it all figured out write the books. Now that has changed.

Writing this book has forced me to think about every aspect of my life and my career. I don't have a textbook solution to anything. I will merely spend some time talking about winning. Take, for example, the PGA golfer Jim Furyk. He has the ugliest golf swing on the PGA Tour, but I'll wager you a round of golf at Pebble Beach that Jim doesn't waste a single calorie trying to mimic the eight steps to a perfect golf swing. He just takes what he has and goes out and gets it done.

Twenty minutes into this project I was crying, and I'm not normally a crier. A good friend told me that writing this book would be a cathartic process. He was right. So while the journey of my life has been incredible and the rewards too extreme to comprehend, the number of brushes with failure and even death have forced me to admit that luck and the grace of God do factor into it.

I'm not suggesting that if you do what I did, you will be successful. I am merely telling you that the simple formula of "work hard, treat people decently, and always tell the truth" will get you close to your goal.

I believe that beyond his upbringing, a person defines himself by the external conditions that affect his life. The response to those conditions is what counts. It's not where you came from that is essential. It's what you do with your potential.

I will tell you where I came from, what I experienced, and how I got from a really distant "there" to a very present "here." I don't candy-coat my stories, so some parts of them are hard to tell, even hard for me to look back on. But you should know about those parts because of what each story represents and the messages it sends about success and failure in a challenging, complicated, but fascinating world.

I believe that my story is a model for what can happen over time when lots of hard work is spliced into an unyielding quest for excellence and a passion for victory. You can never lose sight of the importance of those things. No one ever got to the top of anything by planning a leisurely, indifferent ascent to reach the middle.

Play to Win

I've never walked onto any playing field, any court, any course, planning to lose. I can say the same for any position I've ever held: no matter the challenge, I've always played to win.

Sometimes people become phenomenally successful through no fault of their own. Those are flukes in the history of business, and not something anyone can count on. Your story is yours to build. The fact that there will be obstacles along the way is not as important as what you do to overcome them. No matter the challenge, the only thing that matters is your response, because that is the one thing you can control.

It would be so easy if there were a clear pathway that guaranteed success. That doesn't exist. But in its place is a reliable, tested strategy that will always work to advance your interests. Because so much of my life has been defined by intense competition, either as an athlete or as an executive, I am certain about the central element at the heart of most success stories:

You have to really *want* to win.

Even when you have been defeated, you still have to want to win. In fact, from the moment that defeat is imminent, you must suit up for the next opportunity. This drive to win will help you know yourself and understand your mistakes. (There will be many.) It is the fuel that will help you get back into the contest, which, fortunately, never really ends. Losses never deter people who want to win. They are not embarrassed or humiliated by defeat. They learn from it.

The only genuine defeat happens when that desire to win isn't there anymore. That is when you know the game is really over.

So, if you want to know what is inside my story of business and success, here's a simple description of where everything starts for me:

I always want to win.

I want the basketball with the game on the line. I want the bat in my hands with two outs and two on in the bottom of the ninth. I want to have the baton in my hands at the beginning of the race. I want the tough job assignments that no one else wants. They are tests of your character and are real-life experiences that can be more valuable than reading case studies in a library because these challenges will shape you. They give you the knowledge, competence, and confidence to step up the next time, maybe to an even bigger challenge. They are the doorways that lead you beyond your own world.

My Bridge

As 2010 began, I was in Mexico City with Ricardo B. Salinas, the chairman of Grupo Salinas, helping him with the transformation of his remarkable family business, which he has grown and diversified into a multibillion-dollar conglomerate.

I learned a lot about Ricardo in the first five minutes in his office. When I entered, I could not help but notice the stacks of books on his desk, coffee tables, and conference room table. Unable to restrain myself, I asked him if this was a new decorating fad or if he was searching for something in all those books. He responded, "Neither." He picked up a book and quickly began telling me about ideas and concepts it had given him. He picked up another, and the explanation was the same.

Salinas is a learner.

Every time I meet with him, he pulls out a pad of paper and takes notes. He studies businesses around the world and is unashamed about taking an idea, a best practice, and implementing it in Grupo Salinas. It is this thirst for knowledge that gave me the chance to work with him in the first place. He became aware of the work Tichy had done at GE, Ameritech, Intel, and other companies and wanted to meet him. That meeting led to a multiyear engagement for Tichy. I've known Tichy for almost twenty years, and he asked me to join him in the work with Ricardo. (Ricardo wanted my assistance for one of the Grupo businesses, the wireless company Iusacell.)

What makes Salinas and others like him so intriguing to me is also their ability to teach. I've seen him in forums with his plaza managers teaching them how to read their P&Ls or how to grow their store portfolios or how to coach and develop their people, and these are priceless sessions of CEO leadership. Then you witness his thirst for knowledge, and it becomes clear that the really great CEOs are leaders, teachers, and learners. Over the course of our time working together, I have heard many stories from the Grupo executive team about how Salinas consumes information constantly. He is always benchmarking. Working with Ricardo was like going back to school to learn how another part of the world thinks about business. His insight and his diligence left their marks on me, proving again that learning never really ends.

Grupo Salinas is a noteworthy venture for many reasons, not the least of which is Salinas's belief in providing easy access to everyday products and services to the lower and middle classes. In a way, it's one of Henry Ford's lessons moved south of the border. Ford knew he needed to help create the economy that would build demand for his automobiles. He knew how important the lower and middle classes were to his business. So does Salinas.

The United States, a beacon of great opportunity to impoverished Mexico, plays a big role in his plans. Too much of that relationship has been defined by the troubling cliché of drug trafficking, which is creating havoc on both sides of the border. Salinas knows how important it is to tackle that problem. In an address given on March 22, 2010, to American business writers at the Walter Cronkite School at the

University of Arizona, he argued that the relationship between the United States and Mexico should not be defined solely as a long-running struggle over drugs. Both countries had too much to offer to allow that kind of poison to wreck opportunity.

"The issue isn't one of pointing fingers, but of finding a solution to this cancer together," he said. He said he wanted to build bridges between the United States and Mexico, not fences.

I like that bridge-building metaphor. It presents a very good model for my own life and career, an image that helps explain how things played out for me. The bridge I built stretched from a world of disadvantage and the racism that defined the United States in the mid-twentieth century; into a transformation accomplished by education and the competitive challenge that is at the heart of all sports; and then, quite naturally, to business.

If you could walk back across that bridge, there would be points at which you would find me underground with phone company cable splicers, or rambling around my territory in my phone company truck to visit with my installation technicians as they stopped at people's homes. That has always been one of my defining behaviors: learning everything I could about how my business worked, how my workers approached their jobs, and how they worked through their challenges.

If you are expecting stellar performance from the people around you, knowing something about their jobs will help you. I have learned how to perform my employees' tasks, and that gives me a keen sense of how to improve the function and help my organization serve customers better.

Ricardo Salinas shares my interest in the workers' jobs. He keeps his foot on the gas pedal. He knows how every one of his businesses works and he is an expert at retail, banking, telecommunications—at whatever he takes on. I'm certain that this point of view is not embraced by some leaders, but it has been essential in my journey and Ricardo's. Each job has its own language, and it gives you a great advantage as a leader to know how to speak it.

Just showing up is not enough. We are the engineers of our lives. How we use our skills, our experience, our values, and our diligence dictates where we go next. In business and in life, there is no point at which we are finished with this immense construction project. But let go of either the drive to win or the focus on quality, and the building stops.

You risk building a bridge to nowhere.

Ricardo Salinas's company, Grupo Salinas, consists of a retail bank, a wireless company, around a thousand retail consumer electronic/household goods stores, a television network, and several more diversified entities. Each company has its own senior executive team, but they are all united by Grupo's emphasis on rapid growth, strong results, and world-class performance. The array of services involved is broad, stretching from cell phones and television networks to motorcycle sales. As principal of my consulting company, Eagles Landing Partners, I've worked with Ricardo Salinas to address an array of challenges his many companies face as they improve and expand their businesses and develop the next generation of leaders.

I am also working with Tichy at a large conglomerate in Thailand (CP Group), where we are helping the chairman with several strategic initiatives while simultaneously developing the company's next generation of leaders.

We are working in Brunei, too, in an effort aimed at improving the country's 256 schools. The challenge there is that Brunei schools are already good. The country is one of the wealthiest on the planet, and 99 percent of the citizens return to Brunei after studying outside the country. But the rich oil reserves will dry up in the next twenty to thirty years, and the country has to define a new economy. Entrepreneurism and private industry need a jump start, and the children in the country have to have a world-class education. Just as it matters everywhere else, leadership is crucial in education, too. That is how we will help the Ministry of Education improve the capability of Brunei's children, by helping Brunei create great principals.

I'm also working with a small software company in Jacksonville, Florida (Meridian Technologies), which was founded eleven years ago by a brilliant guy named Chris Pillay. He picked up the phone one day and called Ross Perot to ask him some questions about how Ross had founded EDS. Ross called him back, and the rest is history. Pillay and his wife, Monteen, have developed a very special business that is poised to go to the next level, and I'm having a lot of fun working with them on their journey.

I'm also working with a fascinating firm called Avanade and its CEO, Adam Warby. Avanade is an IT firm that was started more than ten years ago as a joint venture between Accenture and Microsoft. I've been a customer, so I'm very familiar with the firm's capabilities. Adam is a great CEO who has guided the firm through some impressive growth years, and I expect it to perform even better as we exit the financial downturn of 2009/2010.

Suffice it to say that I have a variety of clients who keep me busy. More important, they keep me challenged.

My career will never escape these kinds of challenges. I don't want it to.

I have spent much of my life building the experience and skills I need to help governments, institutions, and companies excel at what they do. Yet I think if I had to rewrite my curriculum vitae to put it in the clearest terms possible, it would simply say, "How can I use what I have learned to help you?" And in that question, the word *learned* would cover a vast collection of executive experiences.

I didn't start out at the bottom in the first phone company I worked for, Indiana Bell, but it was pretty close. A few years after I joined the company, I had the good fortune to be at the beginning of the vast transition in which the twenty-two Regional Bell Operating Companies that made up AT&T were broken up. Indiana Bell and a handful of other Midwestern Bells were consolidated to become Ameritech.

The learning in my early jobs was constant, not only about my own responsibilities but also about how corporations work—not what they *say* they do, but what they *actually* do.

Mine, of course, are the same credentials that many successful businessmen and consultants carry into the field, references to their years in banking, in retail, in communications, in technology. They might also point to their backgrounds, how they were raised in cultures or in families that put a high value on success at business.

Only a piece of that is my story.

There was nothing in my culture, particularly in my earliest years, that would have led anyone to believe a business career would eventually unfold for me. My first preference for college, after all, was divinity school, but it would have taken a big leap of faith for me even to fathom that college would be in my future back then.

I have been blessed in so many ways (and I am not reluctant about using that word or believing it) that I am shy about listing them. I have a beautiful family and lovely places to live and visit. I have a whole army of friends constructed carefully over a long career. People I thought I might grow to despise have frequently converted me. And I have converted people who thought in the beginning that I could not get out of their lives quickly enough.

Having the kind of career where friends will follow you wherever you may go is priceless. The question "Who is with me?" should play a central role in the thinking of every executive, not in the sense that you are looking for loyal supporters and trying to avoid enemies. It's deeper than that. If I left tomorrow to go do something else, who would pull up stakes to come along with me? Who would want to keep learning and developing and conquering new things? Who would want to keep that relationship alive? Particularly when you have been working hard at transformation, at genuine change and reform inside a company that is full of challenges and complexity, you want those kinds of people with you. That they want to be there, too, makes the relationship all the more valuable.

You are, after all, building the bridges of your lives together, and what could be more important than that?

The real lesson of transformation is that it happens not in companies and not in offices, but in lives.

An Unlikely Place

My story starts in an unlikely place and then climbs—sometimes because I made it climb and sometimes because people I hold close to my heart reached down and grabbed my hand and helped pull me up, or at least gave me a little boost. What those people did was more valuable than favoritism or nepotism or special advantage. They shared advice. They showed me what I needed to know.

I came from a part of town that was not much associated with success of any kind. It was an unlikely place to start building a big bridge. Many of the black children born in my generation were never able to break away from that difficult, impoverished beginning. The slope outside the front door of the life I was born into was so steep it kept most people from making the climb. And once you started slipping—maybe with drugs or alcohol, crime or hopelessness—the plunge to the bottom was swift and unforgiving. It left people who may have been full of talent but short on opportunity crushed at the bottom.

A blessed few of us—and again I use the word *blessed* knowingly and with intention—became exceptions because of hard work, diligence, and an unyielding focus on our goals. We had no idea in the beginning what we would be. We were just kids, black and American and as full of spunk as anyone else our age. But we were at the forefront of an era of sweeping social change that would redefine where we fit in the complicated ethnic and racial patchwork that was America. We would enter that era as an aggrieved class that could trace its injuries all the way back to the days of slavery, and we would leave it with the same legal standing, and the same opportunities, as everyone else. There was no way we could know how that period would touch our lives until many years had passed.

A Hard, Happy Childhood

There is a protective beauty in the joy of childhood.

You are never really aware of your circumstances, because they are the same as the circumstances of everyone around you. We had no television, no radio, no telephone. We spent a lot of time just playing in the backyard. Mostly just kids in the family were part of that scene, because no one was allowed to visit when my mother wasn't home. She cleaned people's houses during the day.

My mother's name is Geneva. I am one of the last six children she had. I come from a family of thirteen brothers and sisters (eleven with whom I share a mother, two who share my father) spread across a couple of marriages. We lived in Kokomo, Indiana, until I was in the third grade. My mother and father, Robert, split up when I was in the first grade, at which point my father, who worked in a steel mill and who struggled with an addiction to alcohol, went to live in Grand Rapids, Michigan.

I recognize that this might all sound chaotic and might also evoke images of a deprived, troubled childhood. True, I had floppy-soled shoes I had to hold together with my toes. But I wasn't the only one. Most of the kids I knew had hard-luck stories. When no one you know has much of anything, there is no shame attached to having nothing.

It would be easy to take those circumstances and turn them into a story of deprivation, loss, and aching need. But there was something stronger at the center of my childhood, at least for me. Hard times and difficulties aside, I deeply loved my mother and father. Because of that I thought I had a great childhood. I delighted in helping my mother and happily anticipated every minute I could spend with my dad. There are important lessons there about embracing what you have, not fretting about what is missing.

Long before the era of bass boats and fish-locating sonar, there was just fishing. It was a discipline as much as it was a sport. Patience, knowledge, and, yes, even strategy came together in catching fish. That was true on the Sea of Galilee in the Bible and it was true of the best places to fish around Kokomo.

What could be better for a young boy than lessons from a father in reading water, in knowing where you were likely to catch crappie or largemouth bass? My father taught me everything there was to know about fishing, from harvesting night crawlers after the rain (free bait!) to cleaning fish. I never ate what we caught, because I have an allergy to fish, but my family did. We would head as often as we could to the Mississinewa Reservoir, Wildcat Creek, or the Wabash River to fish. Sometimes we caught so many catfish and bass that I would have to drag them on the stringer to the house. There were nine of us living in the house at that point, and the fish were important. Sometimes we would fish two times in one day, once at dawn and then again in the evening.

I lived to come home to see my dad. Everything about the joy of life as a young boy swirled around him. He was a soft-spoken man and rarely had much to say. But sitting on the banks of rivers, he would tell me things about life and about what was happening at home. He tried to help me understand what was going on.

You never forget those talks and lessons. Even our difficult moments sometimes presented revelations. I knew that he loved my mother. He told me he hated their arguments and that he felt he could not please her.

I remember the day my brother Bobby Cecil, the one I injured in the backyard baseball game, was taken to an institution in Logansport, about thirty-five minutes from Kokomo, because of his mental disorder. To me, the institution seemed really cool because the place had rolling lawns and real baseball diamonds and I had never seen anything like that. That was probably the first indication I had that there was a life outside of my neighborhood in Kokomo. That awareness came with a hard lesson. In what became a lasting heartbreak for me, Bobby Cecil died of cancer when he was fourteen.

My Father Leaves

One Saturday my father took me fishing and told me he was going to be leaving our family. I will never forget that day. I didn't understand.

"Will we go with you?" I asked, and he said no.

"Will you be sleeping at Grandma's house?" I asked, and he said yes.

Then I told him I didn't understand why we couldn't come and sleep at Grandma's house, too. He explained that it was time for Mother and Father to live apart because they did not get along very well anymore. Nothing he said made any sense to me.

I got to see him a lot at first, because Grandma was just six blocks down the street. We still went fishing. But from Mom I gradually came to understand that he wasn't ever coming home. He finally left and went to Grand Rapids, Michigan.

An interesting thing happened at that point. I shifted all of my attention to my mother. She became the center of my universe.

This was about the same time that the family went on welfare, which in Kokomo in that era meant you got some food. It was simple stuff. Macaroni. Blocks of cheese. Cans of peanut butter. Processed meat. I never thought much about the welfare food, but I thought it was strange that we had to go to this building to get the food rather than to the A& P grocery store.

I would watch my mother make bologna sandwiches for all of us. She made certain everybody had a sandwich, but it didn't take me long to notice that there was no sandwich for her. The very first time I noticed that she didn't have a sandwich, I decided I wasn't going to eat mine. She asked me, "Junior, why didn't you eat your sandwich?" and I told her, "I'm not hungry, Mom," and she said, "Well, you need to eat anyway." I told her it would make my tummy hurt. She said okay, but she wrapped the sandwich up for me to eat later. That was not what I'd expected, so I told her okay again and began to eat the sandwich. When I was done with half the sandwich, I told her I was full. When she was cleaning up later, I saw her eat that sandwich I'd left on the table. I had it figured out now. She would first make sure all of us had food, but there would always be one or more of us who wouldn't eat all of our food, so she would eat what was left over. If everyone ate everything on his or her plate, that meant our mother would go without food. I kept watch on this and would eat slowly to make sure I left something if my siblings ate all of their food. To this day I still eat slowly, and often when I'm at dinner with friends or a client and I'm the last to finish, this memory of my mom going without food comes to mind. It's a constant reminder of those tough days.

I used to go with her to the welfare office to pick up the food. I would pull a little wagon to use to carry it home. We would get two boxes of flour, four cans of processed meat, two cans of peanut butter, powdered eggs, a block of cheese, and other brown boxes. The cans and boxes had plain labels, so I didn't know the contents.

I will never forget the day my mother stopped going to collect the welfare food. She asked the guy behind the counter if she could substitute more peanut butter for the second bag of flour. "You wouldn't be in here begging for more peanut butter if you didn't have all those kids," the man said. My mother swore off welfare at that point and we never went back.

Even after my father moved to Michigan, I continued to catch fish to bring home. I would walk over to Wildcat Creek and catch a nice stringer of them, then bring them home, clean them, and watch my mom cook and eat them with pride. I also helped my mother clean the house. I wanted to be a good boy. I know that sounds a little precious today, but the alternatives in that era for young black boys were not acceptable.

I saw relatives and friends dropping out of school and using drugs. A lot of them ended up dead or in prison. And I didn't want to be like that. Sitting on the porch at my grandmother's house, I would hear stories about the dysfunction within the broader family. Most of my relatives were not doing well. But there was one role model: my cousin Mary Lou. She was the first in our big, big family to go to college. Mary Lou was older than me, but not old enough to ignore me. I loved visiting her.

She would occasionally come out into the street for a game of kickball, but as we grew older, the attention she paid to me and her younger brothers and sister began to dissipate. But I was paying attention to her. Mary Lou didn't drop out of school like everybody else. She was active in her high school and church, and I could see that she had goals. I wanted to be like her. When she told all of us she was going to Ball State University, that seemed like another world to me. Only years later did I realize that Ball State was only sixty-one miles east of Kokomo. When she went off to college, I carried her senior picture around in my wallet and showed it to everyone. I had a cousin in college! I decided I wanted to go to Ball State just like Mary Lou. To this day, she is still a special role model for me.

Going to Work

After my dad left and when I was in the third grade I started getting jobs.

I delivered the *Kokomo Tribune*. It was actually my brother Aaron's paper route, but he let me have it because I was always up between 4:00 and 5:00 with my mom anyway. I don't remember how much I made doing that, but I put every dime of it on the table for my mother.

Sometimes I would go to meet her when she was done with her work at the Conkles' house. The Conkles owned a car dealership in town. I thought they lived in a mansion because their house, like the houses in their neighborhood, was so big and the lawn so manicured you just knew not to step on the grass. I remember taking a ride through that neighborhood a few years ago and realizing that those houses weren't mansions at all, just modest homes.

The Conkles would give my mother clothes, toys, and books for us. I read a lot as a child. I loved it. What we had available to read from the Conkles' donation of books to the Knowling clan was the Nancy Drew mystery series. I read all of them several times. I know all about Ned and Nancy and Hannah. My brothers used to tease me about it, because I kept all the books in the room where all of us boys bunked.

I went to Willard-Douglas Elementary School in Kokomo, where I was just an average student. My earliest years in school didn't leave many strong impressions, but there are some strong memories. One happened in the first grade. I had just one pair of shoes back then, and the sole of one had come apart. The shoe looked like a mouth when I walked, and it would make a flapping sound.

My teacher, Mrs. Whitacre, asked me about that sound one day, and I just said, "What are you talking about?" She told me to wait for her, but I walked away, using my usual trick to stop the flopping noise, holding the sole with my toes. Two days later she asked me to stay after class. When all the kids had gone, she pulled a box out of her desk. In the box was a brand-new pair of Buster Brown shoes.

"Tell your mother it was a gift from me, so she is not upset," she told me.

I went home and told my mother and she cried.

Learning at the YMCA

The YMCA was my second home. I loved the Kokomo YMCA. It was a great place for kids to go. It accepted kids like me, who had no money, which was very important for many of us. When my mother told all of us that we could go to the Y and that we just needed to enroll, I was the first and only of the siblings to run over there immediately to sign up. I only knew a handful of the other kids there, but that didn't matter because within a short period of time you would know everybody, because that is how the YMCA works. The place was so clean, spacious, and bubbling with exciting stuff to do. I had never played sports and couldn't swim, but I was game for anything that was going on in that building.

My mother never made any of us go to the Y, but I was there every day. Truth be told, I lived at the YMCA. I learned how to swim there, but not through a swimming program. One day some older kids tossed me into the deep end of the pool and I immediately sank and started swallowing water. I knew I was going to drown, so I started fighting and fighting and quickly realized I was going nowhere. I sank to the bottom again and then very calmly pushed hard off the floor of the pool and immediately made my way to the top. Once I got there, I started to swim and I have never stopped.

The Kokomo YMCA built an academic and religious foundation for me that would stay with me all my life. The Y is where I learned about values, about Christianity. There is a reason for the *C* in YMCA. All of the great Christian values were on display there. The staff exemplified those values every day, so I had great role models. For example, before you could play anything at the Y, you had to complete your homework.

These days those kinds of contributions are viewed as, perhaps, quaint. But they were very important for me. The training and program experiences at the YMCA gave me the foundation to meet the challenge I'd set for myself to be a good boy. My mother's guidance and courage inspired me, but the YMCA gave me the environment and opportunity to grow as a young man. I have tried to return those favors by helping the Y throughout my adult life.

The YMCA leaders I have had the privilege of knowing over the years have included Jack Lund, the CEO of the New York City YMCA, with whom I worked in Chicago before he sprouted as a leader; and Tom Massey, who was with the YMCA of the USA as a field leader and later became CEO of Triangle 2, a consulting firm that caters to YMCAs. Over the years, I've watched Jack and Tom progress and make a difference in the lives of disadvantaged kids. Along the way, my friendship with them has kept me grounded and never too far from a larger obligation in life: "For those of us to whom much has been given, much is required."

The Y was a place, then, that gave me values and friendships that have followed me all along my journey. It is as crucial in the development of young lives today as it was so many years ago, when I was working my way through the challenges of childhood and looking for good behavioral models to embrace.

Reunited with My Father

When I was in the fourth grade (I was nine) it was decided that I would go stay with my father for a while in Grand Rapids. I've never asked my mother why she gave in to my constant plea to see him, and I'm not sure I want to know the answer, because she allowed not only me but also my two younger sisters, Freeda and Trudy, to go to live with him. That left my older sister Ruby; the twins, Darlene and Charlene; and my younger brother Danny with our mother.

While living with my dad, I attended Sheldon Elementary School. That's where I found out I could be a very strong student and a good writer. I wrote great papers, and you could always count on me to have the answers, because I did the homework. I also got what every young man needed: a teacher to look up to. It was in the fifth grade at Sheldon. Her name was Miss Brown and she was the first and only black teacher I have ever had.

Being close to my father again was great for me. He introduced me to sports in Grand Rapids. We would go to see the Detroit Tigers play. I got a chance to see Al Kaline, Willie Horton, and Norm Cash on the field. Before long, I could recite the whole lineup.

I got into the Boy Scouts in Grand Rapids, too, but that was boring for someone who had been fishing since he was three. I told my dad I wasn't having any fun at it, and he said I didn't have to go. I told him that I loved going to the YMCA, however, so one Saturday he drove me over to the local Y and it was just like being back home at the Kokomo YMCA. That's the universal thing about the YMCA: once you've been in one, you've been in them all. Great staff, everyone walks the Christian principles, homework before fun, and a great environment to promote "healthy minds, bodies, and souls."

I look back on my time with my father in Grand Rapids now as a three-year love affair. The only downside was that he had a girlfriend who lived with us and who mistreated my sisters. This awful woman berated and spanked my sisters so much that it seemed like a daily thing. Years later, my father said that if I had told him about how this woman had been treating us he would have stopped it. I was disappointed in myself after I told him about the mistreatment. Watching him get very emotional right in front of me, and he was not an emotional man, I realized that this was something I should have kept bottled up. My father is dead now and telling him about that problem was something I believe I should have taken to the grave. As a father, I should have known that. What positive outcome could I have expected by telling him? What was I thinking? There are not many things that I want to take back in my life, but this is one of them. I'm glad I never revealed to him the details of the mistreatment.

I remember when I decided I was going to stop the abuse myself, an experience that taught me a lifetime's worth of lessons in a few minutes. When you see injustice, you have to act against it. After she spanked my sister Freeda one day, I confronted the woman with a knife. (Freeda was a good kid and never got into trouble. To this day she leads with her heart and tries to do good all the time. If you knew her as a child or an adult, you would never understand why anyone would want to hurt her.) I was ten years old at the time and decided that this woman would never touch my sisters again. I don't think my father's girlfriend was actually afraid I would use the knife. But I could tell that the confrontation frightened her, and I know that she feared I would tell my father about her physical abuse.

After that, she never mistreated my sisters when I was around. The experience changed my behavior, too. I was so worried about my sisters that I stopped going outside to play. I hung around to make sure they were safe. I had taken on a responsibility that was a big burden for such a young boy. To be sure, my sisters were now protected, but protecting them meant that my own possibilities were severely limited. I don't know how my two sisters think about those days in Grand Rapids, as I've never wanted to revisit the subject; I don't want to pick at that particular scab.

Those years I spent with my father were when I really connected with sports, particularly baseball. I would read the papers, find all the statistics, and memorize them. I would also collect baseball cards and memorize the statistics on the back. Before long, I had a huge collection.

My father had a brother, Uncle Woody, who lived in Chicago. We would go to visit Uncle Woody and Aunt Catherine, and these were very, very cool trips. Like me, my father and Uncle Woody were sports fanatics, and they would allow me to sit and talk with them like an adult. I knew those statistics cold. I didn't know it at the time, but this was the beginning of a long and loving relationship with baseball, basketball, football, and golf. I wasn't yet a player, but I was learning everything I could about the games.

As mysterious as it was to me when my mother let us live with our father, it was even more mysterious when she suddenly wanted us back in Kokomo. One day she drove up and collected us without telling him. We were out of there like thieves in the night. Only years later, as an adult, did I understand the pain this stealth exit inflicted on my father. I was sitting in the hospital with him during his final days when he told me about that incident. He explained to me how much it had devastated him to come home and find his three children gone without an explanation. There he was, frail, staring at death, sorry for so many things in his life, and with only me there with him—he had only a distant relationship with Freeda and Trudy and no relationship with the twins and Danny—with tears trickling down his face as he talked about that day. It broke my heart to hear him describe how that day never went away for him. He stared out the window as he said this, and I was left with the silence of a very raw moment between us. I wanted to reach over and hug him, but I didn't know how to do it. What kept me from doing it still haunts me to this day. I regret I didn't hug my father. The long embrace I gave him in his casket gave me no return.

I continue to lock up from real emotion. I recall one Christmas when my oldest daughter, Jennifer, gave me a Christmas card. For years I would not let the kids buy me anything. That morning, I sat down and read the long note she had written me, and I had trouble finishing it because tears clouded my vision. Then there she was in front of me. She took the card from my hands and hugged me tightly and told me that she loved me. It is one of the most intense and loving experiences I have had as a father. The true magnitude of what I could have done to ease my father's pain was once again right in front of me. I know that he cannot hear me now but I need to tell my dad how sorry I am for not easing his pain. He knew how much I loved him. That is very clear to me. I only wish I had the memory of an embrace when he was going through his most difficult phase.

When my sisters and I got back to Indiana, we learned that our mother had a new husband, an air force enlisted man. He was the guy she'd been dating when we left.

Things were not the same. My mom now lived in a bigger, nicer home on Jefferson Street. This new husband had a new car. There was ample food to eat. Clearly things were much better from a material perspective. Still, I cringed with every act of public affection between my mother and this man, and suddenly I realized that I didn't know this woman. The reality that my mother would never again let my father back into her life hurt. I struggled with these new emotions and decided to clam up and stay out of sight as best I could.

By that time, my older brother Bobby Cecil had died. That death, and the new surroundings and change of marital status for my mother, made me think about asking her to let me go to Missouri to help her parents with their farm. My older brothers, Aaron and Jerry, lived on the farm, and Bobby Cecil had been living there when he passed away from leukemia. As the days passed, this idea of moving south felt right, so I approached my mother one Sunday afternoon and asked if she would let me move. For what seemed like days to me, she sat there without responding, but then she smiled and said yes. The move presented an opportunity for a big change in my life.

Picking Cotton and Learning Lessons

My grandparents lived on a farm in Haiti, Missouri. Charlie and Jeanette Spicer were wonderful people who lived simple, difficult lives off the land. Almost everything they needed in their lives came from that sixty-acre farm, which had no indoor plumbing.

The routine at the farm began with chores at dawn: feeding the chickens, slopping the hogs, collecting the eggs from the henhouse, bringing in water for my grandmother to use during the day, and emptying the slop jars. I had no clue what a slop jar was until I was summoned to take care of my grandmother's one morning. It was a porcelain bucket with a lid and handle with newspaper lining the bottom. You went to the bathroom in it in the middle of night, rather than trying to find your way to the outhouse. My chore involved emptying the jar in the outhouse and then going to the yard pump to wash it out. It was an awful duty, but over time I got used to doing it every morning.

After breakfast, we would go into the fields to work. Depending on what time of year it was, we were either chopping weeds with a hoe or harvesting cotton. We picked the cotton by hand; there were no machines. We'd bend over and pull the cotton from the bulbs. Once we'd cleared the husk, we'd put the cotton in a fifteen-foot-long bag that we wore over our shoulders. We'd spend the whole day in the field bending over, picking cotton, and putting it in the bag. It was a harvest ritual that stretched right back to the days of slavery.

We would do this from sunup to sundown, in one-hundred-degree heat. My brother Aaron, who had a darker complexion, would be blue by the end of the day. I was supposed to go to school, Peach Orchard Elementary, but I didn't go about half of the time. When the school bus came to the house—you could see it from afar because of all the dust it kicked up on the dirt road—we would lie down in the fields. The bus would wait for a few minutes, until it was clear we weren't coming, and then off it would go. We lay down in the field because we didn't want the kids on the bus to see us working in the field.

Even though I went to school only half the time, I was still a straight-A student. There were no distractions on the farm. I loved school, and I had nothing else to do.

A Powerful Mentor

My life on the farm and the relationship I developed with my grand-parents was very special. By the time I was in the sixth grade, from watching and listening to my grandfather, I knew all about farming. I could do everything but start the old John Deere tractor he used, his only piece of equipment. (You had to get it started by spinning a heavy flywheel, and I was too small for that.)

My grandfather had a blacksmith station near these huge pecan trees in the yard. I would sit there and listen to him talk while he worked. He would sing and he would preach, in the same cadence Dr. Martin Luther King, Jr., used when he preached, and I would sit there mesmerized for six, seven hours, as he worked and preached and sang.

My grandfather was a tall man, and red looking because he was part Native American.

Each Sunday morning, we would go to church, where he would preach. My grandfather cited the Bible frequently in his sermons, but as he could barely read, it was all in his head. And each Sunday morning, someone would have to walk my grandmother out of the church, fanning her all the way, because she would become so overcome with elation, a kind of spiritual ecstasy that is common in black churches. She was a woman who got so deeply into the Gospels that they were alive for her, and you could see it.

At home she would sit and talk to me about the family, filling in all the gaps in terms of my aunts and uncles, and where my mom fit in. Often she would look at me and tell me something that I still cherish to this day:

"You're going to be somebody, Robert."

I didn't know what it meant then.

My grandmother was never harsh. She was never angry, even under very difficult circumstances. By example, she and my grandfather taught me all about courage and compassion and unconditional love.

Some behaviors of theirs bothered me, though. One of them was my grandmother's insistence on going only to the back doors of the homes of white neighbors she visited. When I challenged this, saying she should knock on their front doors, she would say, "We just don't do it." That is all she would say. It made me angry. It made me feel that I was not worthy to go through people's front doors.

Tin Can Basketball

One time, my grandfather made a basketball for me out of a collection of old cans. He melted the cans down and made me a ball. Granted, it was a heavy ball, but it had no rough edges. Of course, it wouldn't bounce, but you could shoot it like a basketball. My hoop was a big lard can with the bottom cut out nailed to the smokehouse. I am still a very good shooter. It began there, with a tin ball and a lard can and grandparents who were patient enough to put up with an immense amount of noise for hours every day. Glorious sermons and basketball with a tin ball and a lard can—these became powerful influences in my life.

My grandfather's role in my love of sports stretched beyond that tin ball and lard can, however. All the teams at the school I attended were in the junior high and high school levels. As I was only in the sixth grade, my grandfather went to the school and told one of the teachers that I was a pretty good player (even though I had never played a sport before). So they put me on the junior high baseball team; I was the shortstop. I had never played in school, only with my brothers and sisters, but I knew the game, what each position was supposed to do. My first time at bat, I hit the ball out of the park. I was up five times and I got five hits. And when any ball came my way, as shortstop I was the able to throw the runner out at first. I surprised myself by how well I performed.

Then basketball season came along, and my grandfather told the school I was good at that, too. They put me on the seventh-grade team, but after practice the coach came up and told me he wanted me on the eighth-grade team. I think I scored thirty-six points in my first game. My grandfather came to every game and, boy, was he proud. It was heaven having him at my games.

My grandfather had a powerful influence over my spiritual life, too, but not by anything he dictated. He did it by example. I asked my grandmother once about his preaching and praying, and she told me the story of a tornado crashing its way toward their house. When the storm was within a mile, she said, my grandfather went out on the front porch and stood there and had a conversation with God.

"I knew we were going to die," my grandmother told me. "The tornado was a half a mile wide. It was huge." But my grandfather started praying on the porch, using one of his most common pleas: "Please, sir, have mercy!" He prayed and prayed, but the storm came that much closer—and then it veered ninety degrees from the house.

Lessons on the Farm

Despite all the joys, there are some tough memories from those years.

During one period we went for months without meat for a meal. There was oppressive heat and obviously no air-conditioning. We had bad run-ins with snakes and no connection to the outside world except the local news we heard on the radio at dinnertime. I remember a Christmas when my sixth-grade teacher told us to bring in one of the presents we'd received, for show-and-tell. My only gift that Christmas was a new fishing lure that my mother had sent to me. It couldn't have cost more than fifty cents in 1967, but I was eager to take it to school to show everyone.

The day of show-and-tell, a little girl, Mary Jane, who sat behind me, asked what I'd brought. I gave it to her in its plastic case so she could get a closer look. Then I asked her if I could have it back, and she started crying: the lure had become tangled in her sweater. The teacher heard her crying and came back to our desks and asked what had happened. Mary Jane said, "Robert did it," and the teacher grabbed me by the ear and pulled me out of my desk and took me to see Mr. Stewart, the principal. I never had a chance to tell my side of the story.

Mr. Stewart told me that I could have injured Mary Jane. He said my behavior reinforced his belief that it was wrong to have black children in school with white children.

Then he told me to put my hands on his desk and he paddled me maybe twenty times. Then he stopped and unbuttoned his shirt and rolled up his sleeves and paddled me some more. He hit me twenty or thirty more times, but by this time I wasn't feeling anything. He stopped paddling me and left the office for about five to ten minutes. When he returned I saw that he'd merely gone to get a Coke from the machine near the cafeteria. He drank it and started yelling at me again. Then he told me to stand up again, and he beat me for a half hour. He stopped only to wipe the sweat from his brow.

The rest of the day was a blur. I couldn't feel anything in my butt. When I got home, my grandmother noticed I was walking strangely, and she said, "What's wrong with you?" I didn't want to tell her what had happened, but she pulled up my shirt and she saw. "What happened?" she asked. When I told her, she just started singing. Not singing singing, but spiritual singing. She bathed my back and legs with Epsom salts, but the wounds just got worse.

I never looked at my teacher or at Mr. Stewart the same way again, though. And I made a promise to myself. I swore that one day I would come back to Peach Orchard Elementary and show them that they could not keep me down. It was one of the first deposits in this reservoir of adversity that I draw on when I am in stressful situations. It helps me keep focused and helps me reduce to child's play almost any tough encounter I have in my professional life.

The story doesn't end there.

Someone asked me years ago if I ever went back to Peach Orchard Elementary, and I said that I had but that Mr. Stewart had gone. But I'm glad that I didn't have the opportunity to avenge myself on him. There is scripture around the question of getting vengeance. Time heals all wounds, and anytime vengeance becomes your motive, you are only holding yourself hostage. Other people have moved on, and you are the only one still holding the baggage.

A Farewell to the Farm

I never asked to leave my grandparents' farm, but one day my mother showed up with her husband and asked me if I wanted to leave. I felt this terrible conflict, because I so loved my grandparents. But they were getting very old, and my mother said it was time for them to sell the farm. That was one of the darkest days of my life, sitting in the car going down the lane, looking back at my grandmother waving to me. I'm sure she was crying, because I know I was. She moved to Indiana several years later, after my grandfather had a fatal accident. He was out driving his pickup truck when he was hit by a semi. My mother left home to be with him and was with him when he passed away.

I'd left the farm and was moving again, this time into a much more comfortable house on an air force base. I was also about to become a serious athlete, which would carry me into college and the world beyond. Perhaps just as important, I was about to start my own business.

CHAPTER TWO

The Go-to Guy

I was going to live on Grissom Air Force Base, which was north of Kokomo. I had never lived in a house that was so comfortable or in circumstances that were so stable. On top of this, there was something new going on in the family now. We went to church every Sunday. We never used to go to church, but my mother had changed. Her new husband had introduced her to Christianity. She was a born-again Christian.

There was more. In military life, everything must be in its place: cut, polished, and in order. I have always appreciated that kind of order, so that part of life was very comfortable for me. I was a natural at making certain that everything was in the right place. If you could dig down to the roots of how I have behaved in my career, that excavation would lead to this time and place—Grissom Air Force Base and my teenage years— how I handled myself after I arrived, what connections I made, and my first focused efforts at earning money.

I don't want to begin by saying, "I just can't say enough about sports," because that is such a cliché. But in my case, it happens to be true. Still, there is not enough in that statement to encompass what sports meant in my life. To rephrase it more accurately, I would have to say, "I can't say enough about the people I connected with in sports."

I entered high school with no expectations—I didn't know if I would graduate or if I would leave school and home early to get a job—but I ended up encountering four coaches who taught me more than how to play a game: Nello Williams, Joe Goodman, Ben Bowles, and Dick Haslam. All four of those men invested in me. It's ironic that I would put it this way, but it's true. They all had an equity stake in my life because of the value of what they gave me.

I've often wondered how things would have turned out for me had two of these coaches not made the overture to get me involved in sports. Nello Williams coaxed me into coming out for the cross-country team in the ninth grade. I wasn't the best runner on the team, because I didn't know anything about running, but I soon became one of the best. Then Joe Goodman came up to me in the hall one day during my sophomore year and told me that I might like football. I still remember everything about that first day of practice. I didn't even know how to put the pads into the uniform; I had to watch other guys to figure it out. (Luckily no one picked up on the skinny black kid who had no idea how to get dressed.)

Ben Bowles was the legendary basketball coach at the high school. He was an intimidating man. Intense and focused, he rarely smiled. More than anything else in sports, I wanted to play for him and be a part of the highly successful Maconaquah basketball program. I played three years for Bowles, and he brought out the best in me. He was one of the toughest coaches I ever played for, but I went to school every day looking forward to the two to three hours of practice with him. Ben Bowles would find it hard to imagine today how much he was in my head back then. At the free-throw line, most guys would bounce the ball three times and then shoot. I would keep bouncing the ball until I heard Coach Bowles on the sidelines saying, "Okay, son, we need them." Then I would shoot.

We had a dismal junior season and finished in the middle of the pack in our conference, which we'd historically dominated. So Bowles was replaced by Dick Haslam. Coach Haslam had played at Crawfordsville High School, in Crawfordsville, Indiana, and in his senior year his team went to the state finals and he was named the Arthur L. Trester Award winner, an award given to the player in the final four who epitomizes sportsmanship, character, and scholastic excellence. Coach Haslam was a different kind of coach, and one I didn't initially connect with. With seven returning lettermen and four returning starters, we proceeded to lose our first four games my senior year. I was particularly put off by a preseason article in which Haslam told reporters that I was the best player he had ever coached but that in order for the team to fulfill its expectations, I would have to learn to make my teammates better and commit to a team game. I went to his office after that fourth loss for guidance on what to do to stop the embarrassing losses. Coach Haslam was frank with me on the changes I needed to make if we were going to be successful. It would require me to commit to a larger purpose than my ability to score at will. I would have to understand the strengths and weaknesses of my teammates and exploit those strengths. It meant that I would need to understand what parts of my strengths I needed to deploy against certain teams depending on what we needed to beat the opponent.

For example, for a very tall and athletic Kokomo Haworth team, I would need to crash the boards hard all night in order to give our team a chance. Against a slow and undersized Northwestern team, I would need to handle the ball more and get it down low to Lee Barger- huff, to take advantage of Lee's quickness and scoring ability in the paint. Or against a very good Kokomo Wildcat team with very few weaknesses, Mike Fruth and Chris Simmons would have to get the majority of the shots, because I would be double-teamed by some very good athletes. The challenge that Coach Haslam gave me to improve our team was one of the most valuable lessons in my young life, and a life-long lesson.

Oh, and yes, we righted the ship and won the conference.

These four men—Nello Williams, Joe Goodman, Ben Bowles, and Dick Haslam—were not just my coaches; they were my role models and father figures.

People who don't know what sports can do think of it as an endless collection of games with scores and stars and failures and winners and losers. For me, it was the learning of lessons, hour by hour, that I carried straight off the playing field and into my life. My work ethic marched alongside my sports ethic.

It came down to winning in both worlds.

The Lawn Leader

It didn't take long for me to sense some opportunities at Grissom. The air force insisted on having its residential housing properties meticulously maintained, and I was great at this. Mowing the lawn and caring how our property looked came so easy to me that my mother began winning the base commander award every month for the best-looking yard.

I didn't realize I was building the foundation of a small business.

Word of my abilities spread, and soon I was being hired to take care of other people's properties. After a while, there was just too much work for one person to do. So I assembled my own crew. Without thinking much about it at all, I had become a businessman, a manager. I had eight guys working for me in my lawn care business. Even though I was just thirteen and had no driver's license, I would drive around the base in an old car that belonged to my mother to inspect everyone's work. I checked everything that could be checked. Quality control at age thirteen! It was an early sign.

Managing came naturally. I was the lawn leader.

I never spent or kept any of the money I made, and over time it added up to hundreds of dollars. I took it all home and left it on the table for my mother. I wanted to do everything I could to help her.

The lawn service wasn't my only business. The base had a golf course with a lake. I thought there might be some fish in the lake for me to catch. One of the guys at the golf club said there was nothing in that lake but deep mud and thousands of golf balls.

"You guys never take them out?" I asked.

"Nope."

I asked if anyone at the club would want the balls if I retrieved them. The man said he thought the pro at the shop would buy all of them. In that instant, my new business was born. I got an old burlap bag, put on a pair of shorts, and started swimming in that lake. I ran my hand down through the mud and came up with ten to twelve balls each time. I collected thousands of them, and I made hundreds of dollars selling them.

It is true that there are no wasted experiences. The challenge is in figuring out how to apply those experiences. Golf balls seemed like a fine opportunity.

I took that money home, too.

It seemed that Grissom presented opportunities around every corner, and I seemed to have a knack for looking at situations and translating them into money.

I noticed that the Grissom base commissary employed grocery sackers. How complicated could that job be? It was about customer service, logistics, and reputation. I had seen it in my lawn care business as it grew. I would see it bagging groceries, too.

The standard operating procedure was to bag the groceries, put them in a cart, and roll the cart to the shopper's car, where he or she would give you a couple of dollars as a tip. Then back inside and do it again. It seemed to me that a lot of time was spent going to cars and walking around in parking lots.

After watching for a while, I figured out that the potential big dollars weren't in the lines themselves but in getting the purchases out to the cars for the highest number of customers.

Express lanes!

I asked the store manager if I could bag the groceries at the express lane. He didn't understand why I would want to do that, because the customers there would have only ten to fifteen items each and the cashiers bagged those. I told him that I would like to try it. I wanted to show him that I could have the groceries bagged by the time the cashier rang everything up and collected the cash from the customer. That would speed up the process.

The express lane was not a "tip" lane, because the cashier was supposed to bag the groceries. But the customers on that lane tipped me anyway (fifty cents to a dollar). Still, the number of customers I bagged groceries for in an hour was staggering: I was making ten times more on the express lane!

I was meticulous about how I loaded the bags, too. I would double-bag the cans. Double-bag the meats. Keep the fragile things such as chips and bread and eggs in the same bag. I would tell the customers exactly what I was doing and why. They were getting a value-added grocery bagging experience. The housewives really loved it when I explained how I had secured the eggs and kept the bread out of harm's way.

Before long, officers' wives were coming to my lane for checkout even though they had more than ten to fifteen items. They liked the way I took care of them. I was even being requested on the normal checkout lanes, when housewives came in for the heavy-duty two-carts-full shopping they did once a month. And instead of the fifty-cent tip in the express lane, I was now getting tips of two to five dollars. My system was working.

I had become the go-to guy in the checkout lanes.

These first jobs gave me confidence that I could make money and figure out new ways to grow my opportunities. These jobs were the practical parts of my education, the kinds of things you might learn in school about use of time, about finding businesses where other people see only mud and water, about the clear benefit of dedicated customer service.

If you are up to the challenge, being the go-to guy in anything is a good thing. Getting paid for it was obviously very important for a young man who rarely had two nickels to rub together, and giving the money to my mother made those earnings all the more important.

Watch. Listen. Learn. That was a big slice of my education.

Sports Transcends Race

There was no high school on the base. Instead, the kids from Grissom attended Maconaquah High School, a fairly well-to-do place because it was supported by both local tax money and money from the air force. Military bases in the United States helped pay for public education in the schools that base kids attended. Because of this, Maconaquah was not only flush with programs, it was also the most diverse school I'd ever attended.

Thanks to the air base nearby, Maconaquah didn't look like most schools in Indiana. It had the funding and the teaching expertise to provide a solid academic background (which I might not have gotten had I stayed in Kokomo or Grand Rapids or on my grandparents' farm). American military bases were like graduate schools for the free world's military, and those officers and enlisted men usually brought their families along as they underwent American training in an array of technical and military skills. As a result of this, we were the only integrated school in the area, and it made the place strong, interesting, and challenging.

The legal structure that kept blacks apart from everyone else was melting away with the enactment of the Voting Rights Act and Civil Rights Act in the early 1960s, and the "separate but equal" practice that had defined education for so many generations (and that had defined so much of life) was disappearing, too. Still, it was not typical to see black and white students attending the same school. Maconaquah was an exception. Those students from Grissom were pushing diversity onto the school in a state that had a long, brutal reputation for racial problems of all kinds. Rural Indiana had been the midwestern gathering grounds for the Ku Klux Klan, which had a resurgence in the 1920s. A lot of those attitudes die hard in rural America.

This was a different world. Moving into such a diverse school changed the way education felt for me.

Maconaquah is also where I learned that sports had the power to transcend even the difficulties of race. At the point in my life when I entered that school, I was very shy and introverted. I immediately discovered that the kids at Maconaquah were much better players than the kids at Peach Orchard. I would not be moving up to the eighth- or ninth-grade teams here, as there was no capability gap at work now. I performed well and was the leading scorer on the seventh-grade basketball team. The same thing occurred on the eighth-grade team, but there was nothing really outstanding about me.

My eighth-grade basketball coach, Joe Goodman, sat down with me one afternoon and gave me some advice. He told me that if I wanted to be one of the best athletes ever to play at Maconaquah High School, I would have to go down to Foster Park in Kokomo and Maconaquah Park in Peru every day that summer to play with the high school and college guys. If I did this, next year would be very different.

Those parks were ten to twenty miles from the high school, and I didn't have a car. My sister Ruby lived in Kokomo, so I asked her if

I could stay with her for the summer. Every day, I would go to my summer job and work my eight hours, and then, by 4:30 PM, I would be at Foster Park. I was one of the smallest kids at the park, and it was hard for me just to get picked for a team. Then one day my brother-in-law Tommie Glenn, Ruby's husband, came down to the park with me to play. Tommie, a Kokomo High graduate, was a minister in Kokomo who had founded a little church that was growing like a weed. He was young, hip, and a really good preacher. He also loved sports.

On that afternoon when Tommie came to Foster Park with me, Jesse Hillman, the star point guard on the Kokomo High School team, immediately came up to Tommie and embraced him. Kokomo High School is one of the historic schools in Indiana basketball. Every year, they seem to go long into the state tournament. Kokomo was a hotbed for talent. I didn't know that Tommie knew all the current and past players.

Anyway, Tommie was picked to play on Jesse's team. After their second win in a row, Tommie walked over to Jesse and said, "Hey, man, I'm beat. Let my brother-in-law spell me." Normally when I went to the park I'd get in one game, and if we would lose, I would sit around for two or three hours waiting to get into the next game. I was psyched to be on Jesse's team. My first time down the court, Jesse hit me with a great pass on the break, and instead of finishing the play with a strong move to the bucket, I kicked it back to him and almost threw the ball away.

When we went back on defense, Jesse ran next to me and said, "Tommie says you can stroke it. I'll get you the ball. So be ready to knock it down." When he got me the ball a couple of plays later, I took the twenty-footer and hit nothing but the chains. (Foster Park's basketball hoops had chains for nets instead of cords.) I hit four or five more, and a lot of guys around the court started murmuring about the kid with the nice stroke.

It didn't stop there. Jesse worked with me all summer. Jesse was a great ball handler and defensive player and he taught me numerous ball handling drills. He also taught me how to play defense, making it really simple for me.

By the end of the summer I had no problem getting picked for a team, and even when our team lost, the next group of guys would pick me to run with them. I could play all evening and never get tired. This eighth-grader was getting better by the day, and my confidence was off the charts. I took great pleasure in getting the ball with the game on the line and generating the offense either to get the bucket or give it up to the open man for an easier shot.

Getting Better Grades

I was a C student. Worse than that, I was planning to quit school at the end of the ninth grade and do what I thought I knew how to do best: make money. My mother was my big concern. I remember the day I told her I was going to quit. I said I saw how hard it was for her to work two jobs and I wanted to get work so I could help her with money.

She sat with me for the first and last mother-son talk of my life. We were at the kitchen table.

"You are not quitting school," she said. "I am tired of losing my kids."

"But I think I could do so much to help you," I said.

"No," she said. "It's time to help yourself. You don't have a chance if you don't get through school."

And that was all it took. There was no further debate—I never debated with my mother. I also never raised the subject again. I stayed in school. True to what my grandmother once told me, I turned out to be the one who broke that cycle of failure and poverty—and not because I was the smartest. (I was not the brightest bulb in the family. Ruby, Charlene, Darlene, and Freeda were the smart ones.) It was because my mother did that intervention.

Even with that kind of support, I was a painfully shy young man. I never dated. But I was not shy on the playing field. The referee would signal the opening of a football game and I would never leave the field. I kicked off. I played safety on defense. If we held them, I returned the punts. On offense, my main position was wide receiver, but I played quarterback sometimes and running back. In fact, the first time I touched the ball as a running back I scored on a twelve-yard touchdown. If we scored, I kicked the extra point, and I kicked the field goals. I played high school football the way most kids played pickup games on a field in the neighborhood. You did whatever you were good at and you played the entire game.

And I was good at all of it.

In basketball, I set all kinds of school records. I was a phenomenal runner in track. I even played baseball.

But I was not asserting myself in the classroom. It was not that I didn't have the ability. I just didn't see the point. I was pulled in so many directions at that stage in my life that I didn't force myself to pay attention to academics. Being a success at sports seemed good enough at a point when I was just trying to get through school.

Then I had a breakthrough. I was in my second year of Latin with Mrs. Holmes. One day she was handing back papers and as she handed me my F paper, she muttered something. When class was over, I left the room but then circled back inside (I didn't want the other kids to think I was sucking up to the teacher) and said to her, "Mrs. Holmes, what did you mean by that comment, when you said, 'You could do so much better'?"

"Robert," she said. "You are one of the most gifted kids in the class, and what I don't understand is why you don't even try."

That was all I needed to hear. For whatever reason, in that moment I changed.

I walked out of there and I made a commitment. I decided I'd show her I could be a great student. Over time, a C student grew into a B student, and a B student became an A student. I was well on my way.

Once my grades improved, I took my report cards from my other classes to show to Mrs. Holmes. Walking into her class for the first time, I was the young man who'd thought seriously about quitting school. Now I was a convert. She was great at her job.

My Mother Moves

I was becoming very successful at high school when I was confronted with another big decision.

My mother was moving to California, one of those career shifts for my stepfather that was inevitable in the military world. But I didn't want to leave Indiana. I was doing very well in school, and was being recruited by dozens of universities. The question was, "Do I go with my parents or do I stay and maintain this momentum?"

I stayed behind.

But where was I going to live? All my coaches invited me to stay at their homes. Instead, I decided to stay with two of my older white teachers, Estel and Joyce Cook. They had three grown children, Eric, Mike, and Elayne. I went to school with Eric Cook, who was two years ahead of me. Eric and I played football together. Mike was a teacher in the Maconaquah system and a former great athlete at Maconaquah High. So for a year and a half I was in an unexpected place, living for the first time in the home of white people.

There are lessons everywhere, and one of the ones I had missed in my life up to that point was what it was like to live in a house where there is a happy, healthy marriage. Mr. and Mrs. Cook had that kind of marriage, and as a result their household was filled with happiness and stability. The Cooks came to all of my games. Having them at every game was really special. I called them Mom and Dad, and the Cook siblings were okay with their new brother.

My father got to see me play for the first time in his life my senior year, when we played Kokomo High. To this day, I still have the photo from the front page of the sports section of the local paper of me hitting a long jump shot. I hit my first five shots. The first shot I took was from twenty-eight feet. I have never jumped that high in my life. I was probably forty inches off the ground. The picture has me in perfect form. I remember that every time I ran down the court I'd look into the stands at my dad. No doubt about it, I had my high school glories, but I don't think there is anything more glorious than having your father see you hit a jumper from forty inches in the air. It's something you never forget.

Recruiting

If you'd looked at my early high school grades, you might not have been interested in letting me go to your college. What made my high school transcripts work for me were the improvements I made. My grades started out very weak and ended very strong. My progression over four years was where the promise was. So when it came time to pick a college, a lot of great schools were in consideration. Interest came from many of the prestigious conferences, such as the Big Ten, Pac Ten, and even Notre Dame. Then there were scores of smaller schools.

The whole recruiting process frightened me. Remember, up to that point I had never been on an airplane. Having my mother far away in California wasn't bad, because I had at least developed a little independence. But I didn't know what recruiting involved. I had no idea what was okay or not okay. I had no benchmark, and there was no experience in my family that could show me how to navigate this course.

What am I going to do in college? That was my question. What will I major in? More important, what would Shirley Ealy say about my going away to college? Yes, the shy guy had found a girlfriend. She was the most beautiful girl in Kokomo. She and my younger sister Darlene were best friends because they both were musicians and played the piano and organ at my brother-in-law Tommie Glenn's church.

Shirley knew I could have gone almost anywhere in the country, but she wept and pleaded for me to stay close to her. She was going to Indiana University. Meanwhile, Wabash College, in Crawfordsville, Indiana, had made overtures to me, but I really didn't have an interest in that school, until our baseball team experienced an early exit from the state tournament and I found myself with a few free days on my hands. Rob Johnson, the Wabash track coach, called the house, and Mrs. Cook, who was very good at screening calls during this period, said to me, "Son, I want you to talk to this man."

Wabash has been around since 1832 and played an important role in Indiana history. Crawfordsville, Indiana, was a frontier town when the school was founded by a group of men who at first wanted it to be a high school—until the moment it was clear there was need for a college. Caleb Mills, later the father of public education in Indiana, was its first faculty member. The school was modeled on the classic New England universities and has always had learning, virtue, and service as its objectives. It soon developed into a premier liberal arts college—but for men only.

Learning, virtue, and service were not the key elements in play when I arrived at other schools to be wooed. I really liked the schools that would get you dates with the prettiest girls on campus. Some schools would let you raid the bookstore, filling up your bag with whatever you wanted. And I especially liked those schools that gave you a small amount of money to spend over the weekend while you were there. Today I know that these are recruiting violations, but back then I wasn't sure what the rules were. I didn't know any better.

By the time I visited Wabash, I knew what recruiting was all about. But I soon discovered that Wabash was different. What a reception I got in Crawfordsville! The athletic director, basketball coach, football coach, track coach, head of the department of religion (which would become my major), and the president of the university all lined up to meet me. I was struck by this welcoming party. Many of the other schools were limiting me to one sport. Wabash said I could play whatever I wanted. Then they did something really unique.

They knew my mother was in California, so they guaranteed that, a few years out, I would play in front of her there. Wabash made me feel appreciated.

The school also asked me to sit and talk with Raymond Williams, a professor in the religion department. I have had my athletic mentors and my grandfather as a role model in my life, but this was the beginning of a different kind of mentorship, one that put spiritual conversation at the center of my life. To this day, Williams is my mentor on making life choices. He is the guy who helped me sort it all out. When my girlfriend Shirley abruptly left me during my senior year of college, he helped me through that crushing blow. When I was trying to decide whether to play sports after college, take a job, or go to divinity school, he was there for me.

"Robert," he said, "life is about doors, and you never want to take doors off your horizon, so let's keep as many doors open as possible until you have to make the decision." I have carried this advice with me everywhere I have gone, and have distributed it freely to everyone close to me. In America, the doors of opportunity are available to everyone, even though they might not be so easily opened. You have to watch for them and then consider them before deciding which ones to enter.

Add up the personal reception and the connections I forged instantly at that school and you can see why I decided to attend Wabash. The fact that it was a men's school didn't bother me at all. I was still perhaps the most socially inept star athlete in the post–high school world. That would change with time, but not quickly and not easily. Wabash presented an ideal atmosphere in that respect. I could excel at my strengths: academics and sports.

Still, it was not perfect.

An Old Demon

Racism is a virus that spans generations, persisting from grandfather to father to son. In the 1970s it was exacerbated by the fact that when I moved into sports at Wabash, I moved aggressively and upset some key traditions. I was a very good player in basketball and football in my freshman year, so everyone at the school knew who I was. I built a performance record that put me at the heart of varsity sports. And that is where I ran into a fraternity that didn't like me. Basketball was one of its turfs, and several of its members were varsity basketball players. Sophomore year, I became the black person who'd moved in and taken their frat brother's starting job.

The first couple of games, people would boo when I came out onto the court. I'd miss a shot, and they would boo. I would hear racial slurs. That had happened on occasion in high school, too, especially given that I went to school in a rural community. Laws had changed and the official barriers that had defined race relations in America had been removed, but the social barriers had not. Interesting enough, the Wabash coach did nothing to address this problem. My junior year, another black player, Kevin Chavous, made the team; he is now a lifetime friend. Our friendship was natural but it accelerated with the racism we experienced, as each of us became a support for the other. How could the game of basketball have become so painful?

Then Mac Petty was hired as the new basketball coach during my senior year. The change of coaches fixed the racial issue at Wabash immediately. Coach Petty was explicit with every player on the team that they would control their frat brothers, parents, and friends or they would not be wearing the Wabash uniform. Government cannot dictate a change of heart. That comes in time, but it had not yet arrived in

Crawfordsville in 1976. Still, at least for my last year at Wabash, racism was not a problem on the basketball court.

The first week he was on board, Coach Petty sat me down and told me that he had seen me play against Evansville and he liked what he saw, but that I needed to choose to play either basketball or football. He told me with only two seniors on the team, he wanted me to be fully committed to playing basketball. Football would have to go, because the losing at Wabash basketball was over. At that time, I was pivotal to the football team. For three years I had been one of the leading scorers because I was the placekicker and a wide receiver. In fact, I'd never missed an extra point in three seasons of varsity football, so quitting football was not an easy decision.

But Coach Petty had my full attention. He was intense, had played basketball himself in college, and his raw leadership inspired me. I wanted to play for him. I soon considered myself the luckiest guy in the world, because Coach Petty turned out to be the most demanding coach I had ever played for. No matter how hard he pushed me, I wanted more. I felt he pushed me harder than the other players, and when the pushing became unbearable, he knew how to inspire me to dig deeper. Under his guidance, I didn't have the spectacular year I anticipated, but we won more games than we had my first three years at Wabash. More important, I had a coach who was giving me an advanced degree in leadership. He instilled in me the idea of never leaving the gym on a missed shot and always finishing strong, no matter what the score. These are lessons that are with me today.

Aside from sports, I also got a tremendous amount of intellectual stimulus at Wabash. I had never been exposed to black history at any level of my education, but at Wabash I read the works of James Baldwin, Harriet Tubman, and Sojourner Truth, among many others. I also got to hear the many great speakers who visited the campus—and not just authors. I first met Muhammad Ali at Wabash. He came and spoke in 1976 when there were just twenty-seven black students in the whole school and the twenty-seven of us had an entire afternoon and evening to rub elbows with the greatest boxer and one of the most compelling black public figures of all time. Years later I would reconnect with Muhammad. I fondly recall one morning when my good friend Tommie Welch and I were at his Michigan estate when he told me to change my name. He told me to change my slave name of Bob to a pretty African name. He suggested Pharaoh and he said he liked the name Muhammad. His wife, Lonnie, said, "Muhammad, how can you just pick a name for Bob without his input?" The Champ replied, "Because he won't pick a pretty one."

I think there were two components at work in my feelings about Wabash. One of them was racial. Despite the changes on the court, race was still such a problem at Wabash that I don't believe I spent a single day completely untouched by the issues attached to going to a school with only a handful of blacks in the student body and hardly any in the local population. I spent most of my time with other black students in places where other black students gathered, so, in retrospect, it's easy to see how the divide was created. I suspect that's how it was on most campuses in the 1970s. The other component—and this is harder to put a finger on—was connected to class. I struggled to hide the nature of my roots, in terms not of my blackness but of my poverty. I didn't want the people around me to know how tough it had sometimes been for me.

My athletic skills had given me credibility with my peers, but socially I was lonely; I simply didn't know how to be a young college student. I was clueless as to what a black person was supposed to be on campus in the mid-1970s. I did not dress the role. I did not act the role. I did not talk the role. I did not perform the role. The other brothers had suits with flair; I didn't even have blue jeans. They had urban attitudes, language, and presence; I had none of that.

I was just a country boy wearing clothes from Kmart. I didn't fit in among the white students (except on the playing field), and it was a stretch for me even to fit comfortably among the black students, who came from a remarkably different background. I didn't want anyone to know that I had come from such severe poverty, that my life had been defined up to that point by my family's deprivation and dysfunction, and most of all, that I was frightened when I arrived on campus. I cried myself to sleep my first night there, I felt so out of place.

Fortunately, Wabash had a Malcolm X Institute, which became the favorite gathering place (actually, the *only* gathering place) for black students on campus. We could hang there, watch TV, play pool, listen to music, study—whatever we needed to do. In that era, people sometimes forgot that just because black students sat together at public events, it didn't mean we were all the same. We were individuals before we were black.

Deciding to major in religion was a great choice, as it turned out. My intention at that point was to become a minister. Being one of just a few religion majors at Wabash meant I had a lot of one-on-one time with my professors. Raymond Williams became not only a faculty adviser to me but also a father figure, friend, and lifelong mentor.

Wabash was an intensely academic place, certainly much more rigorous than many of the state universities that had been trying to lure me to their campuses. This meant big challenges, the biggest one being a series of comprehensive exams you had to take if you wanted to graduate. It was a week-long process and very intense. There was an immense volume of written work, and then an oral comprehensive review by three professors, one from your major and two selected by the school. You could either pass or fail these exams. You could also get a high pass or complete them with distinction. No matter your disposition, everyone freaked out when it was time to face the comprehensive exams.

When my time came I went to Ray Williams to talk about it. I told him that obviously I wanted him to be the professor representing my discipline.

"That would be the easy way out," he said. He didn't have to explain. I knew what he meant. The comprehensive exams were about rigorous performance, not friendly professors. Wabash had always said that its greatest contribution was teaching young men how to reason. I didn't understand this while I was going to class. I thought it was a weak cliché, something that all schools said: We teach people to reason! It was like the "Knowledge Is Good" slogan from the movie *Animal House*. But Wabash was the real thing.

The comprehensive exams at Wabash rearranged my thinking on that subject. Every question in the comprehensive exams was framed so that you had to put a reasoned position on the table. You had to be able to articulate your point of view and then support it. They even incorporated debates into the exams. One of the professors noted that I had studied many religions. He wanted to know if my thoughts on religion had changed.

I told the trio examining me that I had once viewed heaven as a black-and-white kind of reality: "Here is heaven. Here is hell." But, I told them, I had become convinced that heaven would not be limited to those people who proclaimed their belief in Christ. I told them that I believed we could be held accountable only for what we knew. I went into a description of many religions and pointed out that if all that we knew was Yahweh, or Buddha, or Allah, then who were we to say that we had interpreted the meaning of all these different aspects of belief, and that we were the *only* ones with the right answer? This opened a wonderful conversation about the various religions around the world.

I got a high pass.

Those exams were a culmination of a journey, of the four-year odyssey I spent studying at Wabash. At that school I had learned to think through my positions, frame an argument, have an adult conversation, and above all, reason. I have never abandoned the thought that people are accountable for only what they know. This is an outcome from Wabash that has been reinforced at every level of my career.

After the exams, my assumption was that I had prepared myself well to move into the world of graduate divinity studies. I narrowed my choice of schools to Duke, Yale, and the University of Chicago. I was also a finalist for a Rockefeller grant, of which they give out only a few each year.

I had one foot in divinity school when something happened I had not anticipated.

I was walking across campus to the gym one morning when I saw this very attractive woman in business attire walking nearby. I asked myself, "What would a woman in a business suit be doing at Wabash at seven-thirty in the morning?" I picked up my pace and chased her down. Her name, I discovered, was Karen Vinton and she told me she worked for Indiana Bell. Then I said something inappropriate and very cheesy: "Are there a lot of pretty women like you at your company?" To my surprise, she said, "Bob Knowling, why don't you come and sit and talk with me?"

I remembered Professor Williams talking about all those doors, so I decided I would interview with some companies. I talked to Karen. Then I talked to IBM. I talked to about a dozen companies in all. I got a lot of job offers.

Another choice loomed. Do I go off to divinity school? Do I go into professional sports (because that was an option, too)? Or do I launch a career in the business world? I went to Professor Williams for a series of conversations about these options.

I decided on business.

I was impressed with the number of Wabash men who had built strong business careers. At that time, Wabash men were key executives at American Motors and Whirlpool, and David Orr, Karen Vinton's boss, was far up in the hierarchy at Indiana Bell. Orr and Bob Allen, the future CEO of AT&T, had been classmates.

Obviously, I had something to offer to the business community, because I had done very well in all my interviews.

Some interesting realities came to the fore as I shifted to a career in business. In the world of professional sports, the NFL and the NBA were both so accustomed to black players that race was simply not an issue there.

Exactly why I took an interest in that good-looking woman walking across campus is very much a man thing. Where it led was not. She was an important magnet pulling me toward another one of those doors I had discussed with Professor Williams.

I liked the way Indiana Bell approached me. I felt the people there really wanted me. Dave Orr was instrumental in that decision. He came to visit me twice.

In June 1977, I was about to walk through the doors of Indiana Bell. It is remarkable to me how much my life had prepared me to cope with the challenges and wonders on the other side of those doors. I didn't know it when I signed on, but I was walking into a world where my strengths, my education, and my background would become the granite blocks in the foundation of that bridge I've talked about. I would find a whole new world of mentors, a whole new world of challenges, and, true to the inherent promise at the heart of the American dream, a whole new world of opportunity. And I would start building the reputation that would help carry me through a long and successful career. The term "change agent" was not much on my mind when I left Wabash. I was at the center of my own transformation, and had been from those days in my youth when I decided I wanted to be good when I could have been very bad.

I didn't know it then, but change had always been what Bob Knowling was about.

PART TWO

Working

CHAPTER THREE

The Game Changes

ndiana Bell wanted me, and I decided I wanted Indiana Bell. I had a lot of options, but this one, in Indianapolis, was close to home, which was better for a socially shy small-town guy.

Arriving for work on a Monday morning, I had all of my possessions in my old Buick Electra 225, and the two hundred dollars my mother had given me, but no idea where I would sleep that night. It would be thirty to forty-five days before I received a paycheck, and the two hundred had to last me until then, so the decision was easy. I would sleep in my car and go over to the Fall Creek YMCA to shower and let the steam take the wrinkles out of my shirts. The Y's front desk person had given me a two-week guest pass, so divine intervention was once again on my side. I parked and slept in a park off Springmill Road and was questioned by a policeman only once in the thirty-plus days I slept there.

During recruiting, Indiana Bell had given me two options. The first was to be a business office supervisor. It didn't sound very interesting, and I didn't see any variety in such a job. The second was a position in the plant department, a part of the phone company that was almost completely operational and packed full of crusty twenty- to thirty-year veterans. I knew going in that I would be the only college graduate in the group, maybe in the entire division.

My primary goal was to learn everything I could about my job and the people who worked with me. My second goal was to do my job as best I could.

I became installation supervisor in suburban north Indianapolis, in the 96th Street Garage. Imagine the scene: Lots of compact, efficient telephone company trucks with ladders and collections of tools. Lots of guys who knew the operational side of the phone business from the point at which the wires connected to your home phone to where they connected to the big, complicated panels in the switching centers. This place had all of that, plus a tested system to get all of those technicians moving in the morning and aimed toward their many assignments. In the era before computers, the whole process was manual but effective. The telephone company was good at organization, even organization that depended on a mountain of paper.

My first boss was Dick Murdock, a no-nonsense kind of man who dispensed very practical advice. He was smoking his pipe when I met him. "Well, there's only two things I gotta tell ya," he said. "Make mistakes. It's okay. Just don't make 'em twice, 'cause if you make 'em twice, that tells me you are dumb and not learning. Number two. You gotta show me that you love this job more than I love it."

"Yes sir," I said, without really understanding.

He gave me a crew, and on the first day, I walked into the ready room where they were assembled and started calling out their names and handing out the order packets that had come from dispatch. The crew members took the packets and, as if on cue, threw them on the floor. Dumbfounded, I walked out of there, hearing them erupt with laughter when the door closed behind me. My knees were wobbling. I went into Dick's office to tell him what had happened. He took his pipe out of his mouth and said, "Tell you what, son. You go back in there and open the door and tell them, 'You've got five minutes to get to the trucks and get your asses outta here. Anybody here five minutes from now is suspended. And then walk out."

With every bit of courage I had, I walked back into that ready room and did what Dick had told me to do. I even did it with conviction. Then I went back to his office. He said, "In five minutes go back to the garage. If anyone is still here, you get to suspend somebody on your first day."

Inventing a Better Way

On the surface, it worked. When I walked back to the ready room, it was empty; the technicians were all on the road. But I was not happy. If you had to threaten to suspend people just to get them to work, there was a problem. So I shifted into problem-solving mode. Right away I recognized that I didn't know these guys who worked for me. I didn't know what they did. I didn't know where they went when they left the garage. I just knew that somehow they installed telephones. But I didn't even know how they did that. Also, where had those orders come from? How had they gotten into my hands? Who decided which guys would get which orders? I was lost.

I certainly wasn't going to go ask Dick Murdock what to do about it. That would have been bad form for my first day on the job. I could not go running into his office anytime I confronted a bump in the road. I had already done that once this morning.

Indiana Bell hired me because I had displayed strong leadership skills in college, particularly in sports. I told the Bell interviewers all about it. I was a leader. I decided it was time to figure it all out, where the orders came from, how they got to me, what happened once the men left. Understand that there was no training for this job at Indiana Bell. You just had to do it. They didn't even have an orientation session so you could find out what everyone was supposed to do. They had technical classes such as Pole Climbing and Noise Mitigation and ComKey Installation, for the technicians, but neither Dick nor my district manager, Joe Hall, suggested that I go away for six months of training.

So I did the logical thing. I went to visit Frances, Mr. Murdock's secretary.

There are always people in institutions who know exactly what is going on, and in such detail that, if asked, they could draw a schematic and nail it all down with a PowerPoint presentation. Administrative assistants normally are those people.

"Frances, where do all the orders come from?"

She said they came from the dispatch center at 58th and College Avenue, a place managed by a man named Hap Gillespie. She told me the dispatch center loaded up all the orders the day before, then shipped them over to us so they were ready first thing in the morning. In fact, the storeroom workers came to work around 5:00 AM and were the first to see the day's load for every technician. They unbundled the orders and read each one to determine the hardware, equipment, and phones required for the technician to perform the service called for in the order. They put all of those supplies into a tote box for each technician and placed the box behind the technician's truck. Once all the loads were stocked, the storeroom technicians rebundled the orders and placed them in each supervisor's box in the office. That's how they got to me.

I then went to see Hap and told him I wanted to meet the girls who loaded up my guys. Hap seemed pleased to see me on my first morning on the job and even put his hand on my shoulder as he walked me over to the dispatch center. We walked into a huge room and over to a big old steel wheel full of bins, around which sat women wearing headsets. The walls in the rooms were lined with maps of the streets of Indianapolis, Carmel, Zionsville, and Noblesville. Hap introduced me to the supervisor of dispatch, Bill Bates, who was a friendly young guy. Bill and I connected. He told me to go sit with one of the girls and plug in and see what they did. I saw that there were pegs, red and green, stuck in the maps. I focused on a woman named Cindy. I guess she thought, "Here comes the new guy who needs to learn," but even with a not-so-friendly expression on her face, she taught me how things worked. People will generally do that.

It took a while, but I figured it out.

From what I understood of the system, each peg on the map represented a place where we had a service request to fulfill. Another kind of peg represented the location of each technician in the district at that moment.

"So, you're telling me Mike O'Malia is on Keystone Avenue, just three streets from here, if I understand that peg on the board?" I asked Cindy.

"Yes, and when he finishes that job I'll test it and then I'll take that peg down and show Mike his next job. And I'll move him to that job."

Through that system I could see exactly where my guys were supposed to be working and what kind of installation job they were working on.

"Give me Mike's load for the rest of the day," I said. Cindy wrote down the addresses and I left the building and went to visit Mike O'Malia at work at a customer's house.

When I arrived at the customer's house, I told her I was Mr. Knowling from the phone company and I was looking for my technician. She led me into a room where Mike was on the floor working on a phone jack. He looked up at me.

"What the hell are you doing here?" he said. "I'll bet the other supervisors are not out bothering people. In fact, they are probably at the Bob Evans on 96th and Keystone Avenue having breakfast, but we get the new kid who wants to come bother people."

While Mike's reaction seemed hostile, I found it funny. His tone wasn't mean-spirited at all. Plus, because he was just a few years older than me and a former athlete, I could tell that he was okay with my being there.

He said, "If you promise to stay out of the way, I might be able to teach you something." He resumed his work and started telling me what he was doing. Having no idea of even the basic concepts, I had to pretend that I knew what he was talking about, but I was in a fog. With just a couple of more rooms to finish, Mike gave me the clippers and the pliers and other tools and told me to terminate the jacks. I struggled trying to skin the wires.

"Jeeze oh Pete!" he said. "Don't you know how to skin a wire? Here's how you do it." He grabbed the tool from my hand and showed me.

Word spread. I wasn't there to tell the guys what to do. I was there to learn. I had eighteen installers working for me and, within a week, I had observed everyone on the job at least once—and tried my hand at their jobs. I climbed poles. I crawled under houses. I went down into a manhole when we ran into a cable splicer who was opening cables to enable more lines for service for us; that was really cool.

The guys were impressed that I was willing to do the job with them. If one of them needed something, I would stop at the warehouse and pick it up. It took about thirty days for everyone to warm up to me, and me to them.

I genuinely enjoyed the process, so much so that it became part of my operating method for the rest of my career. Watching how people work, asking them to teach you their job—it begins to spot-weld relationships together. I got to know them and they got to know me.

The Value of Field Work

After working with my guys all morning, I'd often take them to lunch. That is where I learned about the people I was working with, not only how long they had been with the company, but who they were as people. I learned about their lives after hours, their families. That's where I found out about the company softball team. I went out and joined that right away. We would play and then we would go to a bar and they would have beers; I didn't drink.

I suspect a lot of bosses prefer to keep their relationships strictly formal and in the office. For me, that would have meant my never really getting to know my people, because if they did their jobs right, they were never around the office.

At the phone company, the workday doesn't end at five. Sometimes my guys would be in the field at nine, ten, eleven at night. I never went home until all my crew was home. Instead of leaving at five, I would always go find my guys in the field and work with them until the last one was done. I would help them wrap it up so they could go home. I was tough on them when they were not doing what they were supposed to do, but we were building relationships, and with that came improvement in performance.

But not without some help.

All the crews in Indiana were ranked according to sales and productivity, from 1 to 190—there were that many crews. The phone company put a lot of emphasis on this ranking system, because it let everyone know exactly where he stood. When I showed up on the scene, my guys were in the bottom quartile in both sales and productivity. I noticed in the reports that every week the top four or five crews were the ones who worked in Lake County (Gary, Crown Point, and Hammond). So one morning I got my guys out of the garage and at 8:15 I took off toward Lake County. I didn't call anybody. I got to Gary around noon.

I went into a garage and asked where the supervisor was, and was told he was at the dispatch center. I got the directions and went to find him. I told him who I was and said I'd noticed he was tops in sales and productivity every week and I wanted to know how he did it.

I learned from my colleague in Lake County that succeeding in sales was having the ability to spot an opportunity to add to the customer's service. (For example, "I notice you don't have an extension in the kitchen. It would be fairly simple for me to put one in and it's only an additional three dollars and fifty cents per month on your bill," or "I notice that I'm installing two phones today for you, a Princess phone in the bedroom and a Trimline phone in the den. However, we have a great deal on three phones right now, and I could put the third extension in the basement.") He told me that if I could teach my guys to spot opportunities and then help them build the courage to ask for the order, my results would improve. As for productivity, he told me about how he personally helped the dispatch team route the guys when they built the next day's workloads, lining up the right guys with the right jobs.

Armed with these new ideas, I couldn't wait to start sharing them with my guys, a process that began the next morning. I started by going into the dispatch center to watch the clerks prepare the loads. Soon I began to offer them suggestions, based on my personal familiarity with my guys, on how to load certain technicians with specific kinds of work. My numbers started changing right away. Within two months, my crew was out of the basement and into the top ten. In a company that paid such close attention to numbers, this was noticed.

By my fourth month, my results were so good I got a visit.

First, a little education about the phone company in 1978. It had more layers than baklava. I was way down on the bottom, on layer one, a $13,500-a-year manager of a team working out of a garage. My salary was remarkably low because I was a new college hire, whereas my peers, many of them phone company veterans, made on average $45,000 to $55,000 a year. There were twelve management classifications and seven levels of management between where I was working and the president of the company. The bureaucracy was vast.

When it came to career progression, people in the plant department were not aggressive. It could take a long time to shift from level to level in a system like that. Because of this, the visit I got wasn't at all typical.

Rex Smith was an assistant vice president, all the way up at level five.

The day he paid his visit, Rex sat down with a sheaf of papers in front of him. "When you started here four months ago, here is where you were," he said, pointing to a ranking for my team down near the bottom. "Here's where you are today. How did you do that?"

I explained to him how I'd done it—the field visits, the job site education, the strong relationships with my crew members, and learning from guys who were always in the top ten in results. The meeting lasted fifteen minutes.

A day later, I got a call from Joe Hall, the district manager who had hired me. "You're going to run the south district of Indianapolis now," he said. "You'll be meeting with a district manager named Marv Bailey, who's a really bright guy, Purdue grad, and I think you'll like working for him. You are being promoted."

My salary tripled, though even with that bump in compensation, I still wasn't at the minimum for that level of job, but it was the start of a process that would define my years at Indiana Bell and Ameritech after that.

You have to have early wins. I knew how to go in and get the early wins and get the momentum and the confidence going. In every job I have ever had, I have been very astute at assessing the state of the crop. I've known where the low-hanging fruit is, and when I was going to have to bring in the cherry picker to get the stuff higher up. I didn't get seduced by the stuff way up in the trees.

Frankly, I don't do the cherry picker stuff myself. I get my folks to tell me how they are going to get the stuff on the top of the trees, because they know how to better than I, and better than anyone else, too. At the end of the day, the secret to my methodology was tapping into the potential of people and unleashing their power.

It is so simple it's still frightening to me.

Whatever you do, your people have to be part of the process. You have to have their buy-in. I remembered that stretch in high school when we were losing games we should have won. At that point, I learned about being a supporter, about passing the ball and letting other people have the success.

So it came naturally to me in the workplace. I didn't even really have to think about it. I knew the first thing I had to do in any setting was win over the guys and get them on my team.

I learned a lot in my life about what *not* to be, too, and I was very quick to see what *not* to be at the phone company. There was a guy—let's call him Bill—who was doing the same kind of work as I did when I started. But he was a command-and-control type of guy: lots of harsh talk, lots of swearing. I might have taken that route on my first day at work, but it would not have worked. I found out later that my eighteen technicians, not yet my friends and suspicious of the new boss, had talked about what they would do when I first handed out the assignments on my first day. They decided they wanted to teach the college kid a lesson about what is important. One of the guys on the crew wanted to call my bluff when I told them they had five minutes to get to work. But a group of them stepped up and said, "We're trying to put a little fear into the new boy, but if we screw this up, we'll get suspended." Mike O'Malia told me later that my message and then quick exit from the room was the best thing I could have done. He also said I did it right by following up and being part of the team rather than being above them.

I was something of a standout among the supervisors because I spent so much time at work. I was the first in the office in the morning and the last to leave at night. Most of them would get their guys out in the morning and then go to Bob Evans and have coffee, come back to the office to do some paperwork, then get together to have lunch. They had great lives. Meanwhile, at 6:30 in the evening, I was the only guy left in the garage.

Don't get me wrong. There were many outstanding supervisors I learned a ton from. They were well respected by their crews. But I had a different situation going on. I had a hunger and thirst for knowledge, and I didn't want to be a thirty-year first-line supervisor. The other supervisors didn't resent that; but then, I wasn't around long enough for that to happen, because I was promoted six months into the game.

Anxiety, Timing, and Sanctuary

When I think back on those first few months at Indiana Bell and what they meant to me, a whole collection of valuable lessons emerges. Walking around to get to know a job and its people is one of my most important routines, and one I have always done when I've moved to a new position. It also became clear to me very early on that you can't be up to your ears in crises all the time. I felt it was necessary to find places and times of day to renew myself and clear my mind.

I call this "having a sanctuary." It's where you go to revive yourself, to think, to reflect and to slow the music down. It is my refuge. I love being in the sanctuary, getting the job done, being with my guys, and serving my customers without any excuses. Michael Jordan understands a sanctuary. He walks into a gym, any gym, and he is at home. Nothing can touch him there. Emmitt Smith feels the same way on a football field. Having played so many sports, I understand the sanctuary idea from an athletic perspective, but I was surprised at how going out to talk to customers and going into the trenches at work with my guys gave me the same feeling. Getting in a truck with one of my repairmen, climbing down into a CEV vault with one of the cable guys, walking into the frame room with one of my network technicians, stringing C wire with one of my installers—all of that provided me with the same reward as walking onto a playing field provides an athlete. So while I knew even then that my duty as an executive required me to perform a lot of administrative tasks, the real joy in the work has always been going into the sanctuary.

The Adrenaline Problem

One of the big problems in management jobs is anxiety and pressure, which can be brought on by just about anything that is not anticipated. It changes behavior, and this is a lesson I learned well from track coach Nello Williams.

Coach Williams put me into championship form by teaching me that the objective in the 180-yard low hurdles is not to jump but to *step* over the hurdles as you sprint. In my senior year at Maconaquah High I had not been defeated at the hurdles and I had my eyes on competing for the state title.

I'll never forget a particular race that was going to decide the conference championship. I was running against a really good hurdler who had beaten me the year before in the high hurdles but had never been able to beat me in the low hurdles. I'd beaten him in the regular season and I was undefeated at that point. It's worth noting that only a year before, I could not beat anyone with any real talent in this event. I had horrible technique, but because of my athleticism, I won a lot of races.

In my junior year, Coach Williams spent a lot of time working with me on getting better. I remember the day he told me that the only way I would ever master the low hurdles was to seven-step them, which meant taking seven steps in between each hurdle. Sounds simple. I had never been able to take seven steps between the hurdles, probably because I jumped them instead of stepping over them, and I found myself stutter-stepping in between them, which cost me time. While I understood what Coach wanted, I just could not trust the technique. I labored for weeks trying to execute the technical aspect of the hurdles, and had numerous bruises and cuts to show for my efforts. As the season progressed, I relied on my sheer athletic ability and stutter-stepped my way to winning most of the time. I got beat only when I ran against a guy who had the kind of technique Coach Williams had been trying to teach me. Sometimes I would pull off a win against a guy with good technique, but those races had to look pretty funny to the observer. I would bolt out of the blocks with the lead, lose the lead over the first hurdle, then take it back before the second hurdle, lose it over the second hurdle, then gain it back by the third hurdle, repeating that pattern right through the race.

Everything changed my junior year, at the sectionals leading up to the state championship. A funny thing happened. I was bothered by the reality of knowing that I could not win this race with my flawed technique and I hated that feeling. In every sport I played, I believed that we could win every time I put the uniform on, and I didn't like knowing I was a loser even before the gun went off. That feeling made me angry, and in that moment I decided to go all out in this race. While in the starting blocks, I made a mental commitment that I was going to step, not jump, over that first hurdle and then I was going to take seven steps after I crossed that first hurdle, and if I landed on top of that second hurdle, so be it! I'd never had the confidence to trust the coaching, but for some reason that day, I decided to do it.

The race started and, as usual, I was among the leaders to the first hurdle. I never hesitated. I high-stepped over the hurdle and, to my amazement, I had all my speed intact. This was brand new to me. Having cleared the hurdle, I counted the steps. At seven steps, the hurdle looked too far away, but I went for it with a high step and snap-through of my trail leg and—whoa, I cleared it clean! I could not contain the joy of that moment. On the way to the third hurdle I counted seven steps, and the magic happened again. Somehow I forgot about winning the race, I was so in love with the new technique I had just mastered. Hurdles four, five, six, and seven were conquered when reality hit me: I was in the thick of the race and was neck and neck with three other guys. With no worries about my technique, I concentrated on getting to the finish line first. The race ended in a dead heat.

I came in third and qualified for the semi-state event, but more important, I got a boost of confidence that made me want to go back to the starting line and race again. With the new technique, I began to win all my races and came close to setting records.

So, back to that race my senior year, against the guy who was standing in the way of an undefeated season and the conference championship. I knew my teammates had already counted the ten points we would get for my win, and the championship was right there within reach. We also could take third place or higher in the 4-by-100 relay, for which we were the favorites, but I wanted to bring the championship home with a win right here in the hurdles.

When it came to lane assignments, I selected the lane right next to my opponent from Southwood High School. I wanted to be right next to him so that I would have instant feedback on where we were in the race. The starting gun fired. I got a good start and I was sailing. I remember it as though it were happening today. I nearly had the race won, but on the eighth hurdle, something happened I was not prepared for. I was going through my seven count, but the hurdle was in the wrong place. It was closer than it had ever been. I almost hit it. I panicked for a second and then I got to the ninth hurdle, and I'll be darned, that one was even closer. I didn't think I could step over it. I hit it hard but didn't fall. I didn't know what was happening. On the last hurdle, there was no way I could get my foot up to step over it. I had to almost stop. I hit the hurdle and fell to one hand. By the time I regained my balance, the other guy was right there. He beat me in a photo finish.

I didn't understand what had happened.

Coach Williams was the first to reach me. He threw an arm around my shoulders and walked with me. He told me what an incredible job I had done to maintain my balance and finish the race and that I darn near still beat the other guy. He then asked me to replay the race and tell him what had happened. When I finished telling him about the eighth, ninth, and tenth hurdles, he smiled and told me I had just experienced what happens when athletes get their adrenaline up, creating a boost in performance.

"You are a master mechanic. You are a seven-step hurdler now. But you were so hyped and ready for this race, your body actually gave you more performance. And what I haven't taught you is how to alternate your lead leg when you get a boost in performance."

My stride had gotten longer because of adrenaline. The only thing that had changed on the track was my gait. The hurdles were all in the same place. I, on the other hand, was not.

Coach Williams taught me to recognize when adrenaline was at work and how to alternate my lead leg in going over the hurdles when my performance was peaking. That lesson helped me at every sport after that. In the fourth quarter of a highly contested basketball game, for example, when you go to the foul line with the game in the balance, adrenaline can spell the difference between your making the shot and bouncing the ball off the back of the rim. Calming down and maintaining focus is really important. I came to understand that adrenaline can be an asset, if you are prepared for it. It will make you jump higher, run faster, react quicker. I had the second-place medal to show for this lesson, but that medal would prove to be more important than all of the gold medals I won. Many years later, when I was asked to toss out the opening pitch for the U.S. Olympic Baseball Team—my sports fanatic daughter, Aimi, said, "Dad, don't embarrass us"—I made the adjustment for adrenaline and delivered a perfect strike.

It works the same way in business. High-risk, high-reward situations can bring on anxiety. I wear a rubber band on my wrist when I know I will be in a high-anxiety situation. It's there where I can see it, to modulate me, so I can understand what is happening to me and keep in the moment and be successful. Having command of yourself and being able to deliver the "strike" when you are making a presentation to the big bosses or during your first encounter with the analyst community or before a really big proposal cannot be left to luck or chance.

If you think it's all in my head, then you are correct. That is where anxiety is born in everyone, and even though it can have effects all over your body—in your personality, your presentation—remembering that you can handle this problem that starts in your head is a good tool.

That "Pushed Aside" Feeling

My promotion extended my career bridge and immediately carried me into dangerous territory. People often think authority comes with titles, but that's only the superficial part. Real authority comes from relationships in which people trust you and respect you, and those relationships can be constructed only on the basis of performance.

I was in a new world in my new job. I was managing the people who managed the crews now. I had Mr. Murdock's job, but in another district. I was also working at a different level, and was now a peer of the manager of repairs, Doc Miller; the manager of the centers, Hap Gillespie; and the manager of construction, Bud Aldrich. We were all under the direction of a guy named Marv Bailey, a high-energy, college-educated, "new things" kind of guy.

When the five of us would meet, it was clear that Marv was most interested in hearing from the other guys, the older guys, the veterans, and not so much from me. I wasn't being mistreated, but I was being discounted, marginalized. We were meeting a couple of times a week, and I was observing this phenomenon, new to me, taking place. Everything was deferred to Hap and Doc. The success I had had with my first crew at the 96TH Street Garage spread to my new crews, too, but that was getting lost in the conversation. I knew that no matter how much time I spent with Doc and Hap, they would never really respect me because I hadn't grown up on a line crew. It didn't take long, though, for the telephone company to present another one of those opportunities I've talked about.

An Idea Is Born

Someone in the executive suite decided to have a company-wide sales contest for the plant department.

Doc Miller said to Marv and the rest of the team that repair people simply don't sell. "I don't give a shit what the contest is," he said. "We don't sell. We repair things." Hap thought the sales contest was bullshit, too. He didn't want to be a part of it. He saw his job as running the centers. Meanwhile, Marv was hyperventilating about how to get his team to play along with a contest that could very well advance his interests.

While the others were balking, I went home to think about it. I was reading the paper. The last thing I always do when I read the paper is look at the National League baseball standings to see how my Chicago Cubs are doing. The baseball standings in the *Indianapolis Star* comprise a big scoreboard graphic with a kid looking down at league standings with binoculars. This graphic gave me an idea I started working on that night. The thought was to create three-person teams comprising an installer (Bob), a repairman (Doc), and a service center person (Hap). There would be about two hundred teams or so. I would create a season and these teams would compete against one another. Everyone on the team could sell. At the end of the day, the numbers of sales would be aggregated and that would be the team's score for that day.

Then I created standings. I put a schedule together so each team knew exactly whom they would be playing every day. Then I published the results daily, and at the end of the week, I gave a summary of the standings, along with some interesting statistics, such as the overall sales leaders, the installation technician leaders, the repair technician leaders, the service center leaders, the shut-outs, and the lopsided margins of victory.

Of course I asked Doc and Hap for permission to include their people.

"I don't give a shit," Doc said.

"I don't even know why you want my people to participate, because we don't sell," Hap said.

With those ringing endorsements, I set out on a mission to win this company-wide sales contest. I needed to make this crazy plan work, or all the discounting by Doc and Hap would continue. To fall flat on my face would only worsen the "respect" problem I had with them.

I went around to the repair crews and pitched my idea. One technician in particular liked my idea and spoke up in his ready room that he would like nothing more than to smoke those guys up in Lake County. His name was Ron Henson. I made it my business to catch him before he left the garage that morning to pick his brain about the "game" I was going to launch. He told me to be careful not to put more than one naysayer on the same team. In other words, a grumpy installer and a crusty repairman would be toxic together, and the poor service center person on their team would only run for cover.

So here is what played out. The people in the dispatch center started looking for opportunities for the technicians (their teammates). They would look at a customer's level of service and existing equipment, and they would encourage the repairman or the installer to see if the customer might buy the additional services/products they identified. Some service center personnel actually called customers after a repair was complete or service installation was activated and, in the spirit of "following up to see if everything was working okay," would make a pitch for central office features (e.g., call waiting or three-way calling).

What happened after all of my planning and all of Doc and Hap's "I-don't-give-a-shit-ting" was that we blew the numbers right out of the water. The momentum was tremendous, particularly after the teams got engaged. About halfway through the "season," people started to look at the matchups of who was playing and what the results were. Every team had a "game" every day against someone, so key matches were looked at by everyone. Soon people started to get jazzed about whom they were playing each day. Teams would even playfully talk trash to one another. It got so intense that the service center people became lightning rods for a losing team's discontent, as they saw all the activity throughout the day. They were accused of sandbagging sales or not posting until the end of the day. I had to intervene and make people play fair.

Ron Henson's team was hard to beat; they had an incredible record. There were days when Ron would sell twenty or twenty-five items by himself. Ron was the overall sales leader by a landslide. He was so far ahead, in fact, that the only excitement was over who would finish second. Even with his team's big lead, he would not let up. He was psyched about being number one overall, and his motivation for this was crushing the Lake County guys.

We made it an immense amount of fun. But it was also a lot of work. Remember, this was before we had computers and spreadsheets. I had to write up all of this data manually, then get to the photocopier and get it all printed out, then get courier services to deliver the results to the crews.

We won the overall company competition by a vast margin.

At the end we had a huge celebration, which the president attended. Doc Miller stood up to receive an award.

"Let me tell you guys something," he said. "I am a crusty old plant guy. Repair people don't sell! Bob Knowling came to me with this silly idea, and I'll be damned. Repair people have a better opportunity to sell than anyone. You *can* teach an old dog new tricks. I now know that I don't know everything. And while I am up here taking this bow, you guys all need to know it wasn't me, it was that kid sitting over there."

Hap came up and said something similar.

Recognition from the crusty old veterans changed my position within that group. Marv now started to understand that this kid's smart and he's got some real talent. He began to call me and ask me for my thoughts. I became what I view as a "thought partner" with him. He started looking to me as an equal, all because of that silly little game. It got people really connected to the challenge. I know that because on days when I could not get the scoring completed in time, guys would come by my little office and ask, "Dude, where're the scores?"

That exercise provided a collection of object lessons for me, the biggest one being reinforcement of the thought that direct reports and peers are more impressed by performance than by job titles or office alliances. I didn't like the way I was being pushed to the side when I was promoted, just because I was a younger man working with older men who had long careers on the operational side of the business. My new title wasn't going to impress them.

During the awards ceremony, I realized that I had discovered something valuable: once again, a process I could use over and over. The shape that process took, a sports game, wasn't the point (although I have to admit, it worked very well). The important part was thinking out of the box about the game and then using it as a tool to pull everyone together. The process had exactly what it needed: simplicity, competition, quick recognition, and lots of affirmation at the end.

I worked hard at my line job at Indiana Bell for two years. I was learning everything an executive might want to know about how a telephone company works. There are lots of levels of knowledge to point to, but I thought it would be helpful to see everything from how the business was wired to how it treated employees to how it reached out to its customers.

There was yet another development that would change my life, not only at work but at home, too. Marv's boss Ivan Jahns came to me and told me he wanted me to spend some time in human resources. In retrospect, it made a lot of sense, because the company seemed to want to shift me about every two years, and to places where I would confront something I wasn't familiar with that needed to be improved.

Ivan said that in a discussion with Rex Smith and Dave Orr, someone had said, "We need more guys like Bob Knowling in the business."

So I went off to join HR.

By this time I was well aware that when you work for the phone company, you don't have a choice in your career; they tell you when you have a new job. I had figured this out pretty early on, and I was okay with it.

So off I went to colleges and universities as an Indiana Bell recruiter. (You never could have gotten me to believe that three years into my career I would be doing Karen Vinton's job!) The Indiana University stop was brutal. There were so many graduates coming out of that school. I went in with plans to find some strong new employees, but there was one important development I had not anticipated. I came out of that recruiting visit knowing that Angela Thomas, not even an old high school sweetheart and little more than an acquaintance, would eventually become my wife.

The interviewing was tedious: long days spent with candidate after candidate. I had been on campus for about a week and one evening I decided I didn't want to go back to the Holiday Inn, because I was bored beyond belief there. I had noticed a student directory from the university in the office where I was conducting my interviews, so I picked it up and started thumbing through it. I caught sight of the words "Maconaquah High School." I looked at the student's name: Angela Thomas.

And I recognized her.

I hadn't really known her, but I remembered that she'd been a cheerleader. I continued thumbing through the directory. When I got to the *W*s, I saw "Maconaquah High School" again, this time next to the name Mary Williams. She had also been a cheerleader. I remembered her as a very cool gal. I used to go to her parents' house after basketball games to hang out with her. We would shoot pool, watch TV, and eat everything in the house. I called her. As excited as she was to hear from me, she said she had plans to go to dinner with her boyfriend, a soccer player.

Bummer!

I went back to the *T*s and decided to call Angela.

"It's Bob Knowling," I said when she answered.

"Who is this really?" she said. "Because Bob Knowling would never call me."

"No," I said. "It's really me."

I asked her if she was free. She said she was going to the library to study. I said, "After that?" So we went to dinner at the Holiday Inn.

I knew within five minutes of sitting down for dinner that I could certainly take her home to my mother. She was very chatty during the meal, but it wasn't all about herself. She had a very broad perspective on what was going on in the world, in politics, economics, and so on. She was intelligent, personable, and focused on subjects that reached beyond her and, just as important, beyond me.

About halfway through dinner, I told her I was going to marry her.

Later she told me she thought that was the "most stupid thing" she had ever heard a guy say. I gave her a ring about two months later, while we were having dinner with some good friends in Indianapolis. When the waiter was bringing out the desserts, to distract Angela I said, "Can you believe the dress that woman has on?" She turned around to look, and when she turned back to me, the ring was in front of her. Five months after that, we got married. More than thirty years later, I can say with complete honesty that I knew I was going to marry her. I just knew.

I had recruited a wife!

While all this was happening, the recruiting process for the phone company continued. Contrary to Indiana Bell's instructions, I did not seek out people just like me. True, I went looking for athletes, but I'm not talking about real athletes, but rather the kind of people who would be good athletes in the company. I went looking for people who did not need defined boxes to live in. I wanted self-starters who were internally driven.

When I met someone who had his life scripted out, it didn't excite me. I recognized that the person was probably going to be successful, but I was looking for people who wanted to make a difference, who had a passion about work, about life, about learning.

You don't find people like that by asking standard questions. So I depended on open-ended questions: What excites you? What would an ideal day for you look like? What does success look like and feel like to you? How do you deal with failure? Tell me about when you failed and what you learned from it?

I also picked up one of the most valuable interview techniques, and from someone I interviewed. A young woman I was interviewing turned a question back on me that rocked me to my core: "I need you to tell me why your company deserves someone with my capability. What is in it for me?"

I actually got hooked. I answered her question.

She looked at me and said, "I don't think we're a good match."

I was so impressed that I took that tactic and put it into my own interview tool kit. I have used it many times.

The Black Managers' Association

I got a long string of very good jobs at Indiana Bell over time. They were all new and exciting, such as running the Network Technical Support Group, or the Network Switching Organization. I was learning a lot, but I also noticed that my white peers, who had less experience, were being promoted more quickly. My "new assignments" were all lateral moves.

There were some telling experiences. When I was promoted at six months into the company, I was actually one level higher than the guy who was the manager in the business office whom I would have worked for had I chosen the business office job. When we ran into each other one day and reconnected, he jokingly called me "a big suck-up" and asked, "Whom do you know?"

I quickly realized how political and hungry this guy was. It also dawned on me that I was sheltered on the plant side of the business, where there were not a lot of guys knocking down walls to get ahead, just a few guys such as Marv Bailey, Joe Hall, and Ivan Jahns. Marv was bright, innovative, quick, and hungry. Joe, who was my hiring district manager, had a lot of potential, and in fact was my first role model and mentor in the phone company; he is still a friend and mentor. He was going places as well, but he was not as in-your-face as Marv. Ivan was cool—cool as in sturdy, calculating, and sure of himself. I so looked up to him. He was also a former basketball player, so we had lots to talk about when there was that rare occasion for us to hang around together. I looked at these guys as the "competition" and the people who would one day run the plant department, but that sense of competition was not overt.

So the business office guy made me realize that the environment was very different in marketing, sales, and Yellow Pages, where scores of people were fighting to get ahead. Incidentally, the guy in the business office took off shortly thereafter. He went from manager to district manager to division manager to vice president in something like three years. He later went to Wisconsin Bell as a vice president and then became CEO of the largest electrical company in Milwaukee.

What was this about?

The more experience I got in my lateral jobs, the more I realized experience was not the issue. It soon became very clear to me that it wasn't just me; it was people like me—black men, and women—for whom the tests were different. I also learned that I was not "managing my career" like other people were. I will give you one example. One day I was leaving the office with a white guy named Jim. He was at the manager level. Indiana Bell had two towers in Indianapolis, one newer than the other. Even though they were beside each other, the only floors on which you could pass from one tower to the other were the second floor, where the cafeteria was, and the ninth floor. Jim and I both worked in the newer building; he was on the seventeenth floor and I was on the thirteenth. The evening I ran into him in the elevator on his way down, he didn't stay on all the way to the first floor. The elevator stopped at the ninth floor and he proceeded to get off. I asked him what he was doing, and he told me that he rode the rest of the way down in the other tower "because all the vice presidents are in the other building." This meant that on occasion he would run into them.

The next day, I started crossing over to the other tower at the ninth floor and riding the elevator down in that building. I ran into Frank Thomas, another black manager and good friend who was working in information technology. He knew I worked in the new building, so he asked why I was going down in the old building. I told him the theory, and he laughed and said, "Damn, that makes a lot of sense." It could never hurt to be seen by a vice president at the phone company. Or at least that was the conventional wisdom.

I really didn't have the process of getting ahead in the business figured out. Phone companies—and many other companies, for that matter—allowed blacks to ascend to a certain level, but they were not going to be welcomed into the corner office, no matter how great their experience, how strong their potential, or how good their college grades. It was more than just a glass ceiling. This was relatively early in the years that followed the civil rights movement. The legal barriers aimed at holding back African Americans politically and socially had been removed, but the extralegal, invisible barriers were still in place.

While this was frustrating, it was also motivating, a reminder that no matter who we are, we are responsible for our own careers. When you define a problem, it is best to move aggressively to solve it. This was particularly true of the phone company's attitude toward race. At that time in 1985, Indiana Bell had three black employees at higher levels. The three were at the district manager level, when there were about *sixty* such jobs in the company. The level above district manager was division manager, with twenty to twenty-five of those jobs. After division level we had assistant vice presidents, with about a dozen of those jobs, and finally vice president, with about eight such positions, and then the president.

Frank and I put our heads together on the question of advancement. We knew that having just one woman and only two black guys at the district manager level was not sufficient for the company. They were good folks, but they had the same characteristics: They never caused trouble. They always followed the rules. They did not advocate for people of color or women. In street language, what the few brothers in the company would tell you is that to get ahead, you had to kiss a lot of ass, keep your head down, and not rock the boat. That may well have been true, but Frank and I knew it wasn't right, that if there was going to be advancement for women and minorities, it would require some conversations with the people at the top.

How would we do that without appearing self-serving? I believed that a support organization might help. That is when I decided we would form the Indiana Bell Black Managers' Association. What we cared about was not advancement for ourselves, but a conversation with the people at the top about opening some pathways. We looked to existing organizations at the Bells in Michigan and Illinois for guidance.

There were no dues to belong to the association, and anyone who wanted to could join. I had a membership at the Indianapolis Athletic Club, and decided we would go there from 11:30 AM to 1:30 PM, to meet outside our headquarters. We developed a charter. We decided on what we wanted to ask from senior management. I knew when it all began that we had to be really buttoned down.

Cynthia Bates, Frank Thomas, Sheldon Patrick, and Bob Nibbs were all in the room one day when I felt it important to point out something about the work we were undertaking. I told them, "If we are successful, we probably won't be the recipients of the promotions that will occur, and all of us need to understand that. This advocacy cannot be about us. And they will, in fact, promote others. Because of the very nature of this advocacy, we have already violated what is the unspoken profile of what a good brother in higher offices means: noncontroversial, follow the rules, advocate for no one."

We debated this. There was quiet acceptance that if we thought this was all about us, we were in the wrong place, even though every person in the room was a stellar performer.

We were moving into dangerous territory for black people at the phone company. The managers and I pressed for a meeting with the people at the top. That was a very intimidating process, because when you're trying to get people to the table, you can't get them there with a stick; you need to get them there with a carrot. But you also have to let them know that you are serious about what you're doing.

I told the president and the head of human resources that this was a conversation we should have had a long time ago. I told them I believed we were offering them a great opportunity to diagnose the problem and learn how to fix it. Still, I felt nothing but resistance from the president and the head of HR. I told them there were two avenues we could pursue. We could let this play out at this level with a fruitful dialogue, or we could let it play out on the front page of the *Indianapolis Star*, which would be very interested in an article about the obstacles in the way of black advancement at Indiana Bell.

I told them that this wasn't a threat, but rather a reflection of the fact that senior management was just paying lip service to the idea of diversity.

"In the top four levels of the company, there is not one person of color and just two women. And you cannot tell me that we don't have the skill set. In fact, if we don't have the skill set, you go to the market and you bring in someone who does." Basically, I took their excuses away from them. By telling them to go to the market if we didn't have the talent internally, it forced the discussion to be about our profile and track record and not about me and the Black Managers' Association.

These were very difficult and sensitive times at Indiana Bell. While we wanted immediate action and access to information such as compensation profiles, we knew that HR chief Betty Adamson would not embrace our cause if the process became confrontational. We learned from our colleagues at Michigan Bell that the most effective way to communicate with the hierarchy was to threaten to play the situation out in the media. The black managers in Michigan were more than willing to do that. We managed to strike the right balance with Betty, and

eventually were successful in getting our company to redefine its relationships with black workers.

I believe my work on that issue was one of the most significant contributions I made at Indiana Bell, and the changes did come. I felt myself
something of a prophet.

There were only three things we cared about: promotion, pay, and
profile. Over the next year, if there were ten opportunities, the people at
the top would have to prove their commitment to diversity, and show
they weren't just paying lip service, by promoting a person of color
instead of ten white males. They would have to examine the fact that pay
for black people was not in proportion to pay for others. Finally, they
had to show their commitment by what they did going forward and put
stakes in the ground for improvement of our profile at every level.

Still, when the first couple of black promotions came, they involved
people who were in no way troublemakers or advocates. They were the
same quiet black people who had been promoted before. Companies had
figured out a long time ago that if they put one black person in upper
management, it would look good.

I had to continue to tell myself to stay the course. Continue to perform. Yet it was hard for me to handle, to have to go home and tell
Angela I had been passed over for a promotion again. I resigned myself
to the fact that I would probably have to leave the company down the
road. But I thought I had started something worthwhile. Lone rangers
were not going to change things at the top. It took a critical mass to do
that. It was time to start working on a résumé. I had a lot of strong
things to say about myself and I looked forward to putting them down
on paper.

Then something interesting happened.

Judy Myers moved into the human resources job. An avid golfer and
one of the good people in the company, she'd come up in the operations
and technical side of the business, through operator services, the business office, and then the plant department.

"Let's talk about the issue that you've sort of started in the company,"
this astute white woman said in our first conversation. "How are we
gonna get the boys to play right? Obviously they don't want us in the

country club, and they don't want us driving the cart. How the hell are we going to get them to play? I gotta get you moving on this thing."

It was wonderful.

She told me to keep doing exactly what I was doing. Don't turn down the heat. Keep the performance at a stellar level. Don't lose that thought that you are the guy who gets things done. "Leave the rest to me, and don't do anything stupid," she said.

I knew we had an advocate. And I knew I was staying.

CHAPTER FOUR

Big Changes

F ounding the Indiana Bell Black Managers' Association with my friends was not the career killer I had anticipated. It drew attention to the festering problem of race inside the telephone company, to the lack of promotion to senior levels for blacks, Hispanics, and women (basically anyone who wasn't a white male), and started opening up some pathways for advancement for deserving, intelligent people.

I never expected I would be a beneficiary of it. In fact, before Judy Myers talked with me, my plan was to pack up my office and leave Indiana Bell. I decided against that after a lot of consultation with Judy, who seemed dedicated to the idea of fair advancement for everyone.

I was very surprised when I got a call from Norm Cubellis, the assistant vice president of Network. "Robert," he said, "we've never met, but I'm responsible for the Network Switching Organization. I work for Jim Eibel, the vice president. Tomorrow, we're announcing your promotion. You're coming to Network."

That was that. I was promoted to Network.

Network basically enabled all voice and data communications. It was the intricate, almost hidden web of cables, fiber optics, and switching central offices that customers never saw that made people's day-to-day communications possible. I would be the district manager of special services (data communications), responsible for all the technicians who installed and repaired complex services.

———

I made it a point to learn everything I could about the Network central offices, which were the large switching stations that processed all voice and data transmissions, routed the calls/data, and provided incredible billing detail in real time. Learning about the central office switch network was exciting. Still, because Network central office switching was not my job, I had to be careful about how much time I devoted to learning it.

Central office switching took more formal training than anything I had been exposed to, but I was driven to understand how the switching worked. I took several switching courses. Upon completing a course, I would immediately go to the field to try out my new knowledge. I was constantly asking one of my new peers, Bill Overby, questions about what I was learning. A thirty-five-year veteran and former military man, Bill had just recently returned to Indiana Bell after a long tour of duty at AT&T in New Jersey. He was very technical. People just loved him. And he was black.

Bill knew everything about those darn switches, the old ones we were replacing and even the new ones we were installing. I once heard a story about how he was overseeing a very large switch cutover when the technician who was responsible for activating the switch could not get the commands to work. When you cut over a switch, all the cables to the old frame are severed and the switch is now dead. A technician has to type in the new commands, and then the new machine comes online. After several attempts and everyone in near panic mode, Bill moved the guy aside and typed in the commands, and the switch came online. Of course Bill downplayed the event, but that was Bill. It felt good to have him on Norm's team, but I didn't like the way he was sometimes discounted in meetings. I wanted some of his virtue and I really wanted his technical knowledge.

"Knowledge is power" is a cliché for a reason. It does, indeed, advance your interests to know how everything in your purview works. But there are other benefits to learning the systems under your command. Learning all the work gave me two assets that cannot be valued highly enough. First, it endeared me to my technicians. Technicians respect a boss who will come out and ask them about their jobs and how they've installed or fixed things. Everyone knows what it feels like to have a clueless boss. Having a boss who knows what is happening (and, more important, *how* it is happening) advances everyone's interest. If you know what is going on and you ask someone to take a service request that is very difficult and maybe nearly impossible to complete, it sends an immediate message about the level of trust you have in that technician, how much you respect his or her capacity for the work.

But you have to know the work in order to do that.

People talk to one another. When you help them, when you respect them, when you promote them, word gets around. You want the people working for you to understand you, your values, your work ethic, your sense of fairness, and your level of knowledge about their work. You are vested with them in the journey to exceed customers' expectations. It's a much stronger way of managing.

But the challenge doesn't stop there.

Winning Allies

My special services job was a much larger platform, and everything I did was noticed due to the important nature of data services in our business. I was able to win people over in the organization quickly, but I recognized I could not just stop with the people who worked for me. I felt I needed to get my peers to come along with me, too. I didn't want them just to accept me. I wanted them to regard me as a valuable member of the team who performed his job well. It's your responsibility to win your allies, and sometimes you have to give up some of your own power and ego to do that.

Stu Boner was one of my peers and a kingpin in Network. He ran all of Southern Indiana. He was in charge of all the switches. Stu knew more about switching than all of the peer team combined, and he really didn't like coming to Norm's meetings. I think he enjoyed stirring the pot. During one period, a series of thunderstorms in the southern part of the state had left Stu with numerous customer outages, and he was having trouble keeping up with his routine maintenance in his switching central offices and with repairs; he was totally consumed with work. That's not good. These machines were almost like cars. You had to maintain them. If you didn't, you would have trouble down the road. Putting off routine maintenance could eventually impair a switch and that was serious. An impaired switch could shut down thousands of customers' telephone service. The impact of a switching failure is even more profound for businesses that are served by the central office.

If I had to find a simple description for myself, it would be "I am a process guy." I believe you need to understand how everything works in order to determine whether an operation is efficient and whether you can make it even more efficient. The greatest way to improve productivity in an organization is to remove steps from the process. Eliminating or simplifying steps enables the work to be done more quickly. Doing things more quickly and eliminating steps gives you more capacity. The more capacity you have, the more work you can handle. This is really important as a matter of scale; as you get everyone to adhere to the improved process, you get the leverage of the multiplier effect. You can do that without adding a single dollar to costs, just through the efficient use of process management.

My philosophy as a "process man" was about to deliver great benefits to Stu Boner.

I had been paying close attention to process in my organization. I knew what my productivity was: Urban versus rural. Weekend versus weekday. By day of the week.

We had improved the operating performance of special services. Our on-time performance for installed orders was well over 95 percent, and the repair report rate was the lowest the company had seen in a decade. We were getting more done with fewer people and with outstanding work quality.

In a meeting with the team one day, our boss, Norm Cubellis, was beating people up about the service levels. After the meeting, I walked over to Stu and told him I understood he was having some problems in Evansville, New Albany, and Bloomington. "What if I give you a dozen guys? My guys can't do routine maintenance, but we can run jumpers on the frame, diagnose trouble, and do other tasks that consume your resources in the central office. Don't worry about paying for them. I will carry the costs. I'll give them to you for a couple of months."

"What?" Stu said. The phone company was not the kind of place where offers like that came along very often.

"Stu," I said, "you need the help. I've got the people and the capacity. Plus, if you need them longer, I'm willing to extend the time they are loaned to you, and I'm willing to eat any overtime they have to work to help you out."

When I got back to my office, I had a conference call with my two guys who ran special services for the southern territory, Norm Davenport and Larry Voorhees. I told them we needed to give up a dozen guys to help Stu. "By the way, we want to do it right," I said. "Let's send him our stars, because the better the people we send him, the more it's going to help us." Six months later, Stu got in trouble on another project and called and asked for help. "Let me take a look at it," I said. My thought was that even if I didn't have the capacity, I would help him and figure out a way to survive on my end.

Some time passed and I had to sit down with Norm for my first performance appraisal from him. My performance was outstanding, he said. I told him I wanted to know why I was outstanding, even though I appreciated the rating, because I knew all about "evaluation creep," which happens at every company. People are moved along with favorable reviews because it's too uncomfortable to go in the other direction.

"I'm assuming Stu Boner's outstanding, too," I said.

"Yes," Norm said. "Stu is outstanding, but for other reasons. Let me tell you why you are outstanding. It's about all of this capacity you have built and how you have transformed the organization we gave you to run. But more important, son, the way you go and help others, the way you go and take on the mission of the team, you act like you have my job. You are acting like a business owner. And I can't teach that."

And I never knew that Stu had told him about all the help I was giving him. I didn't do it so he would tell the boss about it. There is *always* a quid pro quo. Like Bill Overby, Stu later helped me to understand the switch network. I had never been in the switch network before. "I hope you are picking all this up," he told me at one of our Cubellis meetings, "because one day you're running all of this."

That used to make me gleam. I became his protégé.

Learning What Works

This period of my career was full of practical lessons.

I didn't play golf until I started hanging out with Judy Myers and her friends, but once I got into it, I found out that golf was a whole other venue where important things happen. In a short period of time, I committed myself to working on my golf game and developed into a pretty good player.

Still, I learned to tone down my game a little bit as time passed, because people don't like losing. Of course I won plenty of games, but not all of them. One of the senior executives who was supposed to be a really good golfer once jokingly called me a gorilla on the course after I blew my drive past his drive by about eighty yards.

After watching me go birdie, par, birdie on the first three holes, I could sense his demeanor changing. The friendly chatter was gone. On the fourth hole, I killed my drive right down the middle about 320 yards. I caught the incredulous look on his face, so while walking down the fairway to my ball, I made a drastic decision about how I was going to do in that game.

I held back on purpose.

I doubt that I am the inventor of strategic losing. I suspect it's quite common. Still, I felt awful after I tanked the match. Golf is one of the few activities where the nonathletic person can actually participate and compete. This executive had never played a competitive sport. Yet here I was letting him beat me in golf so I could preserve his ego and advance my interests.

I was disrespecting myself when I lost to make someone else feel better, or when I tried to manufacture a promotion by riding in the proper elevator. I don't have an excuse for that. I did it to advance *myself.* I was really pissed off at myself when I had to eat crow and feign interest in that executive's golf advice after I let him win. All of your learning doesn't come at work.

I was starting to get a reputation as a team player who delivered excellent results.

Good news was right around the corner. My friend and confidante Judy Myers was moved over as head of the Network company, replacing Norm Cubellis.

Judy was respected in every corner of the phone company. Why she chose to help me was a mystery, but when I look at the people she'd supported, one thing was certain; they were all proven performers. I've had several people contribute to my career and life, and it seems that everyone came along at the right time. Dick Murdock, Joe Hall, and Rex Smith were there for me in my early days in the plant department, and now I was getting help from Judy Myers.

Asked for My Thoughts

I was sitting in my office one day after Judy had been promoted when she called and asked me if I had a minute. Her office was on the ninth floor of the new building. She was at the fifth level, an assistant vice president, and she had an office as big as a house, with couches and everything. It was the phone company way. The higher you climbed, the better the surroundings.

In her office she motioned for me to have a seat on the couch and she joined me.

"I have been thinking about some things in terms of how we can really transform Network." Then she started off on an idea, then another, and another, and at the end, she asked, "What do you think?"

At that instant, I realized it was the first time in my professional life that someone had asked me for my opinion. I was soaring when I left that room. You would have thought someone had made me president of the company, the way I looked when I walked out of Judy's office that day. Something magical had happened. Her interest in my opinion made me feel wanted, respected, and valued. What would happen if I started to do that with some of my own people?

That was a big "aha!" moment in terms of enlisting people. Every lesson I had learned before had come from a coach, or from the experiences of handling adversity. But this was different. A coach never asked me what I thought of a play or a plan. This was new for me.

The phone company was changing, slowly but certainly. The independent Bell companies that had operated in each state were facing a massive breakup. They were also facing changes in their business model that would see them abandon the certainty of state regulation, with its guaranteed modest return on investment, for a place in the open market that would test all the old assumptions about phone company investment, even as it created abundant opportunities.

In 1984, under a consent decree reached with the U.S. Department of Justice, the Bell phone system was broken up. We went from twenty-two operating companies to five big regional companies. Indiana Bell was no longer just Indiana Bell. It was one of five companies that became Ameritech, along with Ohio, Michigan, Illinois, and Wisconsin Bell. This was an important change for me, too.

Opportunities

I had a white-collar job that exceeded any and all of my expectations. My first taste of executive management, of working out problems and squeezing bigger efficiencies from whatever I was doing, had started a fire inside of me. I wanted to move up, maybe to the president's office. It was great to understand that there was not some element missing in me that would prevent me from going to the top. The only dilemma I had was that I was a person of color in an institution that was not yet accustomed to advancing people of color to senior levels.

The Ameritech launch opened a lot of doorways. Ameritech had lots of corporate executive jobs in Chicago. Combining all those companies into one also opened the window to opportunities in Ohio, Michigan, Illinois, and Wisconsin. With the consolidation of those companies into Ameritech, I was seeing people leave Indiana Bell and go to Ameritech Services at a much higher level. Indiana Bell had maybe eight vice presidents. But the universe of vice president positions increased by a factor of ten at Ameritech, so now there were a hundred vice president spots. That made work quite exciting.

I knew that in order to snag one of those jobs, it was really important for me to continue to accept positions that were outside of my area of expertise. I took jobs in marketing. I took jobs in sales, where I had my first profit and loss responsibilities. I was always looking for new opportunities.

One of the assumptions I was working under proved to be wrong. I thought that all telephone companies were pretty much the same, at least in terms of culture. What I learned is that Indiana Bell and Ohio Bell had different cultures. And so did the other companies.

Dick Notebaert Arrives

I had an immediate impression about Dick Notebaert when he arrived as the president of Indiana Bell in 1989. He was young. He had energy. He had edge. He filled a room when he walked into it. He oozed confidence. He made you feel that nothing could go wrong that he couldn't fix.

Dick brought the top fifty of us in the company together to tell us his company vision. Then he began setting up breakfast meetings, because he wanted to meet with all of us in small groups. Dick had been around the phone company for a while. More than that, he was a "real guy," meaning about as far as anyone might want to get from the word *elite*. His college job had been washing trucks. He was born in Montreal and grew up in Columbus, Ohio, and went to the University of Wisconsin–Madison. In 1969 he moved into Wisconsin Bell's marketing department. He worked his way up. After he picked up an MBA from the University of Wisconsin, he was named vice president of marketing and began rocketing up the hierarchy. He would be moving to the very top of Ameritech within a few years, and to a successful extended career in communications after that.

Dick's reputation would be constructed around his unbreakable connection with the people who worked for him. He was comfortable talking to and helping out others, from the top of the company to the bottom. Clearly this was a boss who would appreciate an unusual approach from a subordinate. But I didn't know this at the time. What I had in mind was a little risky.

I made a calculated move at this point. When it was my time to have Donuts with Dick (that's what we called the breakfasts), I decided I wasn't going to show up. I had a good reason, I believed. I was responsible for all of the complex services organization, which basically included any business that needed anything from the telephone company. Every morning from 5:30 to 6:00, I was in my service center looking over the day's work and adjusting the workload to where I thought it needed to be (something I learned from Dan Clawson, a service center manager in Indianapolis, and Doc Miller). That wasn't my job, it was the center manager's job, but I was having trouble with him. He wasn't getting the job done the way I wanted it done.

I had a bad habit in those days. I would explain what I wanted someone to do, and if he didn't do it right, I wouldn't take the time to coach him in the work. I would just do the job myself.

That morning, the hour for my scheduled meeting with Dick Notebaert came and went. Dick's administrative assistant called me midmorning. "Mr. Notebaert wants to know what happened this morning and why you missed the breakfast. And he would like to see you in his office."

I trudged to his office. He was on the telephone and motioned for me to sit. I didn't sit. (I really don't like people telling me what to do.) Around the walls of his office were photos from the past dozen years of executive retreats. Every year, the president and the president's direct reports would go away to French Lick, Indiana, for strategy meetings. On one of the days while they were down there, they would get into their suits and ties and pose for a picture.

They were among the whitest corporate photographs I had ever seen.

I was looking at these photos on the walls of Dick's office when he completed his phone call. "Bob, Dick Notebaert," he said, extending his hand. "What happened this morning?"

"What do you mean what happened?" I replied, playing dumb.

"Well, you missed my meeting."

Then I explained to him what I do in the morning. I told him I had made the decision I was going to serve my customers, because I assign all the work to my technicians.

"I like you," he said in response. "And I even like that bullshit answer."

I sensed an opening. "Look, Dick, I'm on board. Wherever you're going, I want to be on the bus. I heard what you said when you came on board, and you need to know that I am a breakthrough leader. I don't need to be told to take the hill. I just want somebody to tell me I am on the right hill."

Dead silence.

Sensing another opening and a chance to change the subject, I asked him if he planned to keep all of those photos in his office. He said he had not thought about it. I told him I thought he should take them down right now, today.

Dead silence again.

I told him that every president who had used his office who had allowed those photos to stay up there was basically saying with a loud voice, "If you are a woman, you can work here, but you can never work *here*." I told him that he was telling every person of color, "You can work here, but you can never work *here*."

And with that, the friendly, outgoing, full-of-life energetic disposition disappeared from Dick. He became sullen. His whole facial expression changed. I could see that this was the first time he had ever been confronted on an issue like this. I had made him a part of the problem.

Then something unexpected happened again. Those pictures disappeared from his office and from all the other offices on that floor. Several days later, he asked me to come back to his office, and he did something very similar to what Judy Myers had done.

Bob Knowling, Sounding Board

"What do you think the problems are in this company?" he asked me. "If you were me, where would you focus first?"

I became one of his sounding boards. This changed my perception about my role in the company. It was no longer about how I could get ahead. It was about how I could help Indiana Bell. Nowhere in my career had I ever thought that way. And I had not seen many other people thinking that way, either. It had always been about me and my plans for getting the next thing. But watching Notebaert and thinking about how he did his job changed me. He gave me corporate consciousness, and I began to forget about my own career. I don't mean "forget" in the sense that I stopped working. I mean "forget" in the sense that my job became something bigger than simple career advancement.

Notebaert made it his business to change what happened to women and people of color at Indiana Bell. He had a rule: If you had an opening for a district manager or higher, he wanted to see your slate of candidates. And if that slate wasn't what it was supposed to be, reflecting opportunities for all kinds of good employees, he would send people back to the drawing board. None of this was coming down from Ameritech.

Michigan Bell was advanced in this area, but Ohio and Wisconsin were just as bad as Indiana in terms of the jobs profile. Some people argued that Illinois and Michigan should look different because they were pulling from a different population base. I don't think so. I think it was advocacy that led to change in these companies, and Notebaert was most certainly an advocate.

Judy Myers was a pioneer sitting in as assistant vice president of Network, and by the time Notebaert was promoted to president at Ameritech Services, our profile for minorities and women was two, perhaps three times what it was before he arrived and made his commitment. I give Judy a lot of credit for doing the right thing for people, but Notebaert took it to an entirely different level. It was a profound change for women and people of color, and it was a profound change for me, too, because I picked up my first real senior executive mentor in Dick Notebaert.

Attacking a Big Fear

I knew that I needed my public speaking skills to improve, as speaking in public had always been my greatest fear. As comfortable as I was getting close to my technicians, sharing their good and bad times and their stories, the thought of standing onstage in front of hundreds of people and trying to make a point made me shudder. Notebaert recognized this when I spoke at meetings. He told me he would help me fix this problem. Not surprisingly, my experiences in sports would come back into play as I struggled with this challenge—and believe me, it was a struggle.

In staff meetings, knowing that I would have to speak, I would feel the tension build inside me until my turn came. My voice would quiver. The words would not come out. Put me in front of twenty thousand people and give me a ball, and I was okay. But put me in a room, even a small room, and ask me to speak, and there would be big trouble.

Human resources reached out to a company called Communispond and got me a coach, who worked with me day in and day out, and I kept that coach for two years. I learned to master the challenges of public speaking and quick thinking. This was all crucial for me, because Notebaert had decided I should leave the world of technology. He was going to put me in one of the most public places of all.

"You're Running Sales Management"

He promoted me to general manager of all sales and services for Indiana Bell. He didn't sit me down to lecture me on how important it was. There was no "I'm depending on you." He just approached me in passing and said he was making some changes the next day. "You're running sales management," he said.

I had a great reputation as a performer inside the phone company, but there was more than a little resentment when this big job went to the black guy from Network. I was an outsider, so I got snubbed. People didn't return my phone calls.

I couldn't let the negative stuff get in my way, though. I had to learn how to talk and I had to learn how to sell. The first thing I had to do was get over the fear of public speaking. Every session I had with Communispond was on video. One valuable thing I learned from those videos reached straight back into sports. The question was simple: Whom did I see when I walked onto the playing field of an arena holding twenty thousand people? I told them I didn't see anybody. "The game was what was important, not the crowd," I told them. And they told me, "That's still the case. It's the game that is important, not the crowd." Then they taught me a simple method that fixed a lot of the problem. Pick a spot, left, right, and center, no matter how big the crowd. All you have to talk to in that crowd are three sets of eyes, no more. They drilled that into me.

We would be practicing an investor pitch and when I had to stop, they would say, "What are your three spots?" And I would say, "Darn." At first it was kind of easy. Pick out colors, left, right, and center. I still do that. Over time, it worked. And it worked well. Ten, a hundred, twenty thousand—I can talk to whatever size group I have to speak to and that fear is gone.

Sales was a different matter.

Not So Awful Joe

By now you know the pattern I followed in my previous jobs: go out, observe the work, meet the people, bond, learn everything you need to know, and use it in your job every day. I had planned to do it the same way in sales. But my approach changed due to a man I despised so deeply that I wanted to fire him immediately. His name was Joe Devich and he would become one of the most important people in my career.

But not in the beginning. In the beginning, I wanted to whack him.

Joe was one of those obnoxious, perfect guys with the good looks of a young Steven Seagal (complete with the ponytail, which I despised). He was arrogant as hell, and he was a terrible athlete. That's how I first knew him, from my Network basketball team days, where we regularly kicked the stuffing out of everyone. I also ran into him at the company softball games, he played on the marketing team, which was a very good team. But they would hide him at third base. Despite his mediocre playing skills, he would come out on the field wearing all the gear and looking like an ad campaign for Nike or Reebok. In basketball, he was just as terrible, and I went out of my way at every opportunity to score on him or to block his shot, because I despised him so much.

When Notebaert promoted me to head all of sales, Joe reported to me. On my second day on the job, I called him in to meet and told him he would be gone in thirty days.

After I gave Joe his notice, he started to walk out of my office. Then he turned around and said, "But you haven't given me a chance."

I told him I didn't give chances to guys like him. "I have seen your actions. You are a despicable person," I said.

"You're probably right, but don't you believe people can change? What if I show you in thirty days I can be a different Joe Devich?"

"Well, sure," I said. "But Joe, you have to understand something. I'm not the brightest bulb on the string, but you aren't going to be able to bullshit me. You are a bad guy, and I really don't want bad guys in my organization. You don't care about people. You step on people. You grandstand. It's all about you. My job is to make our company success- ful. We are basically on the front line of every dollar of revenue that comes into this business, and I need people who are winners. People who are team players. I don't need grandstanders."

Joe walked out of my office.

The Conversion of Joe

Well, Joe transformed himself, and every time I changed companies, he came along.

I believe that, until me, nobody had ever been so brutally honest with Joe. Within days of my giving him that talking-to, a couple of people came to me and said, "I don't know what you did, but this guy is not afraid to change; he's seeking help on what he needs to do. He wanted to know what he was doing that was wrong and how could he change."

That was the first sign. The second was his behavior. Suddenly I saw a helpful Joe Devich. I saw a Joe Devich who wasn't all about taking credit. I saw him stand down from assignments that he used to use for showboating. Once, he sent me with one of his account executives to visit Bank One instead of going himself, which the old Joe Devich would never have done.

Thirty days passed and there was no doubt in my mind that Joe was on my team. We became inseparable. When I didn't know something, he and I would go to a whiteboard and he would explain it all to me. Joe knew our products and services better than anyone *and* he had a deep knowledge about our technology

I had had him pegged as superficial, but he understood everything about what we did, how we delivered it, and what the right solutions would be for our customers. In a way, Joe had been on his own journey to know his craft, to be the smartest guy in the room. He was good at it, really good.

He fundamentally changed. It's a rare thing.

But he still sucks at sports.

Learning Sales

In the beginning of my time in sales, I was very weak on knowing exactly what products Indiana Bell had to sell, particularly to its business clients. I wasn't clear on whether we should be selling a client a PBX (Private Branch Exchange) system or a Centrex, but Joe was. So with him as my resident expert, I had to start my learning journey again.

I learned the same way I had learned the technology side of things: I watched my sales teams at work and I had Joe as my sounding board. The sales personnel had the knowledge and they had the connections, so you had to let them lead in the discussions with customers. There would come a point in the conversation when an executive might want to chime in, but I knew to be careful about timing my comments. In fact, my guys loved that I didn't go into a room with a customer and hog the conversation.

I worried about how clients were going to view us as an entity with a black sales executive, and I knew there would be some resistance on the part of my sales teams, but the telephone company was about as good as the U.S. Army at handling that kind of thing. They didn't have to like me as their drill sergeant, but the stripes on my arm gave me the authority I needed to guarantee my employees would follow my orders. It was not about me in particular. It was about telephone company culture, in which you respected the person in the position above you. You didn't have to respect the person, but you did have to pay attention and give respect to that position. Insubordination was never tolerated. Hierarchy was the order of the day. I think that is part of the history of any organization that depends so heavily on technology. You need discipline to make certain things work properly. If you are in charge, then people respect the position regardless of how you got there.

I was surprised and somewhat disturbed by what I learned about the sales side of the phone company as I moved through the same process I'd used in all my other jobs, learning from my visits to the field. I learned that it was a toxic environment. It was an environment and an organization that had huge integrity problems. It seemed to be almost above the law in terms of the way it operated.

It spent way too much money entertaining people at golf events and dinners. It made promises to customers it could not keep. Its people simply avoided meetings or showed up late. It was full of bad attitudes and acted like that was some kind of badge of honor. And I had a sense that women were exploited.

Sales was a different kind of environment from the technical side of the company. On the technical side, there were very few people with college degrees, and anyone who had one was likely to have gotten it in engineering. In sales, however, almost everyone had at least an undergraduate degree or a master's in business administration.

I think I was biased from the moment I moved into the sales structure. I didn't like what I saw and I wanted to reform it.

I feel good about what I did. I was one of the first executives in that part of the company who came in and started pruning. I also knew I had to model the right behavior. And I knew that establishing a set of values for the organization would be critical. I wanted people to know how they would be evaluated, how they would be paid, and I wanted them to know the consequences for poor performance and nonadherence to the company's values. I used the same kind of standards in recruiting people.

I didn't address individual cases in this process of setting the standards for the organization. In those few cases of exploitation or harassment, I used the human resources people to resolve matters after an investigation. If someone was guilty of bad behavior, they had to go home. You set expectations and make them clear; you model good behavior; and you send a message of zero tolerance.

I didn't remove anyone from the business based on speculations about their behavior. I removed people from the business based on their performance. Performance is the catalyst for everything.

The Recruiters Call

When you have never been outside your work environment (remember, Indiana Bell was my first and only job after college), you don't really know how you would perform someplace else. You simply have no benchmark. So I was flattered when I began to get attention from executive recruiters.

I went out and interviewed a couple of times. That was a little frightening. With all the confidence I now had, I was surprised when those little shadows of doubt appeared, and I began to question whether I could actually do the work, even with all the successes I had piled up.

So I took measure of what I had achieved.

I had very few enemies or detractors inside of Indiana Bell. Even though I'd straightened out a couple of its organizations—sales in particular—and had had to take some tough stands, my reputation at this point was that people still wanted to join my team. Black colleagues viewed me as a pioneer because I had reached a level that a person of color had never achieved at Indiana Bell, and it appeared that I was headed even higher. And employees in general knew that I appreciated stellar performance and that I took people with me when I got promoted. I was not afraid to create real opportunities. This was happening when most managers in a position to hire people of color were just hunkering down and promoting people who were not going to push for change. To this day, that's a problem. I've talked with a lot of CEOs who lament that they can't find anyone of color to advance. I take them to task when I hear that. I tell them they must not be serious, then, about finding those people.

The problem is that people of color haven't been given access. The noise about lack of experience and qualification is old thinking these days. Having said that, I believe people have to make their own breaks, especially women and people of color. I would not be sitting where I am today if I had not been willing to take some risks. Waiting for the hierarchy to come and knock on your door—well, that's not going to happen.

Still, there is a sliver of the black population who say they aren't waiting for anyone, that they are going to get ahead and create their own opportunities. I guarantee you that makes the difference.

One aspect of this has nothing to do with gender or color. It's something in the DNA that says, "I am charting a course. I am taking a hill." It may sound arrogant, but these are people who know what they want and who go out and make their own breaks and their opportunities. Many don't reach their goal, but they persist in going for the gold medal, and that is the difference.

It's all about seizing the opportunity. Above everything else, performance is what will decide whether you succeed. At the same time, you're not always going to get the reward you deserve (or maybe the punishment, either). At some point, you will have to decide whether your company is ever going to do what it is supposed to do for you if you have consistently delivered a stellar performance. And if it is not, you can't be afraid to leave.

It's also interesting how after you have had various experiences and great results, you will reach a point where you have a moment of clarity about yourself and your ability. You will realize there is not much for you to master. That happened for me after two years in the sales job. I knew then that I could run anything. From the crotchety old plant and Network departments to marketing and sales and all the other jobs in between—there was nothing I couldn't handle at Indiana Bell.

All the recruiting calls I received at this time were from other Bell systems. Word was out about me, I suspect, because of the role I had played in deploying AT&T's new operating system into the network organizations across the country.

AT&T, which owned all twenty-two Bell Operating Companies, had made a significant investment and spent years developing a new operating system for installation and repair operations called the Loop Maintenance Operating System. It was a huge project that changed how we managed installation and repair work for customers. With it, we went from a paper system to a mechanized system, and Indiana Bell was where the new system was pilot-tested. Along with three other people, I was selected to go to Basking Ridge, New Jersey, the AT&T headquarters, to work out the bugs in the system and to install it nationally. The three other people selected came from Bell South, Southwestern Bell, and Southern New England Bell. I became very good friends with the guy from Bell South (Wayne Smith) and the woman from Southwestern Bell (Shelly Forbis).

The assignment was a great opportunity for me. I got to meet very senior people from all over the country. I got to pick my own team. Best of all, I got to select where we would implement the system first. I chose Sacramento, California, where my mother lived. That way I could see her every day. We got the system up and operating, and through that work, I developed a pretty good reputation as a smart guy who really understood this new application.

In 1986, Pacific Bell had a division-level Network job it was trying to fill. I decided to take a look at it. They made an offer, and I met with Dave Orr, the vice president of human resources at Indiana Bell, to discuss the Pacific Bell opportunity. He told me I was a known quantity at Indiana Bell and that I was on my way, that I would do great things in the business. He knew I wanted to be near my mother in California, and this job with Pacific Bell would put me within eighty miles of her. He asked me about the potential I would have at Pacific Bell. He asked if I had considered how I would be able to navigate to the assistant vice president and vice president levels at that much bigger company.

I hadn't thought about that.

He said a move to the corner suite right there in Indiana was highly possible with all that I had done at Indiana Bell. With the resources I would have as a senior officer in the business, I could afford to go see my mother anytime I wanted.

In that instant, I made another one of those decisions that would change the course of my career. I turned down the Pac Bell offer, even though it would have doubled my salary and put me way up in the executive ranks at only twenty-nine years old.

I decided to trust my instincts and trust my bosses and mentors.

This would lead me, within a very short period of time, to the very heart of a business that was in deep trouble and needed to change.

Ameritech was not ready to play in the big leagues of the real telecommunications marketplace. We didn't understand competition and we surely didn't have a sense of urgency about anything. A transformation was needed, but there wasn't anybody breaking any glass in Chicago.

I didn't know that Ameritech chairman Bill Weiss was not happy about the company's state of affairs. We were about to undertake a massive transformation that Bill had crafted. Not many people saw this tsunami coming.

I was still in Indiana, but the Ameritech transformation was right around the corner.

I didn't know it at the time, but I, too, would be transformed in the process. I would go into the process a hardworking, honest executive with a drive to succeed, and would come out a different man. People throw around the phrase "change agent" as though it applies to everyone. It does not. You learn this the day you realize that what you have to change the most is yourself.

CHAPTER FIVE

Transformed

C hairman Bill Weiss knew Ameritech was headed for a very rough-and-tumble world where competition would decide who thrived, who survived, and who disappeared. Deregulation did that to everything it touched. It's easy to forget today that the government was once deeply involved in setting rates for everything, from electricity to telephone services to airline tickets. Under state laws, public utilities had an authorized rate of return for phone companies. Remember Lily Tomlin's phone company operator and her message to callers? "We're the phone company. We don't have to care."

That wasn't much of a stretch. For consumers, there was no one else to turn to in the market.

Weiss was prescient in recognizing that deregulation would place Ameritech in jeopardy. The phone company wasn't the first business to face those kinds of challenges. And the changes stretched beyond questions about the impact of deregulation. Market leaders in almost every field were finding their status threatened as economic and political change swept through the business world. Businesses that had seemed "safe" now found themselves facing severe challenges.

When Weiss picked up the phone to make a call to the University of Michigan to look for help in rebuilding Ameritech, he reached out to a man who was redefining the ways companies approached the challenges of leadership and change. University of Michigan professor Dr. Noel Tichy had published hundreds of articles and about a dozen books on management, strategy, and transformation. He was at the heart of change management at General Electric under Jack Welch and had even taken a sabbatical from the university to run GE's in-house management training program in the Crotonville neighborhood of Ossining, New York, a legendary address in the directory of corporate America.

"I need to reinvent Ameritech," Weiss told Tichy. They met. Noting that Weiss was sixty-two, Tichy said Weiss's primary job should be succession planning. He could use action learning, one of the processes offered by Tichy's consulting company, to attack the challenge of change at Ameritech, but picking his successor must be a primary part of the job.

All of this was happening far from the Indiana Bell world of Bob Knowling.

Life was going well for me. That bridge I'd started building in small-town Kokomo, Indiana, had carried me into a successful and comfortable life by the time I was in my early thirties. I was head of sales management, the target of an array of job offers from many other parts of the telephone system, and increasingly comfortable with the success I had created in my career and my personal life.

The Road to Damascus

What I didn't know then was that I was on the road to Damascus, just like Saul in the Bible, and that my life would be forever changed. It was a bolt of lightning that changed his name and direction. It was Breakthrough Leadership that changed mine.

One morning, Dick Brown, the president of Illinois Bell, called and told me I was to be one of 120 people who were to report to the Arthur Andersen Center at St. Charles, outside of Chicago, on Friday night. This was big. Phone company executives never worked on weekends, and beyond that, it was college basketball Final Four time. The University of Michigan and Indiana University were in the Final Four. Asking people to give that up was asking a lot.

The invitations to the meeting set off grumbling all across the five states that were part of the Ameritech system. People in the various companies started speculating on what was happening. We were told to plan for four days of meetings that would start at 7:00 AM and end at

9:00 PM, Saturday through Tuesday. I had the sense that attendance was not optional. I had no idea when I packed my bags that I was stepping into a process that would push me to my limits; leave me angry, confused, and strongly opposed to what was going on; and then . . .

Well, that's for later.

A Broken Company

On Saturday morning in Chicago, Bill Weiss told us that Ameritech was severely broken. This was surprising to hear about a company that was experiencing record earnings. But according to Bill, we had to reinvent ourselves. We were not ready for competition. We had a leadership void in our own business. Weiss called the Chicago initiative Breakthrough Leadership.

Numerous levels of phone company management were represented at the meeting, everyone from vice chairman down to district managers. Imagine how that felt! It was the first time in history that people of such diverse job descriptions and levels in our company had ever even been in the same room together.

It wouldn't be just this one four-day meeting in Chicago, either. Over time, Breakthrough Leadership meetings would consume the company, all aimed at making certain we were focused on our goals of transforming the company and making progress. Deregulation wasn't going to wait for us to catch up, and neither was the Breakthrough Leadership effort.

Bill had been working with his senior staff and Tichy for months on what needed to be done and who would be a part of the effort to find the answers. At that first meeting, Bill divided the group into four teams of thirty members each. Each team included two executives who were not part of the 120 and who would serve as team leaders. They would be the "sponsors" of the teams. But Weiss didn't pick his direct reports for those team leader positions. He reached down a level. Over time, I came to understand what that meant: Weiss was not confident he had a successor among his direct reports. Part of Tichy's succession proposal was playing out right in front of us.

Dick Notebaert was one of the eight selected as sponsors—four of them leads and four assistants. It was a platinum collection of businesspeople. Dick Notebaert would go on to succeed Weiss as CEO of Ameritech. Dick Brown, also a lead sponsor, eventually went on to CEO roles at H&R Block, Cable&Wireless, and EDS. Gary Drook, a lead sponsor from Indiana Bell, later became CEO of Northwestern Energy. Barry Allen, a lead sponsor, was a former Indiana Bell guy who later became CEO at Wisconsin Power & Gas and then went to Qwest with Notebaert many years later. John Edwardson, chosen as an assistant lead sponsor, went on to become CEO at United Airlines and CDW.

I suppose a lot of the people at the meeting expected some kind of training, but that wasn't what happened. Weiss introduced us to Tichy, Patricia Stacey, and David Dotlich, all from Tichy's Action Learning Associates. Then we went through a close examination of the company's profit and loss statements and discussed what was wrong with the numbers we were reviewing. That stripped the mystery out of the questions about how we were doing.

After that, each of the four teams was given a charge.

One team was tasked with figuring out how we should be organized to face the market.

A second team addressed Ameritech's human resources policies under the assumption that they, too, were broken, and discussed how we would manage and develop talent.

The third team, the one I was assigned to, had to figure out how we would achieve earnings freedom and get us off the rate base rate-of-return formula.

The fourth team addressed the newly created Ameritech Network Corporation, and how we would unbundle the elements to open them to competition, which was the quid pro quo for earnings freedom.

In each case, people were assigned to teams that were outside of their core expertise. The Breakthrough launch that Tichy designed took four days, and each team of thirty was broken into five smaller teams. Leaders were then selected for each smaller team.

And we were off to the races.

Keep in mind that while this leadership process was playing out, we all had to continue with our regular day jobs. Somebody still had to run the phone company that *was*, even as we were searching for a definition of the phone company that would be.

We worked our tails off.

We had to have measurable, quantifiable objectives and a project road map. Almost every day, the consultants were looking for status reports. We were being measured and watched all the time.

It would not take long for the teams to understand that there would be consequences for those teams and individuals who failed.

Bloodletting

Before the start of the second workshop, which was about forty-five days after the first session in St. Charles, something traumatic happened that had never happened in our company. Three senior executives were sent home, fired. Some of the 120 invited to be a part of the Breakthrough Leadership process were also sent home. For the first time in history, we were not told that they'd left to spend more time with their families or pursue other interests.

"They were not Breakthrough Leaders," Weiss said. "They could not make the change."

These firings got everyone's attention. Vice-chairmen-level people and the president of Michigan Bell had been sent home!

I was thinking, "Boy, they are really serious. We're not in Kansas anymore!"

The first night of that second round of meetings was a golden Tichy moment in our company's transformation. He told us that we didn't give each other honest feedback, we lied about performance, and we shuffled underperformers off to work in human resources or procurement when we should have been firing them. Weiss reinforced Tichy's message and told us that those days were over and that we were going to be honest about personal performance. With this as the frame, Tichy told us that we were going to do a team assessment exercise in which we would evaluate our five teammates. There were about five to seven categories, and we had to rank each other, from first to fifth, and explain why we'd ranked people the way we had. This exercise required us to give explicit feedback to our teammates, to explain why we'd rated someone last at helping others, for example. We also had to state why we'd ranked someone first in a category.

I didn't think much about the process until I got the forms. It contained some very hard-hitting instructions. Among them:

1. Please evaluate your peers on the contribution and quality of their ideas to the team's work.
2. Please rate your peers on the level of help and assistance they give others on the team.

We were all going to be sharing this feedback. Because some of the 120 had already been sent home, I knew I could be in trouble. I knew my problem: Show me the goal line, and I'm going to get there. If you can't help me, I'm going to do it myself. That worked well for me in the old phone company. But it had no place in the company that we were creating. I knew that. I felt that.

It put me in a very bad mood.

That night in the hotel bar, I got Dick Brown, Notebaert, Drook, and Edwardson together, and in ten minutes I persuaded them that this feedback process was the worst thing that anyone had ever done in our company. At the end of the day, I said, you are the leaders, but I don't think this is what you want. Why would you artificially insert dysfunction into this process when all of us are still slaying dragons in our day jobs, notwithstanding the fact we are reinventing the company? We already know this is serious. Many people have been fired.

Notebaert said to me, "You're making some very good points."

I went to bed happy.

Word came early the next morning: Notebaert was looking for me. When I found him, he said, "Hey, we need to be open to this process and I want you to go into this session with an open mind. The difference between you and me, Bob, is I'm willing to open a book even if I don't like the cover. We're going to do this exercise this morning and I'm going to ask you to give it a shot. If at the end of this we don't like it, we're not going to do it anymore."

I told him okay.

Years later, I learned the context. Dick had approached Tichy and told him we were not going to do it and that the other team sponsors had agreed with him.

"As far as I know, Bill is expecting us to do this in the morning," Tichy told Dick. "He'll be here. And it will take Bill Weiss telling me we're not going to do it. I would encourage you to have this conversation with him."

I learned from Tichy later that it was even more complicated than that.

When Bill appointed the four team leaders, he told them they were all contenders for his job. He told them they would be playing together and going through everything the 120 were going through. He also told them that if he saw anyone not playing well with others, that person would be out.

When we went into the session that morning, we were given envelopes that had everything in them: all the scores, the rankings, and lots of individual comments. We were told to go find a private place (Arthur Andersen at St. Charles is huge) or go take a walk and read our feedback. Alone.

They told us to think of the name SARAH to help us understand what would be happening. Some of us would be Shocked at what we found in the envelope. That would lead to Anger. Then there would be Rejection. Then a few of us would get to Acceptance and those who did would find Hope.

I Am the Problem

There were some gut punches in my feedback that I had anticipated, but there were categories where I received the top scores of one. The explicit comments from my colleagues were stingers, though. My Lone Ranger behavior was called out by just about everyone on the team, and there were even some surprise negative comments that I hadn't anticipated. I experienced a big growth spurt when I read those responses in the privacy of my hotel room. I was having another "aha" moment.

I recognized that I was the problem. And I resolved to fix it.

After we had had a chance to review all that feedback, we gathered for another meeting. Weiss asked if we had any questions before we moved on. There was a long silence. Bill looked out over the gathering as if anticipating a response.

"Bill, I have something to say," I said. I had recently had knee surgery, so I had to use my crutches to stand up. "I now understand what Bill is trying to do to create a new company. I was afraid of this process. I didn't sleep much last night because I was afraid of getting negative feedback. I was afraid to have my faults pointed out. And I just want to let everybody in this room know that the guy that was afraid and the guy that was fighting this process is the kind of guy we're trying to get rid of in this company, because we don't need people like that. We need people who can accept feedback. We need people who are willing to grow. We need people who can be courageous leaders."

"I now know what you are looking for and I think I can be that, and I want you to know that I'm signing up today to be a Breakthrough Leader."

To this day I don't know why I decided to stand up and say that. There was no time set aside at the phone company for public confession. You did everything you could not to be exposed. You could not raise your hand in our company and say, "I need help." You could not say, "I don't know."

It was perhaps the first time in my career when I had no control over what I was going to do. People I did not know were making decisions about my work, looking at my personality, my aggressiveness. The process was frightening for me.

Before that instant, I had had control of everything in my career. I had received my assignments and nailed every job I'd done. Eventually, my employers in Indiana had to deal with my level of performance. But now I was in an ambiguous position. I didn't know why I had been picked for it. I didn't know how I had been picked. And I had watched as some people who had been invited were fired.

To be sure, we didn't know exactly what Breakthrough Leaders were at that point. We were made to reach conclusions about that ourselves. In retrospect, I think Ameritech was looking for people who epitomized team play, fresh ideas, the embracing of new concepts, a willingness to change, and a willingness to challenge each other in healthy ways.

What happened to me in this process was something like Saul's Road to Damascus experience. I needed to cleanse myself.

During a break, Weiss came up to me and said, "Well done, son," and he hugged me. No one had ever done that before.

None of them realized my state of mind when I stood up to speak. I believed I had already achieved more at the phone company than I had ever thought humanly possible. I was in rarefied air just putting a tie on in the morning. But that moment when I stood up at that meeting, if you had told me I would be out of Ameritech within two days, it would not have mattered. I knew that I was a Breakthrough Leader. I knew that I had had another growth spurt, that I would never again be afraid of feedback, afraid of hearing about my weaknesses.

Sometimes someone has to stand up to change the outcome.

Our Own Crotonville

I knew I was going to get a new job, but I didn't know what it would be. My track record was not just sterling, it was platinum. I had mastered the intricacies of the field, learned the network inside and out, and cleaned up sales like the sheriff cleaned up Dodge. If you asked me to write a list of what job I might get next, running a school would not have been on that list.

But that was what I was about to do. I was going to something that didn't exist yet: the Ameritech Institute. It was Bill Weiss's idea about how we would continue the process of Breakthrough Leadership. It would be where we worked out all of the strategies and processes we would need to make the transformation successful. Each new hire would start out there. Instead of sending our future executives off to Northwestern or some executive management development program, we were going to create our own GE Crotonville facility.

The idea was great, but I was not happy! Making me take the job of running such an institute was like telling Michael Jordan he could pick the players on the Chicago Bulls and design every play, but he couldn't take one step onto the court. The institute was going to be at the heart of what happened at Ameritech, but I didn't care about that. It would be the development arm and the group that would be advising and consulting with the eleven business units and the chairman. I didn't care about that, either. It would be the institution the chairman used to ensure that he had the right kind of culture driving an era of quantum change at Ameritech. That's a very important assignment, but I couldn't see that at the time.

I had two tough weeks. Would I take this assignment, becoming in essence one of three leaders assigned to this little business university, or would I leave Ameritech? The mental process in making this decision was excruciating. Wasn't I good enough to run one of the eleven business units?

Topping all of that, Notebaert became the heir apparent as chairman at Ameritech. A man I viewed as a mentor was going to run the company, so why was I going to be plugged into running a kindergarten for new employees? Why would they do this to me?

Notebaert gave tremendous weight to Tichy's role in the process. The members of the Ameritech Institute team were going to report to Notebaert but be developed by Tichy. This meant I would be reporting to a consultant who had never managed anything in his whole life.

I had never been so unhappy about my situation in my career. I simply could not decide what to do.

That's how the Breakthrough experience ended for me: with my being named as a member of a trio, with Dennis Carr and Judy Raica, assigned to set up what I viewed as a gussied-up training center.

It turned out to be a much better position than I first realized. The structure—with three people at the top—was wrong for many reasons, a primary one being that one of the people on the team was not suited for the job. Dennis Carr was a terrific person and an authentic guy, but this was not the right role for him. Judy Raica, the third team member, was courageous, and everyone knew how aggressive I had been.

Head the Institute

And it happened. Dennis was moved over to be chief financial officer of one of the units, and I was put in charge of the institute.

Most of the early days in the institute were training for us by Tichy's team. Grueling sessions were the norm. Long days of introspection, learning how to diagnose an organization, receiving feedback, and planning the work that needed to be done in the business. Tichy and his associate Patti monitored everything we did, and we were not allowed to fly solo on the work until they felt we could facilitate in a workshop or provide coaching to an executive.

The institute became the internal consulting arm of Ameritech. I divided up the eleven business unit presidents and we split the clients up for my direct report team. My clients were Notebaert and Bob Hurst, head of Ameritech Network and the only African American on the executive staff. I also consulted with Karen Vessely, who had the pay phone business, and Jim Firestone, who headed the consumer unit.

Being in this key consulting role put me in a better position to address one of the problems I had been working on: the poor representation of women and people of color in Ameritech's executive ranks. By that time, I had expanded the Indiana Black Managers' Association into the five-state Ameritech Black Managers' Organization. I had also helped form the women's and Hispanic organizations, by providing a blueprint for how advocacy groups should be organized and work. I was the president of the Ameritech Black Managers' Association and interfaced with Martha Thornton, the head of HR for Ameritech Corporate, who reported to Bill Weiss.

I told everyone the same thing: advocacy is about having meaningful dialogue around data and the response to data, because all we can control is the response. In one of my first meetings with Martha, I told her that there were only three things I was concerned about: pay, profile, and promotion. I suggested we put the data on the table and look at the profile that was created. Then we had to look at the pay attached to those positions. Typically what we found was that when someone had finally done the right thing and given someone an opportunity, the pay was still disproportionate. These employees had reached an advanced level, but their pay didn't advance much with them.

This issue had been playing out before I became head of the Ameritech Institute, and it was one of the most important items on my agenda. I had always worked to advance the cause of diversity at Indiana Bell, and now I was soon going to be in a position where I could be more aggressive about that at Ameritech.

One thing that Martha and I agreed on was the need for diversity training, because the company's level of awareness about the problem was poor. She asked me to look around for good diversity consultants. I settled on a group called J. Howard and Associates, to come in and take some of us through what it would call its first "step diversity" program.

It took three days to complete the program, which was held in Oak Brook, Illinois.

On the first day of the training, I walked into a room along with some thirty other black executives from all five states. I was the lone representative from Indiana Bell. We were asked to state our names, what our jobs were, and what we wanted to get from diversity training. We were there to assess the diversity process and then report back to Human Resources.

"I'm Bob Knowling," I said. "I'm general manager of markets for Indiana Bell and I'm not sure what I want out of this program; I just know I am going to be president of the company one day." When I said that, an African American guy sitting across the room sat straight up. The room was in stunned silence.

When we had a break, the guy came over to me and said, "I've been around a long time and I've never heard anybody be so bold. Let me make sure I got you correct. You're going to be president?"

I said, "Yeah."

"I'll be damned," he said, and walked away from me.

His name was Tommie Welch. He was the division manager of Network for Illinois. That was probably one of the biggest jobs in Illinois Bell, with maybe ten thousand people reporting to him.

Martha wanted to make the diversity program a permanent part of our company, but I have to report that it did little to calm the anger among that first collection of African American executives who attended the training session. Tom was an angry guy. You could tell he had a chip on his shoulder. When somebody in the class said something stupid, he would react. There was a lot of anger in that room. This probably isn't fair, but it wasn't so much a diversity seminar as a gripe session and a pressure-release valve for a lot of frustrated, angry people. Remember, black people could go only so far at the phone company, weren't paid at the same level as their white counterparts, and were expected to be happy about that.

A woman from Michigan looms large in my memory. She got my full attention when she used the word *motherfucker* in describing someone at Michigan Bell. I had never heard a woman use a word like that in a business setting. Her name was Theresa and she was the division manager of all the operators in Michigan; she was intimidating. I was told that she was a stellar performer and that she didn't take crap from anyone. She was one of the most aggressive women I had ever encountered, and you could tell that she had very little patience.

As the session carried forward, the discontent in the room became louder and louder. Remember, this was supposed to be diversity training; we were supposed to be learning how to perform in the competitive environment within a corporation. Instead there was this huge bloodletting going on. It was a profound moment for me, because I had none of that anger, none of those feelings about the people I worked with. I finally understood why the people in the room had reacted the way they had when I said I wanted to be president.

I realized that I was out of touch with a lot of important stuff.

Find a Mentor

I decided I needed to get closer to Tommie for two reasons. The first was obvious: to understand all that anger. The second was practical: I am certain there were dozens of lessons he had experienced that would help me avoid the pitfalls.

Plus, I really liked him.

To this day, he is one of my best friends.

In the beginning, however, I just wanted to get close to him. I talked to him at every break. At group dinners I always found a seat next to him. When a game of bid whist started (it's a little like bridge), I made sure he was my partner. Many of us would get up at 5:00 AM to go play a round of golf, because there was a nice golf course there at the facility. Tom liked golf, and I made sure I played with him. When we got ready to leave the session, he told me he was part of a group that went to Callaway Gardens at Pine Mountain, Georgia, each year. He invited me to go along. I told him I would drive up from Indiana to his home in Chicago and we would go together. We were roommates during that first trip. While we were on the plane to Georgia, I asked him a tough question: "Will you teach me how to get to where I'm going?"

At that instant, his anger seemed to melt. The veil came down and he said yes. He told me about the anger. He told me about the game. He told me about the pitfalls. He told me about how we African Americans were viewed. You can never get comfortable, he said, because at the end of the day, I don't care what you do in this business, it's always going to come back not just to your performance. A day will never go by that the phone company doesn't also remember you are black.

Tommie told me he would be coaching me on some things I would not like. "This tendency you have to bring a lot of minorities and women with you, you have to temper that," he said. "Until you get where you are going, that cannot be your fatal flaw."

The objective is to get the corner suite, he said, because once you are there, it's just you and the board of directors, and you can do what you think you need to do in terms of bringing others along.

From his perspective, he had figured the game out. He just couldn't execute it or, as I found out later, he didn't want to. If you talk to Tommie, to this day he will tell you he didn't get to the top because he was too angry. He went to division manager in just six years, and that was unheard of. He retired early. He said the work just wasn't healthy for him because of all the anger and the politics.

By the time I got to the phone company, I had already decided to leave anger behind. Maybe I left it back at Peach Orchard Elementary where Mr. Stewart beat me so severely. Or maybe I left it in the blacksmith yard where I listened to my grandfather's stories of strife, lynchings, and abuse. Things just rolled off me. I never got angry.

Not Tommie. His anger was deep. A lot of the anger in the room that first day of diversity training was deep, too. Many of them had seen so much injustice in their careers.

A picture developed in my mind of what the successful black executive would look like at those bigger Bell companies of Michigan and Illinois Bell. Some of them had come to speak to the diversity group and I was embarrassed at how weak most of them were.

There were a couple of exceptions: For example, Mike Tatom, Tommie's boss, was the assistant vice president of the Network organization. (We would become good friends and would work together later at another company.) It was refreshing to see him in that senior job, a "technical" executive position. The other exception was Don Goens, a finance executive out of corporate. He and my wife had gone to college together. Don is one of the smartest people I have ever met. He ended up going on to be president of the pay phone unit.

Everybody else was far below the bar, however. It was almost shameful to see these black executives parade into our diversity session given how intimidated they were just talking to us. Their presence seemed to draw out all the anger in the room.

I found a great mentor in Tommie. To this day, I wonder what my life would have been like if he had not helped me. I think it was divine intervention.

What Tommie had to say to me was revealing. He told me that he wished he had known someone like me earlier in his career, back when he still cared. "I can't get to the top. I don't want to get to the top, but it could be fun helping you get there," he said. I asked him why he couldn't get there. Clearly, he was very intelligent, knew how to deliver results, and was a strong leader.

"Too many scars," he said.

He had been passed over. He did a brilliant job but was disproportionately paid. He had to fight for his ratings in his appraisal sessions.

Attitudes like Tommie's had been building—with justification, in most cases—for many years. Something like that doesn't change right away. The advocacy group we created helped to improve the numbers and the pay. Notebaert's arrival in the CEO's job helped change everything, too, because he was committed and he made diversity a requirement. He held every officer accountable for the results and the profile. But a lot of the people in that diversity session ended up retiring and carrying their anger with them. The new group that arrived over time came in with a different attitude. Things were changing, after all.

Choosing to Get Above It

I understood their anger, because they had something to be angry about. I just chose to react to it in a different way. It's almost like the expression "You choose success." I chose to get above it. Still, I had every right and every reason to be angry about things, too. For years, I had watched people with no experience being promoted ahead of me. I knew about the unfairness in salaries. It was a variant of what I had run into at

Age six months

My second-grade school photograph

Playing against archrival Kokomo High, making the perfect jump shot in the first and only game that my dad got to see me play

My mother, Geneva Reynolds, at age eighteen

Playing basketball for Wabash College versus Southern Colorado State College, 1975

With Estel Cook, on the steps of Chadwick Court at Wabash College

My graduation from Wabash College, 1977

In the Indiana Bell technical training center, 1977

Working in the Indiana Bell business office, 1986

At a J. Howard & Associates session with Marc Wallace *(right)* and John Porter *(center)*

Joking with Sue Parks
in Tokyo, 1997

At the President's Club in Hawaii with Kim Sharp *(center)* and Tommie Welch *(right)*, 1999

With daughter Audrey *(left)* and son Robert Jason *(right)*, Sarasota Beach, Florida, 1988

With the Reverend Jesse Jackson *(right)* at the Martin Luther King, Jr., Celebration week at Havens Auditorium in Kokomo, Indiana, 2000

Meeting with then president Bill Clinton at the White House, 1999

Knowling Fieldhouse
at Wabash College

The ribbon-cutting ceremony for Knowling Fieldhouse at Wabash College; *left to right*, my wife, Angela; my daughter Aimi; my son, Robert Jason; Wabash president Andy Ford; my daughter Jennifer; and my daughter Audrey, 2001

Wabash, when the fraternity brothers reacted with boos to the announce-
ment of my name in the starting lineup. It had been a conscious decision
then to ignore them, and it was a conscious decision now at the phone
company to rise above it. I could not allow myself to wallow in my own
self-pity.

My mother's advice comes to me. When you spill a glass of milk, you
have two options: cry over it or clean it up and move on. You have to
move on with things or you will be miserable, inhibited, and constrained. No, I refused to build barricades on my bridge.

And I knew where I was going.

Transforming Ameritech

I had a great relationship with Dick Notebaert.

My job was to push the envelope, to break some glass. But my job
also was to serve as a coach to him, as unusual as that sounds. Clearly
Dick had more experience, more insight, and more acumen than I did,
but I could coach him by providing him with insight on how he'd come
off in a meeting, the way he'd handled a given situation, or how he'd
performed in a debate with a group of new hires.

I remember the day he called me in and said, "You must not be doing
your job. Nobody's asked that you be fired this week." Then he laughed.

I enjoyed my conversations with him about pushing the organization. That was the nature of my work. I was to become the catalyst for
making the executives at Ameritech the best leaders on the planet. That
meant I had to understand their leadership inventories, their strengths,
their weaknesses, and help them become better leaders.

Over time my reputation took some hits. When you are reporting on
how other people are performing, you are automatically suspect in terms
of what you might be telling the boss (Notebaert). I would work hard to
convince people that I was not reporting everything about them, but it
takes an extremely confident person to trust you in such a situation.

Still, it was a great job. I got to sit above the fray. It gave me a platform
to advance my own agenda.

As with most of my jobs, I was a sponge at the beginning, absorbing
everything. I was amazed at what I was seeing. One of the first idols that

fell for me was the mystique of the corner office. The people in those offices did not magically have their pants put on each day. Just as we did, they had to step into them one foot at a time. Their weaknesses were just as prevalent as ours.

I also reached an important conclusion about deficiencies. The cliché had been that black people had one set of deficiencies and women another. That's not right. People just have deficiencies. White men have just as many deficiencies as black people. There are technical deficiencies. There are decisiveness deficiencies. There are financial acumen deficiencies. There is no diagnostic that says white people have this kind of problem, women have that kind of problem, men have this kind of problem, black men have this kind of problem. We are all flawed!

The Breakthrough Leadership effort and the diversity session were combining to launch me on another stage in my career. My bridge was getting stronger.

True to form, circumstances continued to put me exactly where I wanted to be, high up in the hierarchy of a big company wrestling with transformation. The learning just would not stop.

CHAPTER SIX

Naked Emperors

was moving into a level at Ameritech that would give me a close look at the strengths and weaknesses of the people who ran the company. The thought that the higher one climbed, the more one knew simply evaporated. Most people at the top, I quickly learned, were isolated from what was happening in the business below them. These realities reinforced my instincts about knowing everything I could about my job and the jobs of the people working with me.

Breakthrough Leadership implied accountability, and what could be more accountable than knowing your particular business from top to bottom? I was in the opening phases of what would be a three-year immersion in how Ameritech ran. As the head of the Ameritech Institute, it was like having front-row seats; I saw everything happening with a very clear view. I had initially resisted the assignment at first, but once I got into the job—way into the job, actually—I found it was just the place to build my knowledge and help the company with its immense transformation.

Where it led surprised me, and I suspect it will surprise you, too. I went in as a skeptic and came out as a convert and widely recognized change agent.

Thoughts on Diversity

I had some lingering thoughts and concerns about what I experienced during the diversity session. The depth of the bitterness displayed by many of the black executives had been nothing short of shocking. I'm certain that this bitterness (if played out on the job) was a limitation in their careers. I also knew, from a critical assessment on my part, that many of those executives had gone about as far as they could go.

I never believed that institutions such as the phone company were actively racist in the way they made their decisions. I did not think there was a secret committee that decreed that black people could not advance. The promotion of diversity was not that complex an idea; there were just no black people in the room during the conversations. People have to know you are there, that you are a producer.

I wasn't kidding at the diversity seminar when I said I was going to be president of the company one day. There was no longer much mystery left for me about what happened on that eighteenth floor. I knew I was a leader in the business and I knew I could handle the top job. I had nailed the last three jobs I had at Indiana Bell. I knew I was ready to handle whatever came next.

Some people might have thought that the people in the rarefied air of the eighteenth floor had all the answers, like the Oracle in *The Matrix*. But the more exposure I got to the upper levels of management, the more I realized this was not the case. Also, I had Tommie to thank for helping me realize that some agendas are best left unstated in order for you to obtain greater responsibility and leverage. There is a way to demonstrate your independence and your orientation without being a rebel and without frightening the people who are the decision makers.

Never, ever lose sight of the fact that you have to be the best performer. You have to make it so that every time the decision makers get together, they talk about you because you are the guy who delivers. Then pick your moments. Of course you will get angry, but I don't care how frustrated I am, how many times I have been passed over, I'm never, ever going to play that angry black guy card. Even if it's there, you cannot play it. Because once you do that, you are capped. You can't go any further.

Tommie was combative with his superiors and his peers. Some of the people in the diversity training seminar (which was not what the event turned out to be) seemed only a few steps away from doing something violent. How can you expect to advance when you are harboring all that pent-up anger so close to the surface? This doesn't mean you can't address injustice where you see it, that you can't advocate and support, that you can't do the right thing. You just have to pick your spots.

I applied that philosophy even in matters as subtle as dress. During the 1980s, some black executives would wear clothing to work I would never have worn to the office. A dashiki, a pair of green shoes or red shoes. That wasn't me. It was fashionable in that era for black people to wear Flagg Bros. shoes and colored suits. But I did the IBM thing by design. It's not that I didn't like the Flagg Bros. stuff or colorful suits. Still, I made a different choice. Why make my attire the conversation rather than my results? In my opinion, those clothes were distractions that were not going to get me where I wanted to go. Some black people might call my position here as selling out, being an Uncle Tom. I'm okay with that and would not be offended. There would be some credibility to those thoughts if I shunned my responsibility to assist people of color and women as I moved to higher levels. My track record speaks for itself in terms of how much of a champion I've been for people of color and women.

When you become immersed in a job, you can forget who you are. That can happen to anyone. Sometimes, when I am cruising along swatting flies and making things happen, I will have a moment of clarity when I will have to say, "Wait a minute, Bob, you are getting too comfortable." I never get too far out of touch with the reality that, at the end of the day, I am different. Maybe I get so busy I forget I'm black.

You can't get too comfortable. That doesn't mean you should be paranoid and assume everyone is out to get you. I don't believe that the decision makers sit around trying to figure out how to discriminate against women and black people. The reason they discriminate, the reason they are not inclusive, is that the women and people of color are far removed from their consciousness. In circumstances like that, they merely do what is comfortable. There are black people who hate it when I say things like this. But, in the larger context, I honestly don't think there are scores of racists out there who take a daily pledge to keep black people and women down. I think they just don't have consciousness. And they don't have consciousness because we're just not there.

My E. F. Hutton moment when I told those black executives I wanted to be president of the company indicates that I was terribly naïve about the larger Ameritech culture. I knew other blacks in the company considered me the token black, the kiss-ass, the sellout. That's just how some black people are. I have been around black managers when those discussions have taken place about other people. So I know what they were saying about me: "Yeah, that nigger would not let his mother through the door to protect the Man, to keep his seat at the table."

We can be a vicious culture, even in the professional ranks.

Each day at the diversity seminar someone would go down one of those "how unfair and screwed up this company is" rabbit holes. Marc Wallace, the facilitator, would have a challenge to get the room back on course. It was shocking to recognize that these were the people who would be viewed in the rank and file as having made it.

All of this played out while I was still general manager of all markets for Indiana Bell, so I had not yet advanced into the Ameritech job under Notebaert. After the diversity training, I met with Martha to tell her what I thought of it. J. Howard and Associates had been the first vendor we tried. Its approach was solid and included work not only with the black managers but with the top team. Marc Wallace had been a great facilitator. He had had tremendous credibility with the group, not only because he was African American, but because he had been an executive at Dow Chemical before going into consulting.

In talking with Marc years later I learned why he had been so effective with our group. As regional sales manager for Dow, responsible for the midwestern states, he had had the highest revenue volume in the country. He shared with me that it bothered him that black employees at Dow were always complaining about how awful things were for them. He said, "Yes, there were systemic issues, but I also knew that we carried a lot of stuff in our culture that was also part of the problem. My boss approached me about the training that Jeff Howard was doing for Dow down in Texas and he asked me to go check it out for possible use in the sales organization, where diversity was almost nonexistent. I was in the University of Chicago MBA program, was running the most successful sales organization in the company, and I surely didn't want to sacrifice the precious little family time I had. But I did what any loyal lieutenant would do and went and quickly discovered more about myself and how to address concerns I was hearing from so many people. I endorsed its broader use throughout Dow, which ended up being a breakthrough for many talented people. Shortly after completing the program, I was promoted to economic strategist for Dow. After two years in that job, I left Dow to become fifty percent owner of J. Howard and Associates."

No wonder Marc was able to steer our rowdy group to conclusions. He'd walked in our shoes before.

I told Martha and her team that we absolutely needed a third-party facilitator (J. Howard) for future sessions, because we could not do it ourselves. (I didn't want traditional HR people trying to present this kind of subject matter, as it would have been amateur hour. Plus, black managers would have feasted on the folks from HR.) My final recommendation was that she put in place a diversity council of business unit leaders with an appropriate inclusion of black managers, which she did. Things began to get better. Consciousness was raised, and the right conversations began to take place. We did not become militant about it. Things got better because we moved the issue front and center as an agenda item. But it was no longer an agenda item aimed only at black executives. It was for everyone. The diversity seminar that wasn't actually a diversity seminar turned out to be a most revealing and productive experience. The issue was always on the table.

Equity

Through the diversity training, and from my own experiences at Indiana Bell, I realized that there was a danger that people would equate simple allocation with progress. Allocation is a seductive process because it gives management something to point to: "Look, we have blacks and women in key positions!"

But the problem runs deeper than the allocation solution. We still needed to push for the "three Ps": pay, profile, and promotion. The pay and promotion parts speak for themselves, and I was well aware of the inherent unfairness of paying blacks and women lower salaries than their white counterparts for the same work.

The "profile" part is extremely important. That is where you can hold people accountable for what they do starting right now. It also eliminates placing blame and finger-pointing, because it forces you to consider diversity with every opportunity that arises. These are the moments of truth that count. Everything else is rhetoric if you don't get this part right.

Dick Notebaert was fantastic at it. He knew that if the phone company had ten opportunities at the vice-presidential level, he would not be embracing diversity if he put nine or ten white guys in those positions. He said the only way he could change the outcome, improve the profile, was to maintain a pool of women and people of color to tap for those positions.

That would come to be an another important part of my job: making certain through the Ameritech Institute that we were identifying minorities and women candidates throughout the corporation, because the institute touched every business unit, saw every new hire, and was developing the next wave of leaders.

The objectives for the Ameritech Institute varied, and that made the work exciting. We worked directly with Tichy, who was tasked by Notebaert with developing the team into a core group of change agents. All we had was the chairman's vision.

Bill Weiss and, later, even Notebaert wanted to build what Jack Welch had built for GE at Crotonville: a facility where leadership development and orientation to new levels of authority would be facilitated. The one difference between our institute and Crotonville was our formation of a team that would serve as consultants to business leaders. Perhaps the most exciting initiative at the institute took place when Dick gave us some of the top strategies of the business and selected thirty-six high-potential senior leaders to vet those strategies while simultaneously being developed as leaders. This put me in a room with the highest-level people I had ever dealt with at the phone company.

My one-on-one meetings with Notebaert were stimulating. His sense of the organization and of people was profound. He gave me a lot of ammunition in terms of how to be a leader. That's also where I got strong reinforcement of my philosophy of knowing every aspect of the business. He was one of the few people in my career who had moved so high in an organization but still knew the work. He had the same orientation I had. Show up and get your hands dirty. We used to spar because I thought I was smarter than he was on technical issues.

Heading the Ameritech Institute

My tour of duty as the head of the Ameritech Institute started in 1992, just after I moved to Chicago, and I quickly became aware that the power of the job extended far beyond the title. I had been put in a very powerful position because of the institute's relationship to Notebaert. There were still some vice presidents and presidents of units who were nominally above me, but they all knew I was their equal or higher because of my access to the chairman. I had to learn the hard way how to use that power.

I was in a period of immense growth, but it left its stretch marks that weren't at all comfortable.

I would be sitting with a president who didn't want to use me, didn't want me in his unit, but who had to allow me into all the staff meetings and had to vet a strategy with me. He had to consult with me on any personnel moves he wanted to make. The whole time, he never said it but I knew he was worried about how much of what he said would get back to Dick Notebaert. I was like a spy without the capacity to hide. I was in the open all the time.

The field was also flooded with political land mines. I could get hurt with every step. I could get blown up. There were some presidents who had getting rid of me on their agenda.

But my job was not to be liked. It was to transform these men and women into the best world-class leaders I could. On the other hand, I was working with a lot of people who were scared to death of me, but knowing that I had been imposed on them, they had to comply. About half of them eventually got it, embraced it, and saw the growth.

When a Dog Bites

Did I have to be in people's faces constantly? Once again, I turned to advice from my mother. No matter what its size, she told me, a dog doesn't have to bite all the time. People only need to know that the dog *can* bite. From this, I took away that you have to be about 5 percent horse's ass to be an effective leader. People have to know you will pull the trigger if you have to. You just need the courage to pull the trigger and pick your moments.

I learned that from a mistake. I went after a leader.

He was the most toxic person we had in the phone company. He was a bad apple. If you told him the sky was blue, he would argue that it was green. If you told him it was hot, he would argue that it was ice cold. He had to take a different view on everything. He did not like women. He did not like people of color. But he was running a very successful part of the business.

I thought, "Well, I'm supposed to be getting rid of the bad guys, because we're only supposed to have good guys running these units." So I built the case. I lined up all my examples. My thought was that I would convince Notebaert that this guy was toxic and had to be removed.

"I know about that guy," Notebaert said. "And what I do is calibrate. At some point, he will go. But here's the important thing you don't understand. You totally got off mission in terms of what is important and in terms of what your job is. Your role is not to go out and tell me whom to shoot." Then he used a sports analogy. "Let's say we are playing a game of basketball and this guy comes off the bench into the game. Your job is not to make a case of why he shouldn't get the ball. Your job is to help him help us to win the game."

It was crystal clear to me. I had gotten off track. I had lost my way.

Those three years I was a change agent at the Ameritech Institute may have been the most enjoyable job of my telephone company career. I could see tangible results from my contribution to the business. That was because of people like Karen Vessely.

Karen was hell on wheels, and I absolutely adored her. I used the lesson Notebaert taught me to avoid making the same mistake with her. She was a raw uncut diamond who had no idea she was even a gemstone. She was afraid to death of Notebaert, and because of that fear, many of her actions were reactions or guesses as to what she thought might please him. She put her insecurities out there and told me she had been promoted far above what she'd ever expected. She was constantly reminding me that she did not have a college degree. She needed confidence and she didn't have a lot of things in her tool kit.

I saw courage. I saw heart. I saw desire.

As for not having a degree, I have always believed that education is overrated. Give me somebody who has the desire to learn and the courage to take risks and the will to just work hard and we can win. Give me ten street-smart people and I will kick your butt in any industry. Karen was one of the most wonderful human beings I've ever been around.

And a disaster. She would go to meetings always looking like she had just eaten a prune or a lemon. "Give everybody on your team a heart attack," I told her. "Walk in and smile."

All the raw materials were there. She was a good leader and she would become a great leader. I got to coach her and was able to help her hit her stride, find her rhythm as a leader. Soon she became the most special executive I have had the honor of coaching. In the end, those people in the pay phone unit would have followed her to the ends of the world. She came out of the process a much more confident leader, self-reflective, conscious of the environment, considerate of people, and with the understanding that there were more ways than intimidation to motivate people.

Workforce Breakthrough

We had thousands of people to transform. The initial Breakthrough Leadership people, those who survived, were certainly on board, but the vast majority of phone company workers had no idea what was going on. So we created an effort called Breakthrough 1000 that brought in a thousand midlevel managers and took them through a series of workshops where we taught them vision, values, and "workout," in which they were required to pick an initiative in their work environment to change in the Breakthrough 1000 sessions. Typically, these initiatives would be cost reduction, revenue generation, or customer service improvement ideas. Breakthrough 1000 was Tichy's concept and it was brilliant.

Once an executive had gone through training at the institute, he had to go back and take all his direct reports through everything the institute had taken him through. We didn't just send them back and tell them to change their behaviors. We sent them back with everything they needed to teach the whole package to their direct reports and to enlist their team in helping them with whatever project they chose.

We didn't just assume this would happen, either. We brought them back to the institute to check on their progress and do team building. We required them to bring three of their people back with them, and we interviewed those people to find out how well the leader had done it.

I wasn't asking them simple questions, either. In a team-on-team consulting process, we had teams of people talk to other teams about their boss as a leader, about how they were handling conflict on the team, about team dynamics. People would have to talk about how they conducted their workshops. What was the most meaningful thing about them? What was the least meaningful thing? It made it all but impossible to bluff your way through the process. If it was clear you had not done what was required, you were sent home and your boss had to call me.

Remember what I said about the dog biting 5 percent of the time? It took only one or two of those examples before people knew the Breakthrough process was for real.

Notebaert had to be able to go to the front line and hear his message repeated back to him. We had to know that the rank and file was clear on the vision, our values, and our value propositions. Did people understand the culture we were building? Could they play it back to us?

The Breakthrough Leadership effort began paying off. The company's stock price increased significantly. We became much more efficient. Costs went down. Productivity and performance measures were put in place across the company. Before Breakthrough, there were hardly any measures for anyone. After the process, people took ownership all across the company. The more information we spread around, the more people wanted skin in the game. Before Breakthrough, only a few people owned stock in the phone company. After the process, stock was awarded to lower levels of management in the company.

We stressed accountability at every opportunity.

We put value drivers in place that would let people know they were doing a good job. Once we had those, pride in the job soared. People wanted to do their jobs well. They wanted to be the best.

The institute became almost like a doctor's clinic in dealing with patients. We were diagnosing and administering care. But we didn't have any oversight from Notebaert about which patients to treat and which not to treat. That was our call.

What we had was influence and power. A mention of anything in a conversation with Notebaert (and I had many conversations with Notebaert) could cause ripples. I heard about one of them the day Bob Hurst, who was running Network, came to see me. He told me that I didn't realize how much power I had.

"What are you talking about?"

"I just got off the phone with Dick, and I'm in a little trouble," he said. I asked him why, and he fed back to me some information about Network that I had commented on in a conversation with Notebaert. "Why didn't you just pick up the phone and give me that information?" he asked.

"I have been giving you that information for a long time," I said.

"Bob," he said, "make me hear the information."

What I learned from that experience was that anything I'd discussed with Notebaert that had to do with someone else I should relay to that individual himself—the context, the issue, if there was an issue. I wasn't very comfortable with that part of the job, but they were my clients and I had to build trust with them.

In short, there are no comments made in passing to a CEO.

This led me to develop a contract I shared with all of my business unit clients. I told them I was their coach and their consultant and that I would not take anything to Notebaert that I had not discussed with them first. I asked them to understand I had clients going both ways, with them on one side and Notebaert on the other. At the end of the day, I said, Dick was my ultimate client.

That was one of the more uncomfortable parts of the job. At the same time, the fact that someone was having trouble generally wasn't a surprise to anyone. I knew who my problem children were, and they knew they were problem children, for whatever reason. My job was to make people successful until Dick decided it was time for them to leave the team. I was never troubled by that.

I told my team we could never become the chairman's listening post and merely report information back to him. At the same time, we were always picking up information about the business that might be of value to Notebaert and we needed to be sure that the information we shared was something useful that would benefit the company.

A Big New Job

I sensed I was going to go to a big job after running the Ameritech Institute, but what came along exceeded my expectations. I was asked to go to the biggest technical job in Ameritech: running Network. I would be replacing Jim Eibel, who was legendary because of his knowledge about how everything worked. It may have been the coolest job Ameritech had to offer, especially for an executive who didn't mind getting his hands dirty.

The title was vice president of Network operations. It was an officer-level job in the corporation. I could hardly believe I was at a rare sixth-level job. The only job level higher in the company was business unit president or vice chairman (which didn't exist under Notebaert).

To prepare me for my new post, Notebaert told me to go spend some time with Jim Eibel before he retired in a couple of weeks. Jim sat me down with a stack of binders and told me in great detail about everything that mattered to him. Jim was an Indiana Bell guy. I didn't know how he felt about me, but I heard that he was an intimidating guy whom people adored but feared. I was very pleased that we became friends.

This new job was a good one for me. I lifted the performance of the operation to levels people did not think possible. But a lot of the improvement I made was due to my introduction to some folks from Ernst & Young, who were working in various parts of the Network Corporation. Gary Vanderlinden was the lead partner, and his two side-kicks were Sue Chevins and Rob Stamer. I was impressed with their intense focus on process improvement. Obviously E&Y was not cheap to hire, but it had piqued my interest. I have always felt myself to be a process guy, but these folks had a more focused approach. They brought with them a lot of tools that I bought into immediately. Rob Stamer and I forged a great relationship. He nearly lived with my team for months while helping us understand the methodology and focusing the efforts of every division of my organization. We found instant success. Service levels were improved and significant cost was taken out of the organization.

Rob's concept of a "program office" was key. He felt I could take performance to the next level if I carved out a separate group to manage the process initiatives. I didn't need him to twist my arm. I put together a group that I named the PIGs (process improvement group), a team made up of great young talent. I anointed one of my best direct reports, Steffanie Abruscato, to lead the PIGs. I learned later that Steffanie and I had gone to the same high school. Her fantastic team helped the entire organization improve its performance. The PIGs were responsible for spotting many issues that may not have reached my attention. For example, why were switch maintenance procedures being performed in the middle of the day, especially when a procedure went wrong, affecting service to customers. That's the kind of thing you want to do in the middle of the night, when there is very little traffic on the network.

When I challenged my switching guys about this, they raised questions about how the union would feel about our rescheduling this work, which was typically performed by the more senior technicians. Senior guys, I learned, had earned the privilege of picking the popular 8:00 AM–5:00 PM shift. I told them we should show the union how much revenue we were leaking by taking eighty-five thousand customers offline in the middle of the day when a procedure went bad.

I recall the day a switch died in Royal Oak, Michigan.

First, a switch can't die. It has a backup. It has generators. It has batteries. But someone missed all the signals and alarms, so the switch lost AC power and then the battery was drained. Getting that switch back online was no easy matter. It took almost an entire day, and it had to be done very carefully. What are you going to tell the pizza shop owner, the florist, those eighty-five thousand customers without service?

That's what happens in an operating environment when you don't have an orientation around the customer. You miss a lot of the everyday things that become crucial down the line. And you end up with transactional managers who respond to fires and disasters. Those things are going to happen, of course, but if you don't have control of your operating environment, you will live in crisis hell.

The phone company is spectacular at responding to disasters.

During his tenure on the job, Jim Eibel became a hero when a switch in Hinsdale, Illinois, burned to the ground. There were more than fifty thousand subscribers working out of that switch. This should have been a one- to two-week service interruption for those fifty thousand–plus subscribers, but Jim brought in a temporary trailer and restored service in a couple of days.

When the Royal Oak switch went down on a Saturday morning, I jumped on an airplane and was there by 2:00 PM, and I didn't go home until the switch was up and running. I remember that there was a slow response from AT&T technical support, so I called up and asked to speak to an executive. Eventually, I got the number to the person who ran all of AT&T technical services, and was pleased to see it was someone I knew, Carly Fiorina. I took her to task for the tech support ineptness, but she reassured me that they would get me through the crisis. The week after the Royal Oak crisis, she showed up in my office. She offered no excuses. She wanted me to understand that things would be very different on her watch and she committed to immediate changes. I was impressed at how quickly she fixed things for me. That was the beginning of a long relationship with her.

My boss in the Network job was Gary Drook, one of those four key guys in the Breakthrough process who had been lined up for the chairman's job. (He'd lost out to Notebaert.) He was put in charge of the Network company after Bob Hurst unexpectedly passed away. Drook came from an area in Indiana close to where I went to high school. He was a smart guy and a friend. He gave me complete autonomy to run my business and was a tremendous supporter. But I knew his days were numbered.

On the day he was fired, he called six or seven of his direct reports into a room. He said he wanted us to know that, effective that day, he was leaving the business. We all knew that this was code for being fired.

Gary's departure meant there was going to be a new leader, and my assumption was that it was going to be me. I never campaigned for the job, but it made sense. I had all the results to show it. I knew Notebaert respected my talent and was comfortable with me as a leader. And anytime he wanted something done, he reached right around Gary and grabbed me to do it.

Then Notebaert threw a curveball.

He reached out to Bell Atlantic and brought Tom Richards in to replace Gary.

I had karma with Tom because he, too, was a former ballplayer (University of Pittsburgh). He was competent and smart and looked just like an executive. He'd played at Pittsburgh with Billy Knight (who went on to star with the Indiana Pacers in the NBA), so he wasn't just a player; he was a great player. But Tom made a big mistake with me two months into the job.

It was bonus time. In the past, Notebaert had always given me my performance appraisal. Even when Gary Drook was my boss, Notebaert did my review. Going into the performance review meeting with Tom, I thought I was in a strong position. Everyone but Mary Aguina and I had missed his performance numbers. When I walked into the office, Tom said, "Here's your salary increase and here is your bonus." Then he began apologizing.

He proceeded to rationalize the low payout. My brand-new boss not only tried to justify my low bonus with an argument that no one in Network had gotten a big bonus this time around, but he also began coaching me about my career (this after he had been on the job for only two months), telling me I had had an exceptional year and that he didn't want me to be discouraged.

I had never been so insulted in my life. I was just as good as that guy and probably better. I had a performance track record that was second to none. He should have said, "Bob, it's my duty to pass this along, but I wasn't here and what I am interested in is you and what we are going to do going forward. Dick didn't give me any instructions on why the bonus is what it is, but I can tell you I am glad you are here and I am glad you are on the team."

I felt betrayed.

I got to know Tom, and he was a really good leader. As for the bonus thing—after all, he was just the messenger.

As for Notebaert, did I think he betrayed me?

No, I think it was just a question of out of sight, out of mind.

It was 1995 and I had been in Chicago for four years. I was not a happy camper with Gary Drook being fired, Tom Richards coming in, the micromanagement that seemed to be taking place, and this compensation discussion. To make matters worse, I was almost done with my first year of an executive MBA program at Northwestern's Kellogg Graduate School of Management, which Notebaert had endorsed my attending. I actually wanted the MBA more to show my children that you never stop growing, you never stop learning. I wanted them to see me have to study at the end of a long day, to pull an all-nighter writing a paper, and to cram for exams.

With all these things swirling around in my head, I went out and got my phone log and called back all of those headhunters I had been saying no to.

How would I sort them all out? I found a way. I also found it's a lot harder to leave a place you love than you think it will be.

PART THREE

Westward Bound

CHAPTER SEVEN

Go West, Young Man

I needed a method to sort out my job offers.

There were few people I could talk to about this situation because I didn't have a network of friends outside of Ameritech. I obviously could not talk to anyone senior in the company. Then I thought about Gary Drook. I called him, and he invited my wife, Angie, and me to come to dinner at his house on Sunday night.

I was about to learn about the Ben Franklin decision matrix. I was also on the way to adding another long stretch to that life bridge that would carry me far beyond my comfort zone and a great distance away from a company where I had been immensely successful, productive, and, best of all, schooled in understanding all the facets of the business. The opportunity would carry me away from everything that had been so familiar to me—Indiana, Illinois, the midwestern phone companies and how they worked—to a new and challenging executive position.

But not before I figured out which opportunity to pursue.

Gary had a flip chart in his home office. Down the left-hand side of the chart, he told me to list all of the things that would be very important to me in considering a new job opportunity. I came up with a dozen or so important considerations (geography, schools, churches, pay, equity, city diversity, job title, realm of responsibility, CEO succession, etc.). Then we listed all the potential jobs across the top. Then I rated each consideration on a scale of one through five, based on the opportunity. Before we added up the totals, Gary told me to look at the considerations and ask myself if there were some things that were a lot more important than others. In those cells, you give the consideration two times its rating. There were five potential job opportunities. For three of the five, I had a job offer in hand. For the other two, offers were imminent. Using Gary's rating system, I rated the dozen or so considerations for each job opportunity, and when I added up all the columns, I had a clear-cut winner.

US Worst.

That's how US West was known inside the Bell System. The company had had its share of turmoil, and while we never treated them seriously at Ameritech in terms of recruiting talent or getting best practices from them, Bell Operating Companies were very similar in how they were both structured and run. In fact, I felt that my only challenge in joining US West would be just getting to know all the people. My understanding was that I would replace the operations and technology executive vice president. The chairman and board considered me a CEO-succession candidate.

Sol Trujillo had been CEO of US West for six months. He had been in marketing at Mountain Bell before it became US West. In recruiting me, the chairman, Dick McCormick, said he wanted to build a strong bench in the event Sol didn't work out or if he left the company. He warned me that the situation would be a little awkward, because I would be reporting to Trujillo, but I told him that was no problem.

Measuring US West

Building bridges requires you to venture into uncharted waters sometimes. Moving from Indianapolis, Indiana, to Chicago, Illinois, and Ameritech had been a big step for me and my family, but I at least knew all the people. Now I was seriously thinking about heading west to Denver, Colorado, to US West and I didn't know a soul. I decided to give Tommie a call.

Tommie had retired from Ameritech as a division-level manager. Even though he had become a cherished friend, I debated whether I should bother him because I had long since passed the division level and had moved three levels up, into the officer ranks.

Even though we had known each other for only six years, he had been like a father to me. He had helped me understand Ameritech politics and had mentored me. He had taught me how to channel my emotions, how to deal with people, how to understand what made them tick.

My decision to look for a new job did not surprise him. When I called him he laughed and told me he could advise me up to a certain point but this decision had to be made on my own. He could offer his point of view, but I was going places he had never been. He told me he believed I was ready to take these steps.

This created a wave of anxiety in me. I was about to leave an established nest where I was making far beyond the salary I had ever dreamed of making. I was very secure and I had succeeded at every level.

Then there was the other page in the ledger, the one that represented the upside of the US West offer.

First, the company was in terrible condition, so that would give me the opportunity to fix a big operating system. Second, the poor performance of US West was reflected in its stock price. Fix the performance and there could be a great opportunity to create wealth. Finally, there was an outside chance that I would get to run the whole company.

There were some conditions on the ground that were important, too. McCormick and Trujillo came across as very accomplished executives who were consistent in describing the problems in US West. The company had just pushed through a massive reengineering effort that had not achieved its results, and the guy I was replacing was wearing the shirt for that failure. Sol was a solid marketer and retailer but he wasn't involved with the reengineering effort in operations. While McCormick had told me that Sol was the right guy for the CEO's job, he and the board were concerned about the senior management team's ability to turn the company around.

US West's courtship of me continued to the point where I was convinced the people there really wanted me and I really wanted to go. They set up a meeting for me with Tom Bystrzycki, the incumbent executive vice president of operations and technology, the man I was to replace.

I was surprised and impressed by Tom. He was an absolute joy to be around. He was also one of the brightest and most experienced leaders

I had ever met. He knew everything about US West. He told me about infrastructure problems, where the technology gaps were. He knew that the reengineering effort simply had not worked out, but he thought my arrival would carry the company way past that problem and into a happier world on the operational side.

Then he said something that put a knot in my stomach.

He said my joining "his" team would give everyone a fresh chance to start to change the company, because I was a celebrated turnaround guy. I was numb for the rest of the meeting. No one had ever told me I would be reporting to this guy. After all of the energy spent on my recruitment, I was learning now that they were going to bring me in as a subordinate to Tom. Notwithstanding Tom's compelling and friendly nature and undeniable brilliance at operations, I felt that I had been lured into one of those classic bait-and-switch situations, where they offer you one thing on the street to get you inside and then change the offer once you are in the building.

It was a setback, but it wasn't Tom's fault. I was eager to tell Dick and Sol, "Houston, we have a problem!"

When I brought it up with Dick McCormick the next day, he said it was clear to him and Sol that I would be *replacing* Tom. At that stage, I didn't care what the plan was for Tom, but I knew I was not going to leave the comfort and security of Ameritech to go work on "Tom's team."

When I talked to Sol about this, he reinforced what Dick had said and told me I would initially have to report to Tom, but that I would assume the executive vice president's job in nine to twelve months. "Why does it have to be that way?" I asked. Sol then said that Tom and Dick had a long personal relationship. Immediately, I concluded that what had seemed like a good opportunity was being clouded by some silly political decisions. I knew I could fix that company. I knew I could work with Sol. In fact, I knew I could work with Tom, too, but I didn't want to report to him. He was gentle, smart, and decent. He came across as a good manager and leader, an authentic man and a class act. Not once in our two-hour conversation did he make excuses or cast blame on anyone else. But leaving Ameritech to work for him would have been a step backward in my career.

There were red flags all over the place, but I still decided to move forward and take a look at the US West offer. At the same time, I decided to pay attention to a couple of other opportunities, in case the US West deal became even more toxic and alarming to me. Then the US West offer arrived. It looked great, more money than I was making at Ameritech and substantially more equity in the company, which was most important to me.

What to do?

Slow-roll it.

There was still the issue of reporting to Tom. I was not certain I trusted Dick and Sol on the nine- to twelve-month time frame, so I decided to push the issue of reporting and title. I had separate talks with both men, and it became clear to me that Dick had a problem with removing Tom to clear the way for me. It didn't make any sense.

I pondered my situation at Ameritech, too. I would never be the CEO. Notebaert was young and had already reached out to the external market to find a boatload of senior executives as a result of our transformation effort. Even though I owed this guy my career, he had passed over me to select outsiders to run business units. I realized that if I wanted to be a CEO, I needed to leave the nest and venture out on my own.

I really had no idea how things would play out for me at US West. It was the worst telephone company in the Bell system and hadn't gotten that way overnight. It takes a lot of bad decisions to mess up a system that pretty much guaranteed profit under regulation into a bad performer. Important things had to have been ignored, and I wanted to know what they were before I arrived.

There were two sets of doubts at work as I made my US West decision. That first one was what happens to outsiders at US West? Could I run clear of the antibodies that I clearly saw chomping away at Ameritech's imported executives?

The second set was more concrete. I knew I was going into a difficult situation with McCormick in the chairman's seat and Trujillo as CEO. Dick had already told me Sol might not be the right guy. I knew they were going to have their eye on me and others as a replacement for Trujillo, to whom I was going to be reporting once I'd taken over Tom's position.

I knew that work would be my sanctuary from the political situation

I was entering. I could escape the problems (if there were indeed problems between Sol and Dick) by focusing on work. The company was so broken I knew they would let me do what I did best without much interference. But just how broken was it?

It was pretty bad. Phone companies generally bat 90-plus percent in terms of on-time performance for anything—repair, phone service installation, data services performance. But US West was in the 50 to 60 percent area. Data services were all the way down in the 30 percent area. Repairs could take days. It was a mess, but I knew I could fix the place if real authority were placed in my hands.

Why Scale Is Crucial

When systems are big, they work like ships at sea in the sense that a little change in course can have vast consequences. I was reading a report one day that gave me a gentle reminder about how little things can add up to big consequences. One of the airlines decided it was no longer going to put three olives in its cocktails. It would supply just one olive. The cost savings over time would be something outrageous, like a million dollars.

In big organizations, if you understand operating at scale, and you have the discipline to make sure everyone is doing things the same way, you can create a whole lot of benefit. McDonald's is a good example. That standard of consistency and understanding predictable models give you the leverage. You can introduce a new product and know its impact almost immediately. If you are McDonald's, you don't have to wait for Crothersville, Missouri, to catch up to Evanston, Illinois. You know that if you put seven McNuggets in a meal instead of six and charge twenty-five cents more, and that the day for implementing this is October 9, then you know that 99.99 percent of all franchises will implement it the morning of the ninth of October. You can put the algorithm to work and know what the yield will be. That is what a big-scale organization with a disciplined standard operating environment allows you to do.

That's how phone companies work. It was astounding to me that those kinds of efficiencies were not part of the picture at US West.

I think this can be explained as a consequence of living in a regulated marketplace. Think about it. How inventive do you have to be if someone tells you, "Here's what you can make!" with no variation, no marketplace consequence, nothing but a bureaucratic decision based on a lot of cost inputs.

Before deregulation, phone companies were not really competitive entities. Why worry about scale? Why worry about costs? The inefficiencies just become a part of the fabric of things. Ostentatious buildings. A life built on perks. A job defined by the quality and number of perks. If you didn't do things on time, you could get your wrist slapped. The utility commissions at the state level were there to make certain consumers got a satisfactory level of performance. If you failed at that, they fined you.

I learned that US West had been fined tens of millions of dollars over the years by utility commissions in fourteen states. When I asked about those fines and how much money would have to be invested to address infrastructure problems, it was clear that the company had found it cheaper just to pay the fines.

Trying to Quit

I decided to take the job. I was very worried about the meeting with my boss to inform him I was leaving. I met with Dick Notebaert at 5:00 PM.

"I'm leaving Ameritech," I told him.

He slumped in the chair, his upbeat demeanor gone.

I continued: "I've found an opportunity that I'm excited about and I'm effectively resigning today."

"What company?"

"US West."

"What's the job?"

I told him. He asked what was behind this decision.

I pointed out that when he fired Gary Drook, I assumed I would be the likely candidate to fill that job, because I had been delivering superior results running the network, but he'd gone outside for Drook's replacement. (I was careful to praise Tom Richards, though. I didn't want this to be about Tom.)

"But Bob, you are slated to be president of a unit," Dick said.

"I don't know that," I said.

"What else?"

I decided to go for it and tell him everything. I told him my bonus treatment had really given me cause for concern—not the money, but how the message had been delivered to me. The Network company had failed and with the exception of Mary Aguina's (a great leader) and mine, most of the operating units in the Network company were over budget and experiencing service problems. All of our bonuses would be affected. There is no such thing as one or two winners if the larger company fails. I told him that Tom had tried to own the decision for the lower payouts, even though he'd been there only about two months, which was fine. But I said that when he proceeded to coach me on how to advance my career and earning potential, that was insulting to me.

Then I decided to go after another matter that factored into the decision.

"Quite frankly, I don't think I'm important anymore, Dick. I don't think I'm valued. I understand why we needed to bring in all the senior-level talent. I get it. But I also know that I'm as accomplished as any of these new people and can run any unit in this corporation, especially the Network company. I owe everything to you. I am here today, who I am today, because you provided the opportunities. I think I've taken great advantage of them, but you were the enabler."

Then he played a smart card. He looked at me and he did not look away. "Then why would you leave me?"

Damn. He was making it personal.

"I really want to take this job," I said.

"No, you don't," he said. "You don't want to leave me."

He told me he would move me to a president's job. He told me he would fix the compensation. Then he added, "I need you. You hear me, don't you?"

"Yes, sir, I do."

"And don't ever let us get disconnected like this again."

And that was it.

I wasn't ready for it. It was the only card he could have played and he played it so well. As I walked back to my office from the meeting with Notebaert, I felt as though I were blind. What the hell had I just done?

On the way home, I called Dick McCormick and told him I wasn't coming to US West.

Instead of saying, "I told you so," he did a great thing for me. He said, "Well, it was almost too good to be true to think that we had you. The board and the folks were real excited. Who do you know, Bob, that you think I should go after, now that you are not coming? We don't have another candidate. You have been our only focus."

Damn again.

"Let me give it some thought. I am really sorry, Dick," I said.

"Young man, you have nothing to apologize for. I probably would have done exactly what you did."

US West Welcomes Me

Three days after I agreed with Notebaert not to resign, nothing had happened. I had no interactions with Tom Richards, which was fine by me, and not a word from Notebaert about a president's position, about the things he said he was going to do for me.

I also began to have some very strange feelings. I felt as if I had cheated on Notebaert. I had gone out with another suitor and been lured away. I was now back in the fold at Ameritech but feeling very dirty, very disloyal. In addition, I was beating myself up for passing up such a big opportunity. That night I was on my way to a Chicago Bulls game when my phone rang. It was Dick McCormick. We exchanged pleasantries, and then he asked if I had given any thought to executives he might interview for the job I'd just turned down. I paused a moment and then said, "If the job is still open, I'd like to keep my commitment and start Monday morning."

I had played the downsides of the position in my head over and over, weighing them against where I was at Ameritech and where I might be after some time at US West. Notebaert had played his hand well, but not well enough to compete with the lure of a big challenge and the potential for a great reward.

To his credit, Dick McCormick didn't ask me how I would handle Notebaert, and I merely offered him my guarantee that I would not have a problem starting Monday. He offered to send his jet to pick up Angie and the kids Saturday morning and fly them to Denver for an initial house-hunting trip. I called home and left to Angie the task of telling the kids that we were moving, again.

The next morning I called Dick Notebaert's secretary, Pat, and asked her to have him call me, saying it was urgent. Several hours later Dick called. He was in New York, and rushing to Washington, D.C. He asked me to sit tight and said he would call me back in about ninety minutes. When he did, he told me he knew what I wanted. Then he asked me if I had something to write with. I said yes, and he proceeded to give me the following advice about the US West offer:

- Double the equity in the offer
- Guarantee the bonus the first two years
- No fixed number of visits for Angie to find a home
- Severance is two years' salary and bonus and forward-vesting of all equity
- Employment agreement is three years
- Company will purchase the Chicago home if it doesn't sell within a year
- Personal use of the company aircraft

"Don't ever tell anyone I gave you this coaching," he said. US West agreed to every condition.

Of all the people involved, Tom Bystrzycki was great about giving me the space and autonomy to fix the operation at US West. He was respectful. He never once positioned himself as my boss (even though he was). He never entered my space.

Sol reached out to me. He, his wife, Corrine, and Angie and I met socially. We would go to ball games, share dinners, travel together. We became very good friends. I had a lot of respect for Sol. I will never forget the day he called me and said, "Hey, I know you have to get your team in place. Do not feel constrained. Bring in a busload if you have to."

As for the work itself: Poor service. No accountability. Cost over-runs. It was one of the easiest situations to rectify I had ever been in. Here is one way to think of it: "How can you hurt yourself falling out of the basement?"

When we landed at Centennial Airport in Denver on that Saturday morning, we were met by my HR guy Jimmy LaValley, who handed me a thick packet of information and the keys to my new office. Jimmy was very nervous and hyper in that first encounter. I made a mental note to myself that he had to stop drinking coffee, and that he may not be able to handle the ride on this particular boat. He was trying to please. I needed a warrior. I didn't need a Jeep driver.

Well, I was wrong about Jimmy. He was more than up for the journey. If I had been in a war, I would have had no problem turning my back, because Jimmy LaValley would have taken every bullet for me. True, he needed some nurturing, he needed some tough-love counseling, and he needed to be told that he was okay. But he soon became my strategic partner and my trusted confidant. I found out he had a deep thirst for knowledge, and that he knew the operations at US West cold. However, he had never been in a position where he was given total authority to pursue his agenda, where he was asked for his opinion. I broke the seal on something in this guy, and he just flourished. He was like a sponge. He became for me what I think I had been for Notebaert: a guy who could sit me down and say, "You're wrong."

I started asking him questions. "Jimmy, do you think we ought to spend all those millions of dollars and light up that mall and that high-end subdivision with fiber, or do you think the engineers are fudging the numbers and copper wire will do just fine?"

One night I sat down with him and I asked him what he wanted. What would success look like for him? Where was he going? He said he wanted to learn from me and he wanted to run human resources at a big company like US West. I decided I could use him. Also, he didn't melt when I gave him tough feedback.

Jimmy was another one of those cases where I learned to look past my initial judgment of the cover of the book and find out what was really inside. I still have my opinions, of course, and what I seek to do is validate them as quickly as I can, because I can't live with uncertainty. On the other hand, there were a lot more cases where my initial reaction was justified. I have a good batting record on that, too.

Teams and Values

I am a value-centric guy and I don't need a corporate placard to tell me what those values are. I don't need to read the company Web site.

Number one is high integrity.

Number two is you have to be a member of the team. If there is anybody who understands the nature of the team, it's me.

Michael Jordan was great, for example, but people fail to understand that his greatest attribute was how he brought out the best in others. That is really what he and Larry Bird did better than anyone else. They made everyone around them better.

The third thing is passion. Passion around customers, passion around doing things right, passion around winning. Passion is what excites an organization and tells me that you can bring others with you. Passion is infectious.

The fourth thing is a little complicated and a little biblical: the ability to subsume yourself to the greater good. Akin to humility, it's an important leadership trait because it keeps you grounded. A person who is able to subsume himself to the greater good makes it clear that what he is doing is not about himself but about other people.

And the important thing about those four qualities is that they don't play out uniformly in everyone.

A Philosophy of Management

Despite my doubts about the job, I walked into US West full of confidence. After all, up to that point I had never experienced failure. I knew how to unlock that potential for other people and I knew how to build an organization. I also knew how to develop people. That's probably the most enjoyable part of the job. After you do all of the stuff that is absolutely necessary, fixing systems and the like, you get your paycheck. But I get my delight out of working with people. It's a realistic challenge: if

I can unlock the human potential in people, then my job will become easier.

I think these thoughts have more to do with philosophy than with business practice, or maybe in me the two have become the same thing.

At US West, I evolved.

"Watch, listen, and learn" was at the heart of my methodology. It works in sports, it works in life, and it works on the job, too.

I felt there were two ways to drive operational performance. The first way is by using command and control: drive performance, drive results, and you can win. I have a suspicion that this is not sustainable. I also don't believe you can develop people with this approach. What you have is compliance and adherence. An organization that runs on command and compliance will be only as strong as the leader in place. And you'd better hope that person doesn't run out of energy. You don't build loyalty with that kind of process, so you end up with an organization that doesn't enjoy winning. It might well win, but it won't enjoy it.

The other way to drive operational performance is to bring a horde of people along with you, but not with an open, participatory, laissez-faire sort of atmosphere. You set direction. You enable people. Then you get out of the way and turn them loose. Those environments are electric. They are sustainable. They spawn leaders. People want to be there. If it is done right, such an environment can have a life of its own without the leader who created it.

I didn't learn this in one lump of training. In fact, it is a thought that has evolved over many years of watching, of winnowing bad from good, and then imitating what fit my ethical and professional values and seems to work for me.

I learned a lot from watching the people I did *not* want to emulate. I sort of stumbled onto who I was and wanted to be based on all the bad stuff I saw. Early in my career, I used to tell myself, "If I ever get that job, I'm not going to do it that way. I'll do it this way."

All of these developed skills would shortly be coming into play at US West.

CHAPTER EIGHT

US Worst!

My thoughts were all over the place as I approached the US West building entrance. How will it feel in there? How far is the coffee room? Will my office be embarrassingly large? Behind all of those superficial questions was the big one: Am I ready for this challenge?

I arrived at the Mineral Building, where perhaps four thousand US West employees worked, very early on a bright Monday morning, eager to get to work. There were some uncertainties about this new job, issues I would have to work out as soon as I could. But I had succeeded through two decades of Indiana Bell and Ameritech. I was about to be at the heart of the reconstruction of one of America's most important and successful communications companies. I knew what it was like to transform an employee from a worker into a leader. I knew how to identify problems, isolate them, and solve them.

I felt ready for all of that at US West.

It was time to get started.

A Bad Omen

I had given some thought as to how I would enter this new system. Based on the company's really bad service performance, I knew I would be instituting a daily call with all direct reports at 6:00 AM. I wanted to talk about service and meeting commitments to customers. But more important, I needed to hear from the people in charge of this performance. I had twenty-plus direct reports responsible for all services in fourteen states.

The next morning at 5:55, I dialed into the bridge for the big conference call. At first there were seven people on the phone. Then you could hear more people starting to join in. Some of them beeped in as late as 6:15. I was keeping careful notes, asking, "Who is on?"

When I asked that question a couple of times and nobody spoke up, I wrote a note: "Integrity may be an issue."

These were early signs to me of the hand I had been dealt. I was like a dentist probing for sensitive teeth. There were a lot of sensitive teeth here. I knew how to look for them because of the span of that career bridge I had already built.

US West was a different system, of course, with different people, but it was still a phone company, and the laws that rule the workplace—accountability and responsibility—were as legit at US West as they had been at Ameritech. I introduced myself and then told my direct reports that the purpose of the call was for us to get our hands around the volume of work, the resources we had, and to make real-time decisions to start improving our performance with customers.

"Given that there are fourteen state leaders, I would like each leader to share with me your previous day's volume and what level of service completion you were able to accomplish. Second, I'd like to know what your volume is for today and what your plans are for improving performance from yesterday. Who would like to go first?"

Silence.

I wrote a note: "No courage."

I decided to pick the state of Washington to start. From my previous day's review of the numbers, they were one of the really poor-performing states.

The executive in charge of Washington was Bill.

"So, Bill, why don't you start?"

I could hear him clearing his throat. "Well, um, Mr. Knowling . . ."

I hesitated a moment before I responded to Bill's opening. This was my first public interaction with the team I'd inherited and I was very aware that every person on that phone call was curious about me, and eager to see how tough the new guy would be.

"First, Mr. Knowling died in 1986. I'm his son Bob, so Bob, Robert, hey, you! We don't have to be formal in this organization. So, Bill, how was your team's performance yesterday?"

"Well, Bob, I'm not sure what our performance was yesterday. We don't really get those numbers until eleven AM. But I will have those numbers for you . . . and in terms of the numbers . . ."

They had all been told the day before what I would be looking for. I was surprised they didn't have the numbers. I, however, did have the numbers, because my staff guy Jim Castleberry (who would pan out to be one of my great leaders) had collected them for me.

Bill continued: "Today it looks like we have about seven hundred and twenty service orders and it looks like my trouble load is about eleven hundred."

"Any idea of what you are going to complete today?" I asked.

There was some stammering and stuttering. He droned on for a while. Finally, I informed him that I had his numbers from yesterday and that he had completed about 47 percent of his service requests.

I was very collegial, very polite. I did some coaching. I suggested it might be important to size the load first. Why not go ahead and preload 80 percent of the work, then reserve 20 percent of your force to handle work that comes in or work that is caught in the system. Utility players, you know? Whatever needs to be done?

"Yeah, Bob, that makes a lot of sense. I hadn't thought of that."

After ten minutes, I asked, "Who would like to go next?"

Nobody.

So I asked Utah to go next. That area was run by a guy named Phil. It was a bad conversation, with his disclaimer up front that he, too, didn't have his data from yesterday.

When Phil finished his painful review, I told them all that I didn't know how things were run in the past and I didn't care. "But starting tomorrow," I said, "if you cannot come onto this call and present to me, in an intelligent fashion, how you're going to change the outcome for my customers, then I cannot use you in this organization. Number two, my call is at six AM. If you don't have the respect for me and your colleagues to be on at six AM, please do not join my call. Number three, I'm not going away. I'll talk to you tomorrow at six AM."

Making the Cuts

It didn't take long for me to make my first varsity cut. Jimmy and I got on a plane to Seattle, Washington, and in a two-minute meeting, I relieved Bill of his duties and thanked him for his service. Jimmy remained with Bill to help him with his transition. I got back on the plane and went to Denver.

In a communications company, word travels at the speed of light. Everyone in fourteen states knew that Bill was gone. Just as my mother had told me, a dog has to bite somebody only one time for word to get out that that dog can bite. The important thing is not to make the biting the norm and never to make it personal. I knew I needed to send a signal early in the process that everyone was not going to make it. You can't be random about it. Performance is the criterion, not personality.

Within a few days on the job it became clear to me that if I dealt only with the numbers, I would have to send everyone home. That's how deeply troubled US West was. But there are other ways to look at those numbers. Okay, which leaders were improving their numbers, even if only by a little? Which leaders at least had a coherent plan for improving things? Which leaders were getting their hands dirty and making the effort to turn the ship around?

With the exception of Montana, North and South Dakota, and Minnesota, leadership changes were made in all the states. As a consequence of the management changes, the situation in most of those states improved. I had a daily measure of what was going on, what the plan was to resolve issues, and service performance started improving significantly. Leadership changes alone were not sufficient, however. A tremendous amount of coaching was being done on a daily basis.

30-60-90–day Plan

I knew I needed to fix the organization's structure and address the processes, and that change needed to happen quickly. Every time I've taken on a new assignment, I approach the task with a 30-60-90–day game plan. The first 30 days I spend diagnosing the system. The 60-day time frame is for launching the strategic initiatives that are going to turn the company around. The 90-day goal is to align the rewards and the consequences with the proper incentives to drive performance improvement.

All through the 30-60-90–day time frame, people are being assessed, quick wins are celebrated, and I broadcast the vision and values I want everyone to understand and embrace.

My first intervention was built around what I called "Focus: Customer." I will share how that came about a little later. Every metric we had that focused on how we performed for our customers was on the table. We started with baseline data on everything.

This is a lot like what a doctor does. You don't just go into a doctor's office and say, "Doctor, I'm not feeling well," and expect him to start administering treatment. He first must go through a series of procedures to determine what is wrong.

At US West, I found a long list of problems. We were there to deliver service, but we had a lot of different customers. Of those customers, which ones had the highest leverage for the business and which ones would have the most material impact if we fixed their problems? In theory, I needed to fix the problems for all customers, but when you have a burning platform, you have to make hard choices until you can eliminate the crisis.

Phone Company Emergency Room

It becomes a little like emergency room triage. This is an emergency room and I am going to make life-or-death choices. It's that profound. You make a conscious decision about who is going to receive treatment and who is not going to be treated. In fact, you may even have to let someone die.

Most people on my team had a really tough time adapting to this. This was probably the first time they had ever heard an executive say we were not going to serve everybody. With our on-time performance consistently in the 30 to 40 percent range, I made the case that we were equally mistreating all of our customers. But I also knew that just mandating how we approached service improvement would not be sufficient.

I needed to be the leader/teacher now, especially in this broken system where people throughout the entire organization had come to accept failure and substandard performance.

I told them we had to decide where we were going to start having an impact. Then I explained that we would go about our changes in a systematic way. Business customers came first, because they were not only the high-revenue customers, but also the ones who called us every hour or so to see when we were coming out. The typical residential customer, while equally frustrated with our performance, didn't constantly call the way a business customer did.

A data line in a retail store, for example, is a window to electronic transactions. You are the guy who is now calling me at least a dozen times today because no one has come to help you. Take that scenario and apply it across a base of thousands of business customers who have a service problem on a typical day and you can see how that highlights the incredible call volume at my centers.

What if we improved our performance with business customers from 30 percent to 90 percent? You buy a lot of resource capacity if you fix that segment first. With our scale, that kind of improvement was material to our operation.

I explained to my direct report leadership team that there were several interventions we could consider to fix the business, but we had to choose which of those interventions would give us the biggest yield right now, so we could create the capacity to fix more problems.

Here is an example of some of my teaching within the organization. Let's say I have twenty thousand repair tickets that we need to service today where the customer has no dial tone. The phone, the data line, whatever, just doesn't work. Then I have fifty thousand repair tickets that we need to service today where the service is slightly impaired (noise on the line) but is still working. So, let's say I have ten thousand technicians devoted to fixing all seventy thousand of these repair requests. Spreading the resources over the fourteen states the way you would spread peanut butter on a sandwich would give you the same performance for both the customer who is completely out of service and the customer who has impaired service.

But the customer who is completely out of service will call you repeatedly if the service is not restored within a reasonable time, and with business customers the notion of "reasonable" is measured in hours.

The intervention I put in place was Management 101.

Cover every out-of-service request with every available technician for the first four hours of the day. You should be able to cover all twenty thousand out-of-service problems with ten thousand technicians in two and a half to three hours. In addition, any out-of-service repair request that comes in during the course of the day moves to the front of the line for handling and attention.

Fixing out-of-service problems was the first win, as measured by the KPI (Key Performance Indicator) of Out of Service Received Before 5:00 PM and Carried Over (OOS > 24), and there were many more to follow. Every time we turned the corner on another accomplishment, it was like opening the release valve on a reservoir. We were freeing up hundreds of thousands of work hours.

With each win, the management team's belief system got stronger and the customer service satisfaction soared.

I also knew I needed to get ahead of the curve and address preventive maintenance.

I needed some five or six thousand people out there every day keeping the network up to par. When you cut back on routine maintenance, service problems become more prevalent. Acts of nature such as rain, snow, or heat cause abnormal volumes in service outages. These can overwhelm the organization with repair reports. So every time it rained in Oregon and Washington (which it does most of the time), repair calls spiked off the charts. One of the things we liked about the Minnesota, North and South Dakota, and Montana territory was the extreme winters and intense cold. The freezing actually helped us, as the water in the cables froze and the service was thus stabilized. It was the same with the extreme heat in Arizona and New Mexico: it dried out the cables. Water in the network plant is bad.

Because of this, my mood swings were all weather related. Never in my life had I paid so much attention to the weather conditions in my geographic territory. And the weather didn't disappoint. The ice storm in Washington/Oregon in 1997—some say the worst in a century— pushed the repair load beyond one hundred thousand tickets. We sent hundreds of technicians from other states to help with the cleanup. I didn't leave the territory for over a month.

When the Red River flooded in North Dakota, it poured into down- town Fargo and the entire community was evacuated. Our central office had two feet of water in it. We made ABC's national news when a reporter wading through the water in our office told the country that while other buildings, and almost everything else in town, was burning and flooding, the US West central office was still working. He flipped his cell phone on to show everyone he still had US West service!

That day, my technicians bailed water, stacked sandbags, took turns sleeping, and took measures to ensure that our switch stayed online. When the National Guard evacuated the town because of the fires and rising floodwater, my technicians found a boat and went back to our central office. They were heroic. They told me they just felt they were doing their jobs, and I believed them. US West technicians were not to blame for the company's poor service performance. In fact, the techni- cians were the wild card that I was counting on in everything I did in the company. A universal truth about telephone company technicians is their commitment to serving customers.

Now, none of these early wins would have been possible had it not been for a very important visit I made my first week on the job.

My Union Partners

My second day on the job I got into my car and drove three miles to the headquarters of the Communications Workers of America. The union's president and vice president were both there. I didn't have an appoint- ment. The secretary introduced me to John Thompson.

"I'm the new guy," I told him. "I'm here to figure out with you guys how we are going to fix this place."

The union people were totally quiet when I started the meeting. I told them I knew I could not ask them to trust me or blindly sign up with me just because I'm the new guy in the corner office.

"I will never make a decision that affects your people without consulting with you first," I said. "And you are going to help me improve decision making as it affects your people. When there are cases where we disagree, we both will know that we have heard each other, and then we will agree to disagree. I will never disparage you in front of your people. I hope you would do the same for me, but I can't even ask for that."

I told them that leadership was what was required to fix the company and that *we* could do the impossible if they were willing to help me. I told them I had power because I was the leader and they had power because they represented their people. Our ability to work together, I told them, would depend on who was willing to give up power. I told them that no one had sent me. I was there with my olive branch to tell them they could have as much of my power as they wanted, as long as we won for my customers.

John Thompson, the union vice president, was the first to speak. "I'll be damned," he said. "We heard about you from the guys in Chicago. You've got a great reputation. This is a fucked-up company. You've got a bunch of idiots running the place."

I told him that he could say that at union headquarters, but he couldn't talk that way out among our people, because "the idiots is me!" He agreed, and asked what I had in mind. I told them about the intervention strategies I would be deploying and said that I wanted their support of the work. I told them that I planned to go into the field one day a week to visit with employees, to talk to our customers, and to meet with leaders in those communities where we had operations. In addition, I would go somewhere in the territory one night a week.

I told him I needed my field visits for myself, because that was how I got close to the work, met people, and got a sense of what was really wrong. I told them it was where I got my best ideas. I asked John to join me for evening meetings. I wasn't going to pay the employees for attending those meetings, but I would provide a simple dinner of hot dogs and hamburgers. It would be an open forum from 6:00 PM to 8:00 PM. John warned me I would be roasted at those meetings. "Good," I said. "Come with me!"

The first place John and I visited was a small city in Iowa. The company had 61 technicians in that area. We rented a place for the meeting, and 150 people showed up. I asked John who all those people were, and he said some of them were technicians from other areas who'd driven over to see what was happening; some had brought their spouses along.

I began the meeting the way I began all such town hall–style meetings. I told them I was glad to be there and that I was really looking forward to what they had to tell me. I told them there were no sacred cows and that I would answer any question they asked. If I didn't know the answer, I would find the answer and get back to them. Then I just let things happen.

It was an education.

One right after another, angry people came forward to bitch about conditions: the lack of tools, the company's share price. (The stock was at eighteen dollars.) I knew it was important to let them vent. After an hour, it was time for me to stop taking questions and time to be leader/teacher. I told them I wasn't asking any of them to believe in me or trust in me, but that after listening to them I had a good idea of what was wrong. I felt that if I told them my game plan, they would think all this "being open to input" was just a case of bait-and-switch, as I already knew what I wanted to do. Instead, I personally apologized for the condition of the company and told them that my only reason for taking the job had been that I thought I could turn the situation around. Then I told them that for the next thirty minutes they could come up and complain, but the price of entry to voice a complaint was that they had to bring a solution with them.

The tone of the meeting changed.

The next guy up presented his problem with no solution.

"What the hell should we do about it?" I said.

"Well, I really don't know," he replied.

I pointed out that he was breaking the rules. Why would he think I would have a solution to a problem he had lived with for twenty-eight years? "Come on, you've got an answer," I told him. "I'll bet you've got an answer." Then I said, "Did you bring your wife tonight?" He said yes. I said, "I'll bet *she's* got an answer."

The room howled.

Then he came up with an answer. The problem was batteries. The technicians used a lot of batteries for their tools and they wore out. But to get new batteries, they had to order them through a central supply point in the phone company, and it could take three or four weeks for them to arrive.

"Bob, we've got guys borrowing and stealing from everyone because they just can't keep the freakin' batteries. Those batteries cost twenty-six dollars from our supply catalogue. Why can't we just go over to the hardware store and get them for four dollars?"

I looked at Jimmy LaValley, and he said that was correct: everything had to be ordered from a central buying department. I suggested that we just let the technicians buy the batteries at the hardware stores.

John Thompson said, "No, that would be too much like doing something right!"

It was always like this at these meetings.

I never ran into a guy describing a problem who didn't have a solution that was not just intuitively simple but elegant. I believe that best practices don't come from the corporate staff office; they come from the field. The corporate staff should be the disseminator of those best practices.

I have been asked many times how I knew I could walk into the Communications Workers of America office and get them to work with me. While most managers would view that as going into the mouth of the beast, I only regret that I didn't go over there on day one. People like to win and they have an incredible ability to perform if you just let them. At the end of the day, if I am able to win the union over, if they really get it, then we have a legitimate chance to win. What's wrong with being friends with a union?

My relationship with the union became strong almost from the start. And there was a test case that proved it. About my third week on the job, Jimmy told me about a guy who was stealing from us. The telephone company was a loose place if you were a technician, which is the greatest job in the world. You went out every day and you were expected to put in a good day's work. If you needed to stay out until 9:00 or 10:00 PM and put in four hours of overtime every day, no one questioned that. Technicians were always able to make over $100,000 a year because of that.

We caught two guys working their own private business (they did contract construction) until 3:00 PM, and then doing their required work for us and staying out until 9:00 or 10:00 PM. We witnessed one of the guys going into a hardware store, buying supplies, and then going to a residential home that was not on our route. He was running this business on our time. One of the guys was actually on disability and while we didn't see him working this other business, we knew they were in business together. Jimmy told me we had to fire the guys, but he'd talked to John Thompson, the union guy, who said we could not.

I got on the phone with John at the CWA headquarters.

He said it was a quirky situation. Nobody liked the guy we had on videotape working his construction business while on our clock. But the other guy people really respected. John said I could use the group's respect for him and that he had not been caught on video to get that whole group turned around. I bought the deal, and I got a huge lift from it. More important, the union saw I meant what I said, that I was a partner. The union and I could get along.

I didn't feel as though I needed anyone's permission to do anything. I came in with a mission to turn the place around. If everything had been operating smoothly at headquarters, I would not have been needed. So the headquarters people and their attempts to orchestrate policy and procedures would have to be restrained, because they were already diminished in my eyes when I arrived.

I had some trouble with Jimmy's boss, the head of corporate human resources. During my first ninety days, I was supposed to rebuild the rewards and consequences system as part of the turnaround, and that put me right in the face of Jimmy's boss. We clashed on just about everything, although we became good friends later. That put Jimmy in a tough situation, because his boss would tell him the corporate line on things, and then I would tell Jimmy, "That's stupid. We're doing it differently."

Jimmy was my corporate source. He told me I had everyone's underwear tied in knots, that I was really scaring people with what I was doing, to which I replied, "Good. Until somebody tells me I am no longer in charge, we're going to do it my way."

At a certain point it became clear that Jimmy's boss had decided to stop fighting. We were working on compensation programs, and instead of getting in the way, he asked Jimmy what I was going to do. Jimmy told him, and then that became standard operating procedure for everyone in the company. My ideas were practical and were helping people a lot. I was fiscally sound. I was prudent. What I did made sense.

This might sound as if I were the only man who could tie his shoes in a building full of people wearing tasseled loafers, but that's not the case. There were some very smart people at US West. But they were not oriented toward sharing power, listening, championing other people's ideas, or holding people accountable.

I was oriented toward doing what felt right to me. And at the end of the day, I knew that people would benefit and we would yield good results. I wasn't looking for headlines, but I also knew that what I was doing would go viral. It was authentic. I knew it would make my reputation bigger, and that whatever I did with anyone on a given day would reach people in all fourteen states quicker than an e-mail.

Let Go of Power

At the heart of all of this change was the willingness to give up power. I think that is one of the smartest things I have done in my career. I could get anything done. If I had something tough I needed to get done, guess where I went? Instead of sitting with my management team and talking about how to figure a way out of a box, I would go to John, the CWA leader, and tell him what I was up against.

"What would you do?" I'd ask him.

And many times it wasn't even necessary for him to give me an answer, because our relationship was so special that the discussion alone gave me clearer vision. It was not unusual for John to call me days later with an idea or two because he had been thinking about the matter or had gotten some nuggets from a member. He was a partner with me.

Those town hall meetings I held became legendary. The bitching was awful. But in responding to complaints, I never disparaged past management. Every time I went out, I took the hit and I apologized. I told the technicians assembled that I was so sorry for what we had done to them. And I meant it. I knew that in the manner in which I apologized, the noise would be turned down. You just have to tell people that you are sorry and that you care.

The workers in the field got used to me. Sometimes they laughed when I showed up with my work boots and my tool pouch. "Oh, no, you're going to do some work? Don't be slowing me down, man," would be the general reaction.

I would tell them that by the end of the day, they would be struggling to keep up with me. At first everybody had their guard up, but when you spend a whole day with someone, in and out of the truck, in and out of people's houses, under houses, in central offices, you get to know them.

This led to some interesting circumstances.

When I hooked up with one technician, I told him to do what he always did. If the first thing he did each morning was meet up with some other guys for coffee, then he should do that. And he said, "Bob, we can get fired for that." And I said, "Look, if you do it regularly, then do it now. If you don't do it because I am here, you will just be doing it again after I am gone. So do it."

We showed up at the coffee shop and there were seven, eight trucks out back. I walked in and everyone wanted to know if I was going to rat them out, because there was a rule that you went to your initial customer first thing, without exception, and if you were caught anywhere else (like a coffee shop) you would be suspended. I told them no, that I could find this circumstance in any town I visited. "This is happening across fourteen states." The guy I was with asked why we had the rule anyway, and that it ought to be repealed. I asked, "What do I get in return?"

This led to a conversation. I pointed out that their service record was terrible, that on average they were completing only three service requests a day. They told me they didn't respect their management and that they would get paid just as much for three service cases as for nine. I observed that they slacked off because they could and I asked them what I would have to do to get a little extra effort from them.

So I repealed the coffee rule, knowing full well that repealing it would not buy me any more productivity, but that's not why I did it. I told Jimmy we were acting like bad parents who don't follow through on threats of punishment. We weren't suspending anyone for violating the rule, so why was it there?

All the safety rules were still in effect, of course, for obvious reasons. You can take the repealing of rules only so far. One of the highest fatality rates in the Bell System is for electrocution, so we had to be adamant about testing for power under trailers or working aloft. You still had to wear a hard hat, too.

I was riding down a street one day when I saw a US West truck, so I stopped. I almost always did. I looked down the alley and there was a guy up on a pole doing his job. But he was not wearing his hard hat. He didn't know me from Adam, but I went to the trunk of my car and got my hard hat and I tossed it up to him.

"What's your wife's name?" I asked.

"Mary."

"Well, I would hate to be the person to have to go tell Mary you fell and hurt yourself, or worse, you killed yourself because you didn't have your hard hat on." Then I got in my car and left. I could have gotten him in trouble. I could have used his truck number and the time of day to identify him and given him a five-day suspension or even fired him. I didn't. But I don't think he ever went up a pole again without wearing his hard hat. It's no surprise to me that when John and I talked a few weeks after this incident, he knew about the encounter, as word travels fast and I'm sure the technician told several people about it. Anyway, John said, "My friend, you are the real deal."

My guys at US West (and I still affectionately call them my guys) connected with me and I connected with them. I went to bat for them to improve their work environment in a number of different ways. I worked hard to improve their net worth. When I left US West the stock price was at sixty-four dollars a share.

After I left US West, I got a call from a guy in Tucson, Mike Flagg, the president of the Tucson local organization. The union guys were out on strike. It was great to hear from him. I asked him how he was. He told me they were all just sitting in the union hall talking about how long the strike might last. One of the guys in the group told Mike just before they left that night that the strike would not have happened if Bob Knowling had still been there.

Time to Bruise Someone

How did I build that relationship, a connection so strong that this man reached out to me to pass that message along? The answer is rooted in countless examples of partnering with technicians in my quest to fix this huge operating company. Take, for example, the time Sol brought in a new guy to head labor relations. By that time I was in the job I was supposed to have had from the start, executive vice president of operations and technology. I was one of two guys (Greg Winn being the other) to whom Sol entrusted the bulk of the company. So this new labor guy was telling me how we were going to change things. He hadn't been there long enough to understand anything that was happening, but he already had a plan. He barely knew where the bathrooms were located. I chuckled when the guy left my office.

I was in a meeting one morning and Sol ducked his head in the door. "Did you know everyone in Tucson is on strike and out picketing today?"

I said that I didn't know that, but I would take care of it. We finished the meeting and I went to Jimmy.

"Somebody wore an offensive T-shirt," he explained. "The supervisor suspended him, and the whole garage walked out."

I said, "It's not a Tucson strike? It's one garage?" He said yes. It was about 150 guys. I asked him what he had done about it and when my guys would be going back to work. He said Mike Flagg, the Tucson CWA president, had said they would not go back to work until he talked with me. Jimmy told me that the reason the worker had been suspended was that the new labor relations guy had gotten involved and told the supervisor to suspend him.

"The labor guy told my people to suspend someone?" I said.

I walked into the labor guy's office to ask what he did that caused my guys to walk out. He told me that a technician wore an offensive T-shirt, and he advised management to send the guy home for the infraction.

I told the labor guy that since he felt he had the authority to make a decision like this then he should go tell Trujillo when he would have the technicians back to work.

Ten minutes later, Jimmy came into my office and said that everyone was in a dither because I was not doing anything about the problem in Tucson, and because I'd dressed down the new labor guy. I asked Jimmy if he'd seen Sol in my office in a panic. He said no.

"All right. Here's another coaching moment for you. Here's the deal. We've now got to make an example out of our labor guy. We have to make sure that this hurts enough so that he will never, ever make the mistake of doing what he did again."

Then it was time to call Mike in Tucson.

"It's about time you called me!" he said. "Your stupid-ass labor guy told the supervisor to suspend my guy. How long have you been here, Bob? Three years? We don't work like that."

"I know that. So why don't you get them to go back to work?"

"I will," he said, "but I wanted you to know that those labor people are fucking up our company."

I asked him what he needed. He said, yes, the guy should not have worn the T-shirt, which said something unpleasant about US West. He said he wanted to tell his guys to go back to work, but they had to be paid for the time they'd spent picketing.

"Wait a minute, a hundred and fifty guys! I've got to pay them half a day's pay when they didn't work?"

"You've got to pay them, Bob, and I will tell you why. These are the guys who have turned this operation around. Until today this has been the best place in the world to work. They had to stand up for their brother."

I suggested a compromise. I would give the guys their half day's pay, but the kid who wore the T-shirt would have to accept a five-day suspension without pay. I wanted to send a message, not about control or management, but about customers. We don't offend customers with our T-shirts and we don't tarnish our brand. Never.

Mike said he would have them back on the job by noon.

The labor guy came into my office and wanted to know what I was going to do. I said, "What do you mean, what am I going to do?" He said he'd just talked to Sol, and Sol had said I would be getting the people back to work.

"First of all, it's not important what I do," I told him. "I just want to make sure that you understand something. If you ever, ever interfere with my organization again like you did today, even though you don't report to me, I will fire you. The way we work here is the union is our partner, and if you can't handle that, you need to go home. Don't ever do that again."

CHAPTER NINE

Focus . . .

would need some help and some counsel as I pushed to transform US Worst into US Best, and I turned to Patti Stacey, the president of Action Learning Associates, for help.

Perhaps more than anyone else, Patti had helped me climb to a new level of understanding of myself, of customers, of the needs of a business, when I was working at becoming a Breakthrough Leader at Ameritech. It pays to go back to that time now, mainly because I realize how far I had to come and how much I had to change to get to the point in my career where I could fix a troubled company.

I can assure you, no one at US West had to go as far as I had to go at Ameritech, and therein lies the lesson.

The Transformation Trio

Tichy, David Dotlitch, and Patti were a strange trio. I didn't understand what Bill Weiss saw in Tichy, this professor from the University of Michigan Business School and the Action Learning Associates team. I was assigned to the Ameritech Institute team along with two other executives. The assignment started immediately. Dennis Carr, Judy Raica, and I were told to report to a hotel in Ann Arbor, Michigan, for three days. I was not down with the program.

Judy and Dennis were eager beavers in the sessions and I was okay letting them knock themselves out. Any comment I made was typically drawn out by David, who would simply ask, "What do you think about that, Bob?" I would sometimes offer a weak response or just to be a pain, saying, "What do I think about what?" Patti would shoot me a look.

This was not the way my movie was supposed to end. I really didn't want this job.

Privately, Judy tried to shake me up and tell me to get with the program. I remember one of the harsher moments, when she said, "My God, Bob, you are so gifted and talented and you are blowing a once-in-a-lifetime opportunity because you didn't get a business unit job. Get over it!"

After a couple of weeks, and with no improvement in my behavior, it dawned on me that Tichy was talking on a fairly frequent basis with Bill Weiss and Dick Notebaert, and I wondered what he was saying about me.

I really didn't like Patti, who was assigned to be my coach. Her words always pierced me. This was a bad situation, and I didn't try to hide my feelings. Finally, one day at a meeting at the Wyndham Hotel in Chicago, Patti quietly asked me what was I so afraid of, what was driving my behavior. She said that if we couldn't understand it, she wouldn't be able to help me as a leader. Soothing and probing, she reduced me to tears.

For all the mentors who have touched my life and my career, none made the contribution to my growth and development that Patti did. She made me understand my fears. She made me confront my insecurities. She made me find the moral compass I would need for the judgment calls I would be forced to make all the time as a change agent. Somehow she could see right through me. She understood me like no one else ever has.

Later Patti told me that she saw the potential in me, not the dysfunctional behavior. She was determined to get that potential properly channeled. She would not let me cut any corners. She made me work hard on the things I didn't like to do.

She was very good at framing situations and then having me respond. She gave me answers only when I had exhausted my own. Her input always gave me deeper insight into the higher-order thinking I just didn't have at the time. I had never had an executive coach, and I actually used to think that anyone who needed one was inadequate as a leader.

How could I ever have thought that this assignment was a dead end?

Patti was also the first person to get me to open up about my inse-curities and to talk about my fear of failure, my belief that I didn't have what it took to be at a high level, my fear of being exposed as an imposter.

Did I actually believe the stereotype that African Americans didn't have what it took to sit in the corner suite? Patti helped me verbalize these thoughts and work through them. The depth of our relationship was equally exciting and frightening. I never doubted Patti's ability and I totally trusted her insights. I called her with every key decision I was making, to gauge my thinking, to calibrate my thoughts, to check my rationale. I realize how blessed and fortunate I was to have Patti in my life and in my corner. She unlocked my potential and took me to a level of performance and confidence I didn't know I could reach.

Patti's Thoughts on US West

Patti was the first person I called when I accepted the job at US West. Once I had her commitment to help me, I knew I had a fighting chance to win at this new company. Her framework became my intervention strategy there. She told me at the time that she understood my sense of urgency but that the first order of business had to be to stop beating customers up and start improving services. We were debating one day about how hard it would be to get visible improvement in customer results in thirty to sixty days. I argued that with the condition the com-pany was in, we could make a material improvement in customer results in that time frame without question. She said, "Let's go for it."

"Focus: Customer" was born that day.

We would enlist the top 150 leaders in the company to work in teams and take on roles to fix customer service. With the focus on these 150 people, we would cascade the learning and enrollment down to the front-line organization. Along the way, we would find the 50 or 60 per-cent, or maybe even 70 percent, of the 150 who could make the journey with us as leaders.

The answer to the question "What needed to be fixed at US West?" was, basically, "Everything!" But if we had attacked everything, that would have created an overwhelming chore that would have exhausted us.

We needed a process that would allow me to define the problems we faced, isolate the ones that were the most serious and damaging to our business, and create the focused team of executives that US West would need for its transformation.

Patti and I went through an intensive diagnosis aimed at finding the most important, high-leverage, and high-impact things we could do to push US West's transformation along. Did we want to take costs out? Did we need to start with the capital program? There were seven or eight individual initiatives. We decided US West would get the biggest lift if we improved customer service. We weren't talking about survey results; we were talking about real, concrete problems that were damaging our reputation with our customers. Bottom line: we were harming customers by not performing.

How could we deliver on time for them, whether it was a new installation or responding to a trouble report? To do that, we needed to be aligned on the mission, the goals, and the respective roles everyone was going to play in the process of improving customer service.

Adding to that challenge, I was going to have to find out which of my managers were keepers. I decided to bring in those 150 people for a multiday tough-love session where we would talk about the condition of our business, our responsibility for the problems that had gotten us into this trouble, and how to build a plan for changing things.

It was Patti's idea to call it "Focus: Customer."

I would return again to the "Focus" theme as we fixed numerous problems and as the challenge shifted from customer service to leadership and then on to shareholder value. In each case, I was able to collect the right people, get them all on the same page, identify challenges, and create solutions.

As I had anticipated, there were some casualties in the process.

Just as Breakthrough Leadership at Ameritech took on a different tone once it became clear the company would be sending people home who were not Breakthrough Leaders, we wanted to have the right things happen in the right places very quickly, and we needed high-energy performers to do that. In the end, about 15 percent of those 150 executives who were called into the program either opted out or were asked to leave.

Focus: Customer sent the message that this wasn't just another couple of days of what might be called Bonding for Bosses.

Sending in the PIGs

Focus: Customer, Focus: Leadership, and Focus: Shareholder went hand in hand—all three comprised a broad, consistent, and determined effort to get everyone at US West on the same page of the transformational bible. Once I had initiated and completed those efforts, my plan was to unleash my process improvement groups, or PIGs, so I could make certain we were not just paying lip service to change but were aggressively identifying problems and, just as important, developing solid strategies to fix them. But first I needed to go find Rob Stamer at Ernst & Young and persuade him to abandon that track to partner he was on to join me as head of the PIGs. This was no easy sell, but Rob and I had forged a great relationship in Chicago and I trusted his ability and leadership. More important, he was not afraid of me and would challenge my thinking. I remember one day he asked me for my opinion on something and when I offered it, he proceeded to argue with me about it. I told him, "Rob, you can't debate my opinion with me!" He also knew how to lead and how to help me identify which costs we needed to take out and the proper way to fix the underlying business processes systemically. The courtship to get him to say yes was hard, and including his family in the process was the only way I got it done. He is a close friend to this day and I enjoyed watching his boys grow up and turn into fine young men. His son Brian even worked for me for a spell.

I created my PIGs from an unusual combination of selecting bright, young, promising people that I discovered early in the process and searching externally for very bright, very focused people.

Rob and I picked them, trained them, and used them very aggressively to manage our strategic initiatives. I believe that PIGs are mission critical to the successful transformation of every company I have worked at, and I have created and used them over and over, no matter what job I have taken.

Focus: Customer Pays Off

The Focus: Customer effort was remarkably effective. Within days of starting, people all over the company noticed that complaint calls were dropping and problems were being solved much more quickly. The Focus: Customer initiatives were improving results across the entire territory.

US West had magnificent potential, serving twenty-five million customers in fourteen states. Many of those customers were spread across vast territories. The range of weather conditions in those territories was mind-boggling. The Red River seemed to have as its mission in life to flood its banks. Constant rain in Oregon and Washington State and blistering heat in New Mexico and Arizona were all common occurrences. Nothing was simple in the Rocky Mountains when you were dealing with transmission systems. Most of these things were under the control of God alone, so we could not change them. Management, the productivity of the technicians, the mission and focus, customer service performance, cost—those were the variables at US West that we *could* control and, I was convinced, would change.

There were other big problems I had to deal with. We were performing poorly in data services and we had more Federal Aviation Administration circuits to maintain and install than anybody else in the nation. We were routinely causing problems with air traffic control. If you lost a DS3 line (a high-speed, high-capacity transport pipe) in Omaha, it might affect air traffic control over a whole slice of the United States.

This wasn't about pizza shop phone lines or a grandmother being unable to call her grandchildren. Lives were in our hands. The MCI people provided a very large portion of the FAA network in the country, and they would beat the crap out of me every month when they came over for reviews. After four months, it got so bad I had no choice but to make some management changes, because the people I had in place were not cut out for the task. I reached back into Ameritech and asked my good friend Mike Tatom to come help me fix this data organization. Mike was a veteran telephony executive and someone who knew how to slay dragons. Improvement happened immediately when Mike took over the organization.

For the US West Focus: Customer launch, I was very clear about my messaging and wondered only if my organization would understand how serious our situation was. We had a burning platform and everyone needed to understand my case for change.

Our dismal customer service performance record was the one given everyone in the room knew (and many had come to accept), so I told them we were looking at a new day and that all of them were assembled together to start the journey of improved performance. I had a plan and I needed to know who wanted to take the battlefield with me.

I also wanted to make sure that the group understood the focus I wanted. "We're not here to fix the capital problem," I said. "Everybody in the room knows we have that problem. We're not here to fix technology. We're not here to fix cost overruns. Our focus over the next ninety days is to turn the corner on customer service."

Patti broke the group into about thirty teams, with each team given an assignment outside of their core expertise. Most team members were confronted by challenges they had never even thought about before. The team building required some fine-tuning, because we needed an array of skills spread across the various groups.

We didn't have to invent problems. US Worst did that for us.

What do you do about service calls that come in at the close of the day? Do they fall like lumps into the mash, or do we want to take special note of those calls and what we're going to do about them? How do we handle handoffs during customer complaint calls? How do we make certain our customers are not merely passed around? How do we deal with the blizzard of complaints landing on us each day? (We invented something we called Velcro to address this problem. It gave us a way to make certain there were introductions and handoffs along the way so that no customer was lost in the shuffle as we steered them to the proper place to be served.)

The process started racking up good numbers right away, and that meant improved services.

Dick McCormick and I had breakfast one memorable morning, during which he took personal responsibility for the performance of the company, talking at length with me about the failed reengineering effort we had suffered. He said he didn't know what I was doing, but it had been a long time since he'd seen US West service at the improved performance levels we were now delivering.

At the end of the day, I concluded that US West didn't have leaders who pushed the envelope and held people accountable. They didn't have a lot of what Ameritech had, experience at dealing with these kinds of challenges. There were isolated exceptions to this, such as Fran Dolan, in Minnesota, the most outstanding talent I inherited when I took the job. But even in Fran's case, systematic process improvement was missing. There was no reward/consequences structure in place.

Sol was great about letting me do my job. He stayed out of my way and we built a relationship that went beyond the workplace. When Greg Winn was appointed executive vice president of markets, I had a peer who was the greatest business partner one could ask for.

My relationship with Sol was just getting stronger. It had developed into a friendship. Greg, Sol, and I became partners in attacking the problems of US West. It was the best team I had ever been on. With those two guys, it was like playing ball again.

When we shifted to part two of the effort, Focus: Leadership, I wanted to really home in on developing leadership skills and succession planning for the organization. I also wanted to assess the top people in the company. In one of the first initiatives under Focus: Leadership, Patti designed a program where we would bring together thirty-six executives at a time and put them through a series of workshops where they would diagnose and solve strategic problems that I gave them in the business. The teams did a great job on the initiatives, but the real focus was on them as leaders.

I also instituted a series of town hall meetings, which was my attempt to get my executive team to stand and deliver the vision and road map of where we were going, to enlist people, and to tell them why they needed to care about the initiatives we were deploying to fix the business.

Focus: Leadership worked just as well as Focus: Customer. It provided me a platform to get to know where the hidden leaders were inside US West; it created the succession pipeline I wanted, and it gave my leaders and me insight into the kind of people we needed to import to fill out the organization.

Understanding leadership talent, knowing exactly what you have on board, was always the underlying premise of everything I did, even while we were fixing the business. Using the action learning process took what might have been a six-year challenge and compressed it into a very tight time frame for turning the business around.

Finishing with the leadership component cleared the way for the final phase, Focus: Shareholder, which was targeted at one of the most glaring symbols of failure at US West, the failure to reward shareholders for their investment in our company. No one ever talked about the shareholder. Very few employees valued the equity. Focus: Shareholder became a way to teach people about the financial model of the business and how we made money. We wanted to be clear in showing the organization how their improved performance would drive shareholder value. When I walked into the company, the share price had been eighteen bucks and nobody cared about owning equity.

With the help of Professor Larry Seldon from Columbia University, we introduced value drivers, simple sets of productivity metrics that would allow the organization to understand what it did every day that created value in the enterprise. We had used an important benchmark for this process at Ameritech: the Frito-Lay company. From the president of Frito-Lay to the guys who drove the delivery trucks, there was a common productivity metric that told everyone in that company how they were creating value for shareholders. It was called "boxes per day." This simple metric could be disaggregated down to the factory level, where people were actually making the product. How many bags of chips did you put into how many boxes each day?

Everyone in the company understood the same measure, which was why it was so cool. Frito-Lay figured out a way to give someone in accounting, someone in manufacturing, and someone driving a truck a value driver for the number of boxes they needed to account for, process, or deliver every day. Every day there was a measure of how Frito-Lay did by that single, crucial metric. It wasn't the only metric that Frito-Lay paid attention to, but it was one of the simplest.

At Ameritech we used the same model to put in productivity measures each day for our technicians, clerical force, and operators. Everyone had a productivity measure. When you have those drivers in place, you can show people at every level exactly how they are driving share-holder value. Once you have shown employees the basic tenets of the business model, you can show them how they can increase earnings per share by finding ways to be more efficient. The objective is to show the relationship between costs and profits. You teach people those models and then you disaggregate the financials down into what they do every day.

A caller in a dispatch center may have a hard time seeing the link until you define what he does in terms of costs, profits, and impacts on the customer. If you can do that while you are making it clear that the business is *his*, too, all the better.

If you are a repairman and the company average on repair cases closed per day is five, and the new metric you want is seven per day, this productivity increase represents operational efficiency improvement. You can show exactly how that translates into financial results.

We educated everyone at US West on the concept of value drivers and the impact that increased efficiency had on financial performance. The increase in productivity helped to decrease complaint calls and lower costs in operations. Improvements in our organization coupled with great sales performance by Greg Winn's unit was magical, and our stock price started to climb. When the market is as good as it was in the late 1990s you have the given that rising tides lift all ships, but the work we accomplished through Focus: Customer, Focus: Leadership, and Focus: Shareholder and our collaboration with Greg's organization to rid them of our repair complaints greatly contributed to our stock price rise from eighteen dollars a share to more than sixty.

When he came through on visits, Greg Winn would tell my groups that our improved performance actually created more capacity for him in the business office to sell more product, because he was not "wasting" time handling customer calls about service operations. The improvement was material for him, and his organization became a great partner.

Patti Steps Out

I was working on my own set of targets with Dick Stonesifer, the re-tired CEO of General Electric Major Appliances, who was helping me hone my management skills and file down some of my rougher edges. Patti brought Stonesifer to the table after we got started at US West. Some of the tough-love feedback I got at Breakthrough Leadership had stayed with me. But I still needed help with my tendency to take things over and do them myself, or to think of a situation as something I had to repair. People still viewed me as harsh, too direct, too critical of work and effort.

We talked every week.

Just as Patti had been a mentor to me earlier, Dick now took on some of this important developmental work, which was fine with me. He knew I wanted to be a CEO, and he knew what I would have to do to get ready for that kind of advancement, so I felt lucky to have two coaches.

Out of the blue one day, Patti said she needed some quiet time with me. We had also become good friends by then. When we met up later, she told me how proud she was of my development and progress as a leader. Near the end of the conversation she said something that made me freeze. She said she'd known the day would come when she could no longer help me and that she would have to let me go. That day had arrived.

What? Had I pissed her off? I did not want to accept this. I pleaded with her not to do this. I told her that her work was not done yet, that she was leaving me incomplete. She was persistent and then went an additional step to explain that our personal relationship would always be there, but she could no longer provide insight and coaching to me because I needed a different kind of coach. Intellectually, I understood everything she said, but emotionally, I didn't accept any of it. I gathered myself and tried one last appeal: "Patti, please don't leave me. I'm not ready to go forward without you."

I knew I had to keep working on my skills if I was to become a CEO down the road, but this was a curveball that I hadn't seen coming. Dick Stonesifer wouldn't have understood my emotions, so I reached out to Tommie Welch. He would understand and help me get my head screwed back on right.

Tommie listened as I poured out my heart and soul to him. When I was done, he chuckled and reminded me that I had been to this movie before with him. Tommie said that Patti's decision had not been made in haste. He said that she knew the day would come when she would have to push me out of the nest and that her bringing Dick in to work with me was part of her plan to take me to the next level.

PIGs on the Playing Field

About a year into the game, after the Focus initiatives and the continuing transformation, it was time to send in my PIGs—in a formal way.

Earlier, Rob Stamer had deployed a small team of PIGs, but I wanted to go "all in." They would become the intervention methodology for building on the Focus initiatives and continuing the transformation. I was going to need more PIGs at US West than I had used at Ameritech, because it was a bigger organization in terms of functionality and the sheer number of people.

We assigned two PIGs for each officer reporting to me. Mike Tatom had two PIGs. Cathy Hemmer, who was the head of all switch translations and the network operations centers (NOCs), got two, as did every division leader who reported to me. I would meet with Rob and the PIGs weekly.

The officers who came into US West with me understood the PIG process, deployed them, and got a bunch of lift in return. Those who didn't understand the process were highly skeptical. The very smart ones figured out that if you wanted to get ahead of the game, you needed to meet with the PIGs more often than I did. They all knew the PIGs were getting work done, but some of them were afraid to let them see too much data. They would let them into their organizations, but they would not show them where the bodies were buried. Because of that, some of the PIGs were swimming upstream and constantly trying to overcome obstacles.

It didn't take long to figure out who these resistant officers were.

After I met with the ones who were struggling, I would meet with Rob and tell him, "We can do this one of two ways . . . ," and Rob would say, "I know. I know." That was code. It meant it was time for him to deploy and have a "Come to Jesus" talk with someone.

He would say to his peers, "If you cannot open up your organization and work with us, then I am going to give you more help than you want." I have been around Rob for years now. You do not want him in your area helping you fix a problem, and that's not to be interpreted as Rob will break glass or do something sinister. It means he will literally come in and take control, and the situation could get messy. Rob is a fixer. He has an incredible work ethic and he will let nothing stand in the way of getting the results for the company and for our customers.

At that time, we were doing a lot of construction, over $2 billion a year in capital spending. Terry Moya was one of the PIGs assigned to that area. He found out we were deploying a lot of fiber optics, and that's the cheap part of the process, putting the glass in the ground. The most expensive part of deploying fiber is the electronics required to make it work. The engineering organization did not always light up the fiber-optic cable upon installation, which was a good decision, because why spend the capital to light up cable when there are no customers to connect? I actually liked the just-in-time mentality of the organization. Unfortunately, the record keeping was not up to standards, and we lost track of some of the installations. So, in effect, we didn't know where some of the fiber had been deployed.

Once Terry discovered that the record keeping was not meticulous, it became his mission to find this stranded investment so that we could leverage it in our capital program.

This was a home run for us.

Still, we clearly had some problems in our planning, design, and engineering areas.

Rewarding Good Work

About a year and a half into my job at US West, Greg Winn invited me to go to Hawaii with him for his recognition event, which included perhaps seven hundred retail sales–side people at the Maui Ritz-Carlton. This wonderful weeklong celebration was the best recognition program I had ever witnessed. I was genuinely moved by it, because it was grand and because it paid tribute to great performers. I also saw how energized Greg's people were and the sense of pride among those who were recognized, particularly those who were repeat winners. Greg invited me to speak, introducing me against the theme music from *Rocky*. It felt positively electric addressing that audience.

As soon as I got back to Denver, I pulled Jimmy LaValley aside and told him we had to pay tribute to the service people, too. "It will cost us a pretty penny, but we have to do it," I said. I put together my own President's Club and, after inviting Sol and Greg, brought about a thousand people to Hawaii.

You want to talk about lift in an organization?

Some of those people had never been on an airplane before. We told them to invite their spouses or a guest for a week at the Ritz-Carlton in Maui. Not only had most of them never even dreamed of going to Hawaii, but the Ritz-Carlton was icing on the cake.

We weren't there to speak, we were there to wait on those one thousand employees and their guests. We ran out of rooms at the Ritz, so my team and I stayed at the adjoining property, which wasn't bad, but it wasn't the Ritz. It was a hard week of work for the management team. We spent most of our time serving the people who worked for us.

You haven't seen a surprised person until you've seen a supply room attendant who's been invited to Hawaii. It was very special. I allocated so many seats for engineers, so many for repairmen, so many for cablemen. I also instituted something Greg didn't have at his celebration: a president's award. Because I love eagles, the award I picked was a beautiful eagle statue that I called the Wind Walker Award.

The value of the first-ever operations President's Club came to me at 6:00 AM on Sunday, when the buses were leaving for the airport. Jimmy and I got on every bus to say goodbye. I climbed aboard that first bus and I was looking at the most pumped-up group of people I had ever seen. I wanted to thank them, but as I tried to speak, the words were difficult to get out. I tried to tell them how proud I was to be their leader, but raw emotion was the only thing working for me. I stood there, tears running down my cheeks. Somehow I got out "You are my champions," and the entire bus erupted in applause. I turned and walked off the bus. I needed to regain my composure. I looked over at Jimmy, and he just laughed and said, "It's because you care, sir."

Composed, I got on the second bus. One of the Wind Walker Award winners was sitting up front. His award was on his wife's lap. I could see what it meant to both of them. This time it was a total meltdown. I couldn't muster anything. They knew, and they understood. I saw tears flowing from them as well. Something special was happening. It was my high school basketball lesson writ large: Help the others score. That is how to win!

Attention

I was a little uncomfortable with a change that came well into my effort at US West. It started in the local press, with reporters who were impressed by the fact that US West's service had improved so much. Several wrote profiles of me and my role in the process. I was starting to get a name.

Tichy did a long interview/profile of me in *Fast Company* magazine in 1997. My thought was that all of that attention might have made Sol a little uncomfortable. I was shy about my personal work, but I wasn't shy about my support for Sol or my recognition of his brilliance as a boss. Now people were calling me "Mr. Fix It" after an article titled the same appeared.

The *Fast Company* article worried me. Up until that point at US West, I had a free hand to do what I believed I needed to do. On top of that, Sol and I were friends. Our families were friendly, too. I was worried that the adulation I was receiving in the business press would create concern in the senior ranks.

Three days after the article appeared, a copy of the magazine came to my office with a note from Sol.

"Well-deserved praise and recognition. I'm very proud of you," it read.

That was so liberating.

I also was not ready for the "poor boy" aspects of some of the stories, the narrative that focused on my rising from poverty to become such a successful executive. It was embarrassing. And I didn't like the emphasis on my race, either. I wanted it to be more along the lines of "Here is how Bob Knowling surrounded himself with the most talented people he could find and coached them into helping him fix businesses."

But that was not very often the story that was told.

Leaving US West

All of that adulation, and my participation with Wall Street and making speeches and a variety of other appearances, started to draw a lot of attention. I was a target for headhunters. I wanted to be a CEO and I knew that was not going to happen at US West. That company already had a good CEO.

The first offer I entertained came from a company called Nextlink, founded by Craig McCall, who had made billions of dollars when he sold his cellular company, McCall Cellular, to AT&T. He had a venture capital firm out of Seattle called Eagle River Partners. I went up and took a look at the job they were offering.

It was a Competitive Local Exchange Carrier (CLEC) with maybe $100 million in revenue. They were focused on second-tier cities such as Saginaw, Michigan; Rockford, Illinois; and Memphis, Tennessee. The company was growing like a weed. McCall and his brother had built McCall Cellular from nothing, so that impressed me. But I wasn't impressed with the company Nextlink.

CLECs were a dime a dozen at the time. This was one of the bigger ones. They had turned their geography managers into fiefdoms. I thought that was way too much distributed power. I also thought the business would not scale properly because, if it had thirty cities, it had thirty different processes. There was no standard operating protocol. I am a big believer that if you want to be bigger than a popcorn stand, process and process control are really important. You have to be able to replicate. And replication is in direct correlation to having a standard operating environment. McDonald's could not have done what it did without understanding this.

A partner at Egon Zehnder International, the search firm handling this Nextlink placement, called and said he wanted to share his client's thoughts with me, as the dance with me was taking quite a long time. The client, he said, didn't think I was enthusiastic about the business, at least not as enthusiastic as I had seemed during our initial meeting. "My job, Bob, is to determine whether you really want this job," he said.

"Good call. No, I don't want it," I told the partner.

"Can you tell the client why?" he responded.

I told him everything I found wrong with the business model.

He called back later and said the client had told him that my comments were insightful.

Six months after my dance with them, Nextlink went public. Just with what they had offered me, I would have made about $40 million. But the company ran into difficulty, just like all the other CLECs in 2000, and I've often wondered how many of their challenges were a direct result of the problems I was describing. I've never looked back on that opportunity.

I knew I was in demand, and Sol knew it, too. He asked me how long I would be staying at US West. I asked him why he was asking me that kind of a question. He said I had become a big name. I was African American, very well educated, and an experienced Network guy. US West had a corporate policy that any officer wishing to accept a board of director offer had to have it approved by the board, and Sol championed my case when I was offered a director seat on the board of Shell Oil Exploration Company.

"Who wouldn't want you to run their business?" he said.

I told him that when I made a decision, he would be the first person I would tell.

In the fall of 1997, I began getting calls from John Thompson at Heidrick & Struggles. Thompson was persistent about a company named Covad. I did some homework on it. At US West we were toying with the high-speed technology DSL. By January of 1998 that technology had become more intriguing to Sol, me, and others on the senior team. John Thompson never let up on calling me, so I decided I would go out to California and have a look at Covad.

Thompson told me I would make $100 million if I took the Covad job. I had no idea even how to fathom that amount of money. Even though I was making a significant amount of money a year at US West, a person just doesn't think in terms of tens of millions of dollars, or at least I didn't.

So I had a look. Covad had about thirty to forty employees and three very interesting founders who had come from Intel: Chuck McMinn, Chuck Haas, and Dhruv Khanna. McMinn was a business development kind of guy. Haas was the marketing sales guy. Dhruv was a lawyer, so he was general counsel.

It was clear that Warburg Pincus, the biggest investor in the company, wanted a professional CEO. The company had less than $5 million in revenue and a model that really didn't excite me. They were selling DSL to corporations for their employees who worked at home and needed a high-speed connection back to the corporate network.

They had just two customers, Intel and Cisco. I was a little confused about the chemistry among the founders. I assumed they would be best friends, but they weren't. I had to ask myself whether I really wanted to join that company. I also knew that I wanted to be a CEO.

In February, Sol and I had to go to Washington to talk to the FCC about some of our needs. We started with the FCC chairman and then met with each commissioner. Sol told Bill Kennard, chairman of the FCC, that US West was getting killed "around the edges." Then, out of nowhere, Sol said, "Let me tell you about a little company called Covad."

What a feeling. I didn't even know that Sol knew who Covad was, let alone anything about its business model. This conversation happened with each commissioner. I knew I needed to take a hard look at the Covad opportunity and either pursue it with urgency or shut down the conversations by saying no thank you.

I was at another one of those life crossroads.

My relationship with Sol and with Greg Winn was golden. Our results were climbing to unbelievable levels. And we were having a huge impact at US West.

I kept avoiding the calls from John Thompson. I called Tommie to chat about the offer and then I went into my office at home one evening and used the same Ben Franklin decision matrix I'd used to make the US West decision. Covad came up hands down as the place where I should go.

I decided I would leave US West in July. The day I chose to leave, July 7, was the day of the Major League Baseball All-Star Game at Coors Field in Denver. I would be hosting customers in one suite at the stadium, and Greg Winn would be hosting customers in another. Sol, who had to fly to Minneapolis earlier in the day, would shuttle between the two. I told Sol I needed to see him before he left. We met at the hangar.

"Sol, I've decided to leave the company," I told him.

It was even harder than saying goodbye to Dick Notebaert had been. I could not tell if he had tears in his eyes, because I couldn't see that well with the tears that were in mine. He looked at me and said, "You don't really want to leave." And I said, "No, I don't. I have to leave."

"What's going on here?" he asked.

"I have to leave, Sol, because that's my destiny. That's where I want to be." We talked for several hours and it was a very personal and special conversation.

That didn't end the conversation, of course.

Sol was worried that I would be decimating US West by taking his best employees, just as he had seen the migration of talent into US West from Ameritech. I told him I wanted Cathy Hemmer and Joe Devich. He said I could have them. I told him I would call him beforehand if there was someone else I really needed but that I didn't plan to take his people. He said thanks.

I gathered up the family and headed to the All-Star game not wanting to see Greg. He had become my trusted and valued peer, and we were so aligned it was frightening. Around the third inning of the game, Greg poked his head inside the suite door. I went out into the hallway with him. The embrace we had was just what I needed. We spoke in hushed tones. He didn't want me to leave, and I told him that I didn't want to leave but that this was an opportunity I just couldn't pass up.

My family and I were on an airplane to Cabo San Lucas the next morning, as I needed to clear my head and get my mind wrapped around this next journey. The past few years had seen a lot of construction on my bridge; it was expanding. About a week after the All-Star Game (the American League beat the National League 13–8 in the highest-scoring All-Star game in history) I was at Covad.

I had been in the building for about twenty minutes when Chuck McMinn told me there was an offer on the table for one of Greg Winn's key deputies at US West. I sat down with Dhruv, the general counsel, and explained that I had made a deal with Sol to call him about anyone I was going to take with me to Covad.

So after getting Dhruv's advice I got on the phone and called Sol and told him what was up, but I didn't give him the name of the executive whom Covad was recruiting. I told him I had no idea Covad was after the guy but I felt obliged to call anyhow. I asked him if he wanted me to rescind the guy's job offer. He said no.

The guy in question, Bob Grant, accepted the job.

Then the next thing I knew, US West's general counsel, my good friend Mark Roellig, who was a phenomenal leader and contributor, slapped Covad with a lawsuit for the recruitment of Bob Grant. This signaled the opening of combat. I felt that my agreement with Sol not to recruit people from US West was now dead. In hindsight, I should have picked up the phone and called Sol when US West served the lawsuit. Monday-morning quarterbacking is always so easy.

After that, several US West people showed up, and I never felt guilty about it. Months later I got a call from Sol about a regulatory case in Minnesota. They were trying to get permission from their fourteen-state utility commissions to get into the long-distance business and they had a key hearing coming up in Minnesota. Remember, now I was a US West competitor. And if a competitor could come in and talk about how good US West had been at granting me the lines I needed for my DSL business, that was a really good thing.

So when Sol got me on the phone to ask for help, I said sure, but I also wanted to talk about another topic. I told Sol that I had honored our agreement but that when he threw that suit at me, all bets were off. We agreed we both should have been more adult about it. We cleared the air, and I said I would be glad to help him.

That Sunday, Greg Winn and Mark Roellig flew to California and we mapped out a strategy for my helping them. I stayed in touch with Sol and our friendship only grew.

My tie to US West was severed but my friendship with Sol, Greg, and Mark was intact and still is today.

I felt good about leaving US West. I loved that company, loved the relationships I made there, and loved the work I did. I turned it around.

It was no longer US Worst when I left.

CHAPTER TEN

Covad: Rise and Fall

I arrived at Covad in July of 1998. It was a tiny company, but it had the ambition to get ahead of the coming big new thing: high-speed Internet access. The plan to get there focused on giving employees high-speed access to the corporate network from home. I was more interested in getting high-speed access to the masses. So was Chuck Haas, who was in charge of sales and marketing, but we didn't have everyone on the same page with us yet.

It's easy to forget today that there was a time when not everyone had a cell phone or access to the Internet. I viewed Covad as a "present at the creation" kind of company.

The Telecommunications Act of 1996 required existing phone companies to sell access to their copper phone lines to other telecommunications providers. It was the government's way of increasing competition (which leads to more choices for consumers). It would force the various Bells not only to make their copper available, but to do so on very favorable terms.

Covad wasn't interested in providing telephone service. It was hunting much bigger game.

The novelty of being able to use your telephone line to dial up Internet service had long since worn off by the time Covad was founded in 1996. The Internet itself was fascinating to everyone, as were the emerging companies tapping its strength. The more that people became familiar with what the Internet could do, the greater the demand for speedy, powerful service. It took some four hundred years for Johannes Gutenberg's movable type press to lead to general literacy in Europe. The Internet achieved as much in a few years, opening a doorway to knowledge, entertainment, and communication to millions upon millions of new users.

But old-fashioned AOL-type analog services were simply not up to the new challenges of the Internet era. Digital Subscriber Loop (DSL) technology would change all of that. DSL service could travel over phone lines but would operate much more efficiently in providing digital information to computer terminals. The companies providing DSL service (which would always be turned on) would be tapping a vast potential market: the home computer user longing for something a lot faster than analog dial-up.

You might think the Regional Bell Operating Companies (RBOCs) would be eager to get into such a business. They owned the copper and they knew the technology, but coming from that world, I knew that any deployment of DSL on their part would be slow and forced, because that was the nature of the beast.

It would require a lot of capital to add DSL to the network, and the various regulatory agencies would never allow the regional Bell operating companies to cherry-pick the lucrative suburban areas when deciding where to deploy the service. Even though analog service was irritating, it had not yet been shown that people were willing to pay a lot for something better, but the cable operators who were offering high-speed cable modems were getting some traction. The one problem with cable modem service was that your speed would vary depending on the number of users on the node at a given time. When a subscriber was alone on the node or with just a few other customers, the speed via cable modem could be incredible.

The game changed when the cable operators entered the market and the Telecommunications Act of 1996 opened the field to competition. Telephone companies had never been on the cutting edge of technology. They were great at implementing what someone else had already invented, but they weren't interested in risking their reputation or taking chances with how their systems worked. So they dragged their feet.

But not everyone did.

Smelling Opportunity

Among venture capital companies that fuel start-ups, the large private equity firm Warburg Pincus had been researching the subject since 1997, when it was approached by a team of managers who wanted capital to start a DSL service company, beginning in San Francisco and then expanding nationally.

The managers argued that the Baby Bells had been so slow to move into this market that there was a good opportunity to establish a strong national footprint. These managers would control territory in one of technology's most important new products before any competitors entered the field.

These PE-savvy specialists were as aware of the challenges as the Baby Bell people had been. Could the installation price be lowered to a competitive level, and could the old copper lines stand up to the stresses of carrying so much high-frequency information?

The Warburg Pincus analysis concluded that the technology was sound; that Covad had strong management but was weak on telecommunications experience; that the market was ripe for the product; that lots of capital was needed; and that the company would need to ensure sufficient use of that capital to scale the operation.

Warburg also concluded that the new company needed a telecommunications-savvy leader, in particular someone who knew how to develop scale, manage many thousands of employees, and move aggressively into what was an almost open field.

That is where I came in.

My Bridge Grows Again

I was about to add a new section to the bridge of my life. It's only fair to warn you up front that, for the first time in my long career, which had carried me all the way from Kokomo, Indiana, to levels of success I had never anticipated, I was heading for failure. But I would learn that failure, though a harsh teacher, is also a great one.

I finally had the CEO position I had wanted for years, but I was the boss in a world vastly different from US West, Ameritech, or Indiana Bell. Those businesses were all about efficiency, competition, and taking care of your customer base. Covad was about something that did not yet exist: a nationwide DSL network that would be first on the scene, so efficient and so dependable that it would draw customers from everywhere. No one had ever done that before. And getting to market quickly would be one of Covad's greatest assets.

I arrived in Santa Clara, California, Covad's hometown, full of enthusiasm and the sense that we were on the forefront of something important, a new business opportunity attached to a technology that seemed to be changing every hour of every day. It's impossible to overstate the sense of optimism that was surging through the tech economy in the 1990s. We had about $60 million in cash on that July day I walked in, the remaining proceeds from a high-yield debt offering. We believed we could get to the public market in a few months, certainly by November, and our bankers told us that it was a good time to go.

I got an eyeful of the place in my first few weeks there and I realized early on that something was wrong. What Covad had up to that point was the result of a corporate process. They'd tapped some debt, set up a sales force, and acquired some corporate customers. I argued that distribution would be the key to our ultimate success, and one founder was completely in sync with me on this position. I told them we needed other people besides ourselves selling our DSL services, because the object of the game would be a land grab to see who created the most pervasive footprint (network geographic coverage) and who got the most customers first. The company that did that would be the market leader and the market leader gets to set the rules.

We had to talk to some big brands about selling the service for us.

The real game, I argued, would be AOL, Microsoft, EarthLink, and the Baby Bells. The founders and I had some healthy debates about the speed with which the RBOCs would come into the market, not to mention the long-distance carriers and the sea of small CLECs. Someone argued that the RBOCs had so much capital they could burp a billion dollars and a network would appear overnight.

Our great advantage would be the speed with which we could deploy our network and the rapid rounding up of as many customers as we could. That would give us the proof points we needed to validate the big investments we were making to bring the DSL network to the country.

It wasn't hard convincing the board what we needed to do. There were two Warburg Pincus board members, Joe Landy (now the co-president of Warburg) and Dr. Henry Kressel; a guy from Crosspoint Venture Partners; and some angel investors. Having a couple of CEOs on the board would have been great because they lived in the real world and would bring a different perspective to the discussions. My board structure was pretty standard for a Silicon Valley start-up with the exception of Warburg, which was a giant in the private equity space.

We changed the business model and started working on the business-to-business play. Chuck Haas was very good at it. He understood how to segment the market and chose whom we needed to go get. I walked into Covad with a very thick Rolodex, so when we targeted AT&T, it was very easy for me to pick up the phone and call Mike Armstrong, who was running AT&T at the time. It was easy for me to get Joe Nacchio at Qwest, and the same with Garry Betty at EarthLink. I knew them all.

We filed our S-1, for our initial public offering, in October, four months after I arrived, and we soon had secured investments and partnerships with AT&T, Nextlink, and Qwest. AT&T gave me $25 million and said they would white-label Covad as AT&T and sell it in the marketplace as their service. I got $20 million from Qwest, so instead of deploying their own network, they were going to use Covad's national network. Nextlink/Concentric gave us $10 or $15 million. So in the prelude to Covad's initial public offering, we raised in the neighborhood of $60 million.

The bankers were salivating.

Very quickly Covad moved into the fast track. McMinn worked with me on the IPO and partnerships, and Dhruv focused on helping Cathy Hemmer get better cycle time on loops we'd purchased from the RBOCs, and helping John Hemmer, her husband, get access to RBOC central offices so we could deploy our network.

There were many cases of outlandish costs being passed on to us by the Bells just for a ten-by-ten-foot chicken-wire-enclosed cage on their switch room floor. Dhruv was building a great case against the Bells, who were hell-bent on blocking our progress.

We were growing our employee base rapidly. Covad was emerging as a Silicon Valley star, and the tech media of that era were eager to tell success stories. I was the turnaround expert who'd left a dazzling phone company career to help manage the brave new world of Internet connection and communication. I became used to seeing my face on the covers of business magazines.

I assembled my team early on at Covad. There was Joe Devich and Cathy Hemmer. Bob Grant was there. Then we hired Rob Davenport, a Harvard MBA and former investment banker. His vocabulary range was off the charts. I was in awe. I had never heard anyone talk like that. He was the biggest brain I had ever met. And that's what we affectionately called him: Big Brain Guy. "Big Brain Guy" became our Big Deal Guy, and we were making deals left and right. Rob joined us as the head of business development, and soon after our IPO, I moved him into the position of CEO of Covad International.

We didn't have much choice. Our market capitalization reached ten billion dollars.

It was clear to me that with such an inflated market cap, we really didn't have the revenue run rate, earnings, and customer base to support it. I was eager to find as many fixed assets and paying customers as I could to add to our business.

Founderitis

The founders were not a comfortable trio. Two of them didn't get along. I saw that this disdain was one-sided. While one had an ax to grind, the other just wanted to do the job and win. Sometimes I had showdowns with them, too, as I pushed strategic directions I wanted to take or the selection of members for my senior team. To be fair, one of the three founders at Covad was an absolute joy to work with and never gave me one day of grief. Chuck McMinn was a gentleman and a class act. My respect for him has never wavered. One was decent to work with until the end of my tour. But almost from the beginning, one of them made just about every day of my three years at Covad unhappy.

When I had the chance to immerse myself in the work, it was an absolute joy. But that didn't happen often. There I was, making more money than I could count, showing up on the covers of business magazines, and yet I wasn't happy.

Despite these problems, the rising tech tide was lifting a lot of ships, and Covad was certainly one of them. We were doing so well, with everyone making a lot of money, that I decided against having a showdown with the founders. That was a mistake. I have advised many CEOs of start-ups post-Covad about the importance of preventing or curing founderitis. At Covad I was the poster child for handling that particular ailment the wrong way because I ignored the problem and made no effort to bring them into the fold. Equally bad decisions.

You might recognize the symptoms of founderitis.

Founders can be opinionated and set in their ways. They rarely embrace new ideas. They are so close to the business and the process that you can't introduce anything new. They surround themselves with small loyal groups and won't adhere to the protocol you've established for running the business to scale and creating a standard operating environment. They have the sense about them that they are untouchable because they are the founders. It's the job of the CEO to break these barriers down and to bring founders into the team. Founders are not bad people. Their brilliance in developing great companies is something I'm in awe of because so few do it successfully. I also should point out that there are a few exceptional founders who can actually lead, grow, and operate the firms they created. Bill Gates (Microsoft) and Larry Ellison (Oracle) are the great exceptions. It takes an entirely different skill set to lead a business than to found one.

Still, we were doing so well it was difficult for me to focus on the downside. We were riding an external market that was rising quickly, particularly for high-tech stocks. We went to $90 a share, and I split the stock. We had grown from being a little DSL company to a $10 billion–plus market cap company.

We were clearly the DSL provider to watch. While two worthy competitors, NorthPoint and Rhythms, got into the public market, they never approached our success by any measure. According to the metrics that had been set for the industry, we successfully met Wall Street's expectations every quarter. We were riding a great wave in 1999.

Then the air started leaking out of everything.

When the tech bubble burst, all the Internet-related stocks started to fall. It was as though everything people had thought so highly of only a few months before had turned to dust. The idea that the Internet was a place that could produce lots of revenue for everyone slammed into the cold light of day. Search engines were making money. Big sales venues such as Amazon were making money. But the thousands upon thousands of small ISPs and businesses that had assumed it would be easy to tap into the Internet ecosystem were discovering that this wasn't possible when the access to capital dried up.

When trouble hit, everything took a backseat to payroll, including money these companies owed to Covad for the DSL lines we provided for their customers. How do you count money that you are owed? And how long can that receivable be on the books before you stop thinking of it as revenue?

Those would become crucial questions that would affect my position at Covad.

Jesse Jackson, the Clintons, and Business with Michael and Emmitt

Because of my friendship with the Reverend Jesse L. Jackson, one of the doors that my success at Covad opened led to the Oval Office. President Clinton and First Lady Hillary Clinton and I became friends. Visiting the White House gave me goose bumps, not because of the Clintons but because I may well have been standing exactly where Abraham Lincoln once stood.

The contact with Jesse Jackson flowed from my Chicago days. Reverend Jackson reached out to me when I was at Ameritech. He was always looking for ways to draw the business community into the attack on poverty. The reverend wanted a meeting, so I arranged a breakfast with Ameritech vice chairman Dick Brown. We sat down in the Ameritech dining room one day at 6:00 AM.

"We're filling up Cook County Jail," Jackson said. The jail was growing faster than any subdivision in Chicago. He said the problem with Ameritech was that it didn't do enough to help attack the problems that plagued Chicago. It bought suites for the Bulls games and suites for the Bears games and put a new whale in the Shedd Aquarium and sent the Chicago Symphony Orchestra to Europe. Clearly, the problem wasn't that the company had no interest in civic affairs, Jackson said. They were just the wrong civic affairs.

Jackson pointed to the menu cards sitting in front of us on the table. He asked us to take off our glasses and read the menu. Dick started to pick his menu up to peer at it, and Jackson said, "*No*, read it on the table." Dick started laughing and said he couldn't see the writing on the card.

"That's what happens when these boys go to Cook County Jail," Jackson said. "They can't read. You know what it is like if you can't read when you get out of jail? You end up back in jail again. How can you possibly make a contribution to society if you can't read?"

I was so impressed with Jackson that I started going Saturday mornings to his regular meetings at Operation Push, which were an amalgam of church service, political rally, and gospel festival. He is as powerful and compelling at the lectern as he had been that morning at the breakfast table. I started donating money to his organization and forging a relationship with him.

Before I knew it, I was on the phone with him being invited to a meeting with Bill Clinton in Washington. President Clinton and I connected with each other immediately. After I arrived at Covad, I got a call from him. He asked me to be his ambassador for bringing broadband to people who could not afford it, helping to bridge that digital divide.

Clinton was one of the most engaging people I have ever met. Every minute he talked to you, it was as though you were the only person in the world he was concerned about. The First Lady was tough on the outside but wonderfully sensitive on the inside. I loved getting to know her. I remember the day my administrative assistant, Diane Jones, came into my office and said, "Hillary's on the phone." The first lady invited my wife and me, along with six other couples, to the White House for dinner and a private Elton John concert.

How often do you get a call that says President Clinton will have a jet meet you and take you to Washington for an event or a discussion? That happened to me three times, and now it sometimes seems as though it happened in someone else's life.

Once I was in San Diego golfing with some friends in the late fall. I noticed on about the fifth hole that I had missed several calls from my office. I called Diane, my assistant, and she told me that the president's office was trying to reach me. "Really?" She told me that President Clinton wanted me in Little Rock, Arkansas, the next day to be with him for a town hall meeting and then fly with him to Chicago, where he would be giving a speech at a south-side Chicago High School.

I landed in Little Rock and my airplane was ushered over to a hangar where Secret Service personnel came on board. They told me that they would be moving my airplane to a neutral area and that I should gather anything I needed to take with me. The president would be landing within the hour. A couple of big military planes landed and taxied over near the hangar. Three helicopters were unloaded from one and presidential vehicles were removed from the other. Then Air Force One landed. I watched as the president left his airplane and walked to his helicopter. I was led to another helicopter and within fifteen or twenty minutes of his landing I was flying in the presidential convoy. I didn't know where we were going; I didn't know why I was here. I figured I would find out in time.

We landed on a football field and then transferred to vehicles, which took us to a little restaurant for a presidential luncheon. I saw Reverend Jackson and he was the only person in the delegation that I really knew. President Clinton finished his speech and we left to go back to the airport, where we all boarded Air Force One to head to Chicago. I got maybe three minutes with the president on the flight to Chicago. He thanked me for my efforts with ITAA (the Information Technology Association of America) and for my leadership of Covad Communications. He wanted me with him on this trip because he wanted people to hear the name and know the face of one of the leaders helping to bridge the "digital divide."

The stop in Chicago was very similar to the one in Little Rock as we all moved from Air Force One to helicopters. We landed on a school football field and the president spoke to a very large gathering in a high school gym on the south side of Chicago.

Once completed, it was back to Chicago O'Hare for the flight to Washington, D.C. Being a part of this process was something I appreciated only years later. Several months later the president presented me with the Reginald Lewis Trailblazer Award at Reverend Jackson's Wall Street Summit for my work and effort in managing inclusion and helping to bridge the digital divide.

I became a frequent visitor to the White House and was so honored when the president invited me to sit with Hillary at his State of the Union address. I remember calling home afterward. We had been taken back to the White House, so I decided to call home to get the reaction of my kids. Audrey answered the phone. We had a good chat and she said I looked good on TV but she was quick to point out that every time the camera focused on me they caught me chewing gum.

In my early life, I never dreamed I would arrive at a point where I would be meeting the president, visiting the White House, and witnessing a State of the Union address.

There were other unexpected opportunitis, too, surprising to a man who never sought that level of attention that came along with success.

The Chicago Bulls were in Indianapolis to play the Indiana Pacers and my sports fanatic eleven-year-old daughter, Aimi, was going to meet Michael Jordan, one of her dreams.

Tony Prather, an attorney at Indiana Bell, was good friends with Michael and had arranged for Aimi and me to visit the locker room after the game. I laughed at Aimi as she was trembling waiting for her grand moment. Michael was one of the last people to emerge from the dressing room, and when he walked out, he said, "Where's Aimi?" The look on her face was priceless. Michael signed a basketball and a poster for her and posed for several pictures with her.

From that encounter, my friendship with Michael Jordan grew. Other than a few rounds of golf and seeing him at the Ameritech Senior Open golf tournament, our acquaintance had been casual.

Then I met football legend Emmitt Smith, and my relationship with these two megastar athletes intensified. I met Emmitt via Carra Wallace. Emmitt's wife, Pat, and Carra are very good friends and Carra's husband, Werner, was a business associate of Emmitt's.

Over the course of the years, Werner, Emmitt, and I would get together to play golf, have dinner, and talk about business and investment opportunities. In the midst of racking up Super Bowl titles and impressive Hall of Fame statistics, Emmitt had the wherewithal to plan his future beyond football via his investment options. He was always asking questions, and his range of knowledge about various industries was expansive.

Emmitt's competitive nature would come out on the first tee during any round of golf; and I won't divulge the outcome of our matches, but let's just say that one of us needs more time on the practice range. After one round of golf at my course, the California Club, we started talking about all the great new businesses hatching out of Silicon Valley including my company, Covad Communications.

Werner had been advocating that Emmitt, Michael, and I get together and explore ways to work together. The technology industry was in full bloom and after a series of conversations about opportunities to build and create more wealth, we committed to getting all four of us together. We met in Scottsdale for a full day. Michael, Emmitt, and Werner were intrigued with the value and wealth creation that I had accomplished, leading Covad Communications to a very successful IPO and subsequent execution of the business plan that saw the stock price soar and split.

We knew that many high-net-worth people were investors in venture capital, private equity, and hedge funds, and so the questions of which ones you could get access to and which ones had the great track records were central to our discussion. Werner had a more intriguing idea. Why not build our own fund managed by a world-class team? We knew we would want my investment banker from Bear Stearns, along with Werner, to be the general managing partners.

The idea was for us to pool about $100 million of our personal funds, then raise an additional $500 to $750 million through our personal networks. With all the relationships that I had, we could easily get access to deals. We believed this concept, with Michael and Emmitt on board, could have some sizzle to it. The more we talked, the more clear the idea became.

Michael sealed it for me when he spoke in a very hushed tone midafternoon.

"Look, guys, let me be very clear. If we were here talking about owning a hockey franchise, I wouldn't even come to the meeting unless Wayne Gretzky was sitting here with us, leading the charge. Excuse my arrogance, but if we are discussing owning an NBA franchise, my money doesn't go into the deal unless I'm leading the effort. If we are doing this fund with a focus on technology and health care, I'm not in unless Bob Knowling is leading the initiative."

I was set back a moment by Michael's comments. My response was reflective and equally to the point.

"There are three questions that we have to understand before we attempt this bold initiative. First, since all three of you respect my understanding of the space, I need to do some serious due diligence to determine the risk and timing of raising a fund."

It was 2000, and I had seen some softening in the technology sector, and the access to capital was tightening, so I owed everyone a reality check. "Second, I need to find out if my colleague at Bear Stearns is ready to make this leap. He and I have talked about doing something like this. I need to find out if he's ready to leave Bear Stearns, if the stars are aligned for us to do this. And if he isn't ready, I need to find someone of equal talent to fill the role of CFO/investment officer."

"Third and finally, I need to do my own gut check about this venture, because it will require my full attention and I need to decide if I'm ready to walk away from Covad."

I knew that I needed to stay focused and disciplined and not get caught up in the aroma of doing a deal with Michael and Emmitt. When we were leaving the Phoenician, it was a circus watching hotel guests approach Emmitt and Michael for autographs just on that short trip from the meeting room to the limo. We finally got them to the car and headed to the Scottsdale airport. We agreed that I would get back to everyone in thirty days, if possible.

Thinking about what transpired that day, I remember walking up the stairs to my airplane. I was the one trembling now.

The technology sector was walking right into the incredible Internet bubble explosion. We never got the fund off the ground. I kept the guys informed, but it became evident months later how seriously the economy and the sector were crumbling. I don't have any communications with Michael these days, but Emmitt and I stay in touch. I asked him to come out one evening in Dallas to visit with my employees and a group of customers that we were entertaining, and I'm convinced that had Emmitt not done the NFL thing, he could easily have had a stellar executive career.

But I like the title of Hall of Famer better than CEO for him, and I'm sure his fans do, too.

As word of Covad's success spread, I was constantly being called on to speak. One time, I was in Pittsburgh to address the Fortune 500 CEO conference. I got out of the limo at the hotel and I noticed these eight black men, all dressed in formal attire, standing there. I approached them and said, "I got a couple of things I need to do this week. First, I need to get a haircut. Where's the 'hood?" The eight guys surrounded me. One of them said that when he got off at 4:00 PM, he would take me for a haircut. Then I asked them where I could go to listen to some jazz. We bonded. I not only got the haircut, but I also went to listen to music, and I attended church Sunday morning with one of them. It was so cool.

When I gave my speech the following Thursday, there were about two hundred CEOs in the audience—and there, in the back of the room, those eight guys had shown up to hear me speak.

Nothing ever touched me like that moment. I hold it as dear as those precious moments with Jesse Jackson, Bill Clinton, Emmitt Smith, and Michael Jordan.

Covad's Problems Deepen

As troubles deepened in the economy, the high-tech industry Internet stocks were collapsing and the trouble deepened at Covad, too.

By the summer of 2000, Covad's share price had slid from ninety dollars to forty. My competitors' shares were in the teens or single digits, and everything else was sliding south, too. It was getting more difficult to raise money; we were one of just two telecommunications firms to access the markets and raise money in the second half of 2000—MCI at a billion and Covad at over half a billion—after the market went south. Covad was the last in the telecom sector to access the capital markets and get a financing completed.

By June we had just completed the purchase of BlueStar, another DSL company in the Southeast. Dhruv didn't want us to buy it, but one of my board members insisted I purchase it instead of another company in the Pacific Northwest I wanted to acquire first.

By that time, the board at Covad had changed. The two members from Warburg Pincus had departed because they'd bought another telecom asset. I had added three new board members of my choosing, Larry Irving from the U.S. Commerce Department, Debra Dunn from Hewlett-Packard, and Hellene Runtagh, whom I knew from General Electric. Chuck McMinn left Covad to go to Crosspoint Venture Partners as a CEO in residence. Dhruv Khanna and Charles Haas were obviously connected to Crosspoint when they founded Covad, as Crosspoint and Warburg were the early VC and PE investors. I'd gotten along well with the board member from Crosspoint up until this point.

With those potential tensions as a backdrop, I went into the fall of 2000 with an interesting offer in my pocket. Southwestern Bell's Ed Whitacre and I had talked several times. He knew me, where I had been, and what I had done. Southwestern Bell was the only natural place for Covad to be. "Bob, you need to decide where to pitch your tent," Ed said. "And the rightful home for Covad is right here. You let me know if your guys want to make a deal."

I walked into the Covad board meeting and told them what I was up to. Our stock was trading at only twenty-eight dollars. Then a board member said something no one had ever said to me before. "I think you have lost your vision. You guys are getting ready to go on a road show, you're going to raise another half a billion dollars. We'll outlast this downturn. Get back to your vision, Bob."

I didn't like that at all. I was very unhappy. In hindsight, I have wondered many times why I didn't walk away from the company when it was clear that the board and I were not aligned on the endgame. It was one of several mistakes I made, and one of the costliest. I know it was pride that kept me from walking; it would have been too much like losing. Also, I was not working on my own agenda after the first year, and that's a bad compromise for a person who has always had a plan for how to run an organization and how to win.

Without the board support to sell the business, I turned the page. I went to the debt market in September and had a successful $500 million–plus convertible debt offering. The stock traded down under twenty dollars during the road show and didn't recover the way it typically did when we had done other financings.

Fast-forward to October

Covad Communications had not had a misstep in its history, even though our stock price was sliding into the basement right along with the stocks of everybody else in the tech industry. Still, from the day I walked into the company, we had always exceeded Wall Street's expectations by every measure. I was preparing to announce the best quarter in our history. We would exceed every metric that Wall Street tracked for our industry, and I must confess I had played a big role in helping design those metrics for high-speed access companies. As good as these results made me feel, I had a new worry that was nagging me.

It was rooted in some important company history.

When Covad was founded, the business model was very different from what I changed it to when I came on board in July 1998. I believe that selling the product through alternative distribution channels was the right solution for scaling the company. There were a lot of doubters at Covad, but that decision alone, along with flawless execution, put us on the road to market leadership in the DSL business.

In the early days at Covad, we signed up a lot of small Internet service providers who had access to a lot of capital and to bundles of hot ideas to try out as the medium expanded at a speed that was nothing short of astounding. Because Covad and its competitors were basically involved in a land grab at the time, it was hard to assess those smaller companies, even as we were trying to capture the big ones.

Once it became clear that the big service providers were not going to be building their own DSL networks, Covad moved aggressively and seized the lion's share of that business. AT&T, Qwest, XO Communications, EarthLink, and Southwestern Bell were exclusive to me. What could go wrong? In the context of those big companies, nothing.

Month after month, their volume increased and the percentage of my DSL lines consumed by the big brands began to dwarf the monthly lines purchased by the smaller ISPs. We reached the stage at which the big players represented over 80 percent of Covad's revenue and aggregate installed base. They were the most profitable customers we had. But it is hard to overstate the dramatic change that took place when the access to capital started to dry up in 2000. We didn't have enough money.

I still had the doubts I'd carried with me into the company three years earlier. I needed to raise a lot of cash to carry out the plan, but I was not sure that Covad would reach profitability with the money we had in the bank at that time, even though it totaled over $1 billion. My plan saw Covad losing money for four years before it would ever turn a profit. We were now two and a half years into that period and the capital markets had closed down. Covad's need to obtain capital had been the hardest sell in convincing me to come join the company. It was a leap of faith for me then, and now I was facing that leap of faith again.

That is why the history is so important.

The small ISPs would get a Covad bill every month for the number of lines they had purchased from us. They would then bill their own customers for the Internet service and the DSL line. But with the capital market closed down, or available at only a high cost, the small companies had no access to capital. Very few of them would be able to survive. We started seeing this play out in the slow payments we received from some of our smaller ISPs. We had to move many accounts into what was called the "aged receivables" category.

These ISPs were using the funds from their paying customers to cover their payroll costs and keep the lights on. Payments by the ISPs of Covad's DSL bill, typically the largest bill in their accounts payable department, were becoming more delinquent every month.

Still, by the end of the third quarter, we would report record results. We would beat revenue projections by 14 percent. We would beat profit projections by 8 percent. We would beat all of our other metrics by wide margins.

By 2000 the situation inside Covad had calmed a bit. The senior team was as good as it had ever been. The Internet bubble had burst and reality was reclaiming the marketplace, but with over $1 billion in the bank, we were surviving. (This sounds like a lot for a small company, but we all knew it wasn't enough for the business plan we were following.) Still, like everyone else, I had no idea about the magnitude of disaster the technology industry was about to experience.

Bad News from E&Y

In October 2000 we met with Ernst & Young, our accountants, to review the numbers. The external auditor expressed no concern. We had decided we were going to do our earnings call (the quarterly event where the CEO talks with the investment community about performance) from Los Angeles, because I had accepted an offer to appear on Willow Bay's program on Bloomberg Television, and we were still the darlings in the DSL space. The day before the earnings call, I did a favor for my friend Guy Kawasaki and spoke at his garage.com conference, which had about three hundred attendees. The plan was for me to finish the speech, jump on my plane, and meet my guys in LA to go over the numbers again and prepare for the earnings call the next afternoon. After the speech, I noticed that I had received several calls from Mark Perry, my new chief financial officer. My assistant, Diane Jones, said Mark needed to speak to me right away.

"Chief," Mark told me on the phone, "I've been in battle for the last three hours with Ernst and Young, and we have a problem." He told me that one of the local E&Y guys had had second thoughts about our "aging receivables" from the small ISPs and had called the national office for a review. The national E&Y folks had advised the locals to tell us we should not report about 15 percent of our revenue from those troubled ISPs because they had gone beyond delinquent. Mark was furious, because E&Y had already blessed our numbers and our press release the previous day.

I asked Mark to keep talking to them and to tell the local and national E&Y guys to be prepared to talk to me in two hours, when I landed. I called Diane back and asked her to arrange a call with as many of my board members as she could find on short notice.

After a forty-five-minute flight, I landed in Los Angeles and headed for my hotel, where Mark, Nick Kormeluk (my head of investor relations), and Mark Goldstein (my banker from Bear Stearns) were on a telephone conference bridge with the local E&Y team.

It was a hot-tempered call. Mark Perry argued that it was unprofessional for E&Y to have approved the numbers and blessed a press release and then to have phoned the national office for advice on the matter within twenty-four hours of our earnings call. I listened quietly to the argument on both sides for about a half hour. I wanted to make sure the local E&Y guys were listening to their customer. And I wanted to make certain the Covad guys were listening to the E&Y arguments. I thought the decision the E&Y national office had made was a gray area call. From their perspective, we had properly accrued money for these aged receivables, but E&Y believed they were no longer receivables; that they were doubtful. "Doubtful" is a description that defines the ability of an enterprise to collect money from a debtor.

I offered a compromise. "Why don't we report what has been previously approved by you and the national office, but when I report the revenue number, I will explain that approximately fifteen percent of the receivables are getting more delinquent and that if we are not successful in collecting these receivables in the coming months, we will have no choice but to reverse the revenue and treat those debts as uncollectable."

The local E&Y people said the proposal sounded reasonable, so they agreed to consult with their national office. All I asked was that they have the national office people on the phone bridge when they called back in, or at least have the national partner call me. This was one of the most important moments in the life of the company. They owed me that much.

When the national partner called, he was cordial but came right to the point. He said that E&Y should have put a red flag on the matter the last quarter and that I was not the only company chasing ISP delinquencies. He insisted that I had to reverse the 15 percent of revenues and that E&Y needed to sit down with us to understand how much more exposure we had from delinquent ISPs.

I argued with him. I challenged him on the timing. He said they were as upset about this as we were, but there was really no other way around this problem. We spent about thirty minutes talking about the accounting principles, and in the end I could not disagree with him.

I thanked him, and then told my team we needed to prepare for the next day. We would not be recognizing 15 percent of our revenues.

I thought about this for a while. Then I prepared for the board call.

As much as I hated the timing, I could not disagree with E&Y's

decision. There was no one to blame. I was the guy responsible for Covad Communications' performance and I knew better than anyone that if you were bold enough to sit for the cover of *BusinessWeek* and *Forbes*, you had better be bold enough to stand up and take the hit when the company didn't make its numbers.

We had done a great job with Covad. I give all the credit to Cathy Hemmer, Joe Devich, Rob Davenport, Jane Marvin, Mike Lach, John McDevitt, Dhruv Khanna, Chuck Haas, Chuck McMinn, Martha Sessums, Nick Kormeluk, Carra Wallace, Tanya Van Court, Stephanie Mason, Dawn Cain, Rich Wong, Terry Moya, Mark Khoury, Donna Northington, Frank Thomas, Mark Perry, Tim Leahy, Terry Murphy, Bob Grant, Kim Sharp, Al Loges, Diane Jones, Kevin Chavous, Susan Jin Davis, Rob Stamer, and the scores of other great contributors who took Covad to the top.

Now we were going to stumble over an accounting point.

I was the CEO, and it would do no good to point fingers at the departed CFO and accountants and the way they'd measured things, or at bad timing. This failure was mine.

Dealing with the Board

I made the call to the board. Mark Perry and Mark Goldstein were with me. I often think back on the money I made for Crosspoint Ventures, Warburg Pincus, and the angel investors who were on the board when I arrived. Warburg Pincus alone put $8 million into Covad and walked away with net proceeds of over $1 billion for their limited partners. Joe Landy and Dr. Henry Kressel were great board members, and anytime I'd gone to them with a question or needed a door opened, they'd always been there for me. I'm not certain what Crosspoint put into the company, but I know they made a handsome return for their limited partners as well.

When I broke the news to the board about our not being able to recognize 15 percent of the revenue, there was dead silence. After what seemed like a long time, one director told me to fight E&Y on the decision and not let them off the hook.

I told them more about my conversation with E&Y's national

partner, explaining that he had been polite and cordial, that I had presented my alternative, but that they had stuck to their decision.

At that point, the conversation started to go in circles. One board member demanded the name of the E&Y national partner, saying he was going to call him. I was nonresponsive. I warned him that we had pushed the E&Y guys pretty hard and that any more pushing might lead to unintended consequences. The accountants could insist on issuing a letter saying they could not support management's representations of the financial results.

If that was the outcome with E&Y, I said, they would need to find another CEO.

In the wake of those conversations with the board, with E&Y, with my own aides, I was scared. I couldn't let the team see that, though. I needed to get through the earnings call and then move on to rebuilding our reputation, because what was happening to us was no different from what all the other broadband firms were experiencing.

I agreed to amend the financial statements to reflect E&Y's guidance and then asked Mark Perry to rerun the numbers so we could see what the effect would be of not declaring that 15 percent. I wasn't afraid of losing my job. I was more afraid of having to tell Wall Street that I had missed a number. That the story and the rationale for the miss were logical didn't matter to me.

The hours of waiting to make that earnings call were a lot like the hours you spend in the locker room before a big game. The difference was that this time I already knew the score and that we had lost. I struggled to remember a past experience that would help me cope with this terrible defeat. I accepted the fact that when you suffer a setback, you never make excuses. You never rationalize or minimize the loss.

I was a wreck inside. I did not show that outside, though. I knew how to pick myself up and get back into the batter's box. I could not let the investment community see that this was shaking me up, because that would have undermined their confidence in Covad even more. I wasn't the first CEO to miss a quarter, and while I needed to show remorse, I could not let them see I was devastated. Still, I had to be careful not to come off as too bullish about my continued faith in the company. People would sense that I was selling performance, which was not my style. This was going to be a very tough telephone call.

I don't require much sleep, but that night, I couldn't even get the two or three hours I usually got. I tossed and turned thinking about how my employees would react and where the stock price would go. Finally, I got up to make some notes.

I knew I would have to get on the road to Boston, New York, and Washington/Baltimore to visit with Fidelity, Putnam, State Street, T. Rowe Price, Franklin, Morgan Stanley, Goldman, and the other folks who had always come to the table, whether it was debt or equity I was offering to the market. They deserved to see me and to hear why I thought the underlying fundamentals of my company were strong. I was certain they would be wondering if this particular problem was isolated to the ISPs, or if there was something seriously wrong with Covad's business model. I thought through everything I needed to do to deliver my message.

As expected, the reaction to the earnings call was not good. Immediately afterward, in after-hours trading, the stock traded down to something like $2.50 a share. The board asked me to put together a board call two days later. By that time, the stock had climbed to $6.00. It was Thursday night.

The board wanted me to tell them what I was going to do.

First, I said, we are going to starve the network. We're going to stop the deployment of DSLAMs (the servers we install in the Bell central offices that enable the high-speed service to our end-user customers). The more DSLAMs you have, the more customers you can serve, because DSLAMs define your geographic footprint. By stopping deployment I would save those investment dollars earmarked for network expansion, and I would just have to weather the storm created by this lack of geographic coverage. By doing this I would fail on commitments to elected officials who represented rural communities, but I simply had to preserve the $1.2 billion we had in the bank. I told the board that we needed to get to free cash flow break even and pause the national footprint build for now.

Then I told them that in those cases where we had very few customers working out of a particular DSLAM, I would shift those customers to alternative providers. We couldn't afford DSLAMs that weren't paying for themselves. Let's say it took thirty-two customers to make a DSLAM profitable. If I had only twelve for a given DSLAM, I would shift them to Bell South or AT&T.

Third, I promised a new business plan that would get us to profitability

Fourth, I would make a few leadership changes.

The board said it needed time to consider my plan. It took them an hour. They called to say they'd accepted my plan and that they wanted a board meeting on Monday, at which time I could present my new business plan.

First thing Friday, my team and I met and spent that day and the weekend building a new operating plan. Rob Davenport and Mark Perry were spectacular. Scaling back our expansion was logical and the right move, but remember, we were currently operating under a plan that was going to have us in two thousand central offices all over the nation, and I already had spent half a day with Senator Jay Rockefeller of West Virginia convincing him I was going to give as much attention to West Virginia as I was giving to New York City.

Now we had to craft a plan that said we weren't, in fact, going to be able to be in all of the West Virginia counties I had promised Senator Rockefeller we'd be in. And because we needed about $2 billion more to reach the free cash flow break-even point under the old plan, that number would have to be reduced drastically or maybe even eliminated altogether.

That weekend, I sent a long e-mail to one director whom I routinely met with outlining a few personnel problems. He sent a note back: "Sometimes when a team can't come together, change is necessary." Hmm. That's profound. I didn't know what the hell he meant, but I sure wasn't going to spend any time trying to figure it out.

In the boardroom on Monday morning, Rob Davenport began presenting the new plan. He wasn't fifteen minutes into it when one board member started asking all kinds of questions. He was almost picking at the plan, being condescending. Something wasn't right. It got to the point where he was being so rude that I called a time-out and asked the management team to leave the room because I needed an executive session with the board. Cathy gathered up her things. Rob gathered up his things. Mark gathered up his things. But Dhruv just sat there. I said to him, "Dhruv, you, too." And he said, "Well, I'm the general counsel and the secretary of the board." I told him to leave or he would be dismissed. He looked at a board member and didn't move. The board member nodded his head, and Dhruv left.

There was my clue.

"I don't know what's going on," I said, "but you know something, guys? I came here as the celebrated guy who was going to take you to the promised land, and I delivered. We are the standard for high-speed access. We're the best brand in the market. We've raised more money, we have more customers by a factor of ten. Nobody is in our peer group. It's clear to me now that there are other agendas at work and I think you, as a board, need to make a decision." I pointed out that there was no question about my competency, that all my appraisals had been outstanding. Every bonus I had was doubled or tripled from the one before. "What I have done wrong in this company is I have tolerated some dysfunction from the founders and tolerated some interference that I never should have listened to. I missed the difference between 'past due' and 'doubtful' with Ernst and Young. You make up your mind today. You either want me to run this company and to implement the four things I told you about Thursday night—which we were here to discuss this morning until you rudely mistreated my management team—or you find a new CEO."

One director said that sounded like an ultimatum. I told him he could take it any way he wanted to. It was 9:30 in the morning when I walked out of that boardroom. At 3:00 PM, two board members, Bob Hawk and Frank Marshall, walked into my office. I knew it had been a grueling board session, because I had three new directors who supported me. They closed the door. Bob did the talking, and it's important to point out that Bob Hawk was a friend. He was a former US West executive who was retiring as I was entering US West.

"Bobby," he said, "we've decided to take your recommendation and go find a new CEO. We accept your resignation."

I turned around at my desk and took a piece of paper out of my printer. It was a resignation letter I had written on Friday. I gave it to him.

"This is dated Friday," Frank Marshall said.

"Frank, now even you are underestimating me," I said. I had indeed written my resignation letter on Friday and my administrative assistant, Diane, told me later that she knew I was resigning Friday because I'd cleaned certain things out of my office.

Did I fail or didn't I fail? Part of me logically knows I did not fail. Then again, I wasn't the CEO anymore, and I had gone to Covad because of my longtime yearning to be a CEO. What was most disappointing was that I left on their terms, not on my own. When the buzzer sounds in a game and the scoreboard displays your loss, who cares how well you played? You still lost. I failed to manage my board, I failed to integrate the founders into the team and as a result, I was secure as the CEO as long as the company didn't stumble.

Years later, one of the principals at Warburg Pincus, Dr. Henry Kressel (my Covad board member), wrote a book, *Investing in Dynamic Markets: Venture Capital in the Digital Age*, about venture capitalists and the decisions they make. Covad is one of the thirteen Warburg investments Henry highlights in the book, where he gives some background on these investments, good and bad. Enough of the Covad story is in that book that the reader can conclude I did not fail, that what happened at Covad was a function of what was happening in the tech economy and that my leadership of the company resulted in that Warburg investment being the greatest investment in the history of the firm at that time. I'll admit that I did smile when I read the Covad story in the book. Like anyone who has ever lost their job and is not in denial, I know the things I should have done differently. I needed to overcommunicate with my board and I should have been one-on-one with more members rather than just with one of them. I made no real effort to know and understand Chuck Haas and Dhruv. In three years, I never asked either of them to go to dinner, to take in a ball game, to play a round of golf. I never tried to grow the relationships and to get to know them as people. I have never been to Chuck's house and I have no idea what city he even lived in. I did all these things with Chuck McMinn. In fact my great love of red wine was fostered by Chuck. I knew better. In my entire history of leading organizations, I always built good teams and made it a priority to invest in the team individually and on a personal level. It's no wonder these guys didn't support me. Neither they nor I had anything invested. They deserved better from me. The outcome may have well been the same but I would have felt better. To highlight the point, I left the office immediately after my dismissal around 3:30 PM. Starting around 4:30, the gate at my home started ringing and one after another, every member of my executive team showed up at my house. Angie threw together a large pot of spaghetti and we ate and drank wine all night. My banker Mark Goldstein was still in town and he showed up, as well as Tichy. Most of the team spent the night there. There was no crying or whining that night. In fact, most wanted to quit in defiance of the board, but I shut that talk down as quickly as it came up. The point of all this is that Chuck and Dhruv were the only missing members of my team. I truly failed these guys and it is my biggest regret from the Covad experience. It is the sting that has been the hardest to shake off.

I was the adult they brought in to set them on a course to behave like a real company, with real returns and real hopes and plans for the future. To this day, it remains a great irony for me that we built the best of the DSL providers in a very competitive era and yet my tenure as CEO was brought down by this first quarterly miss and the dysfunction that ensued.

PART FOUR

The Best Three Years

CHAPTER ELEVEN

Happy Every Day

I was standing in the middle of the fairway on the par-five second hole at Inverness Golf Club on Saturday morning, waiting for some people to clear the green, because it was my intention to hit the green in two, when I saw my phone flashing. I never answer it on a golf course. For some reason, though, this time I walked over to pick it up.

It was 2002, and my Covad experience was now two years behind me. I had taken another CEO position at a company called Simdesk. This was brand-new technology, and a new experience for me: a plan for a suite of desktop applications that could be loaded on just about any device. But Simdesk was a software company. Other than some central office switch translations, I knew very little about writing code.

Simdesk's software was a thin client application that would allow its user to access files, e-mail, calendars, whatever, from any device connected to the Internet. When I joined the company I was convinced that AOL, Microsoft, Oracle, and others would covet a thin client application like that.

I'd put a lot of my own money into the effort, but now I knew it just wasn't going to work. No one had fallen in love with it. Once it was clear that no one was going to buy that technology, there was no point in staying, but I hadn't started looking for the next thing in my journey.

During this time, I was thinking very generally about which building project I would take on next to extend that career bridge. I had been referred to as Mr. Fix-it and the Agent of Change, and CEO assignments and new board of director opportunities were being presented to me on a fairly frequent basis. The question I had to answer, as I faced the second shot on the second hole, was what I would do next.

Either God or Mayor Bloomberg

Maybe God wanted me to answer that phone. I'm not kidding. I would not normally have done it, but there I was, phone in hand on the fairway. The caller was my friend Michael Brimm, a professor at INSEAD (the European Institute of Business Administration).

"Michael, how the heck are you?"

He told me he'd been talking to one of the young executives he mentored at Goldman Sachs, Ron Beller, who had left Goldman and was now involved with Joel Klein and New York City mayor Michael Bloomberg in a massive transformation project for the New York City public school system. Bloomberg and Klein had asked him for the name of someone who had led a successful business transformation who might be willing to give them some advice on what they were planning to do.

"Would you be willing to talk to Bloomberg and Klein?" he said.

"Sure, why wouldn't I?" I said.

At this point, I want to put the emphasis on the word *talk*, as I assumed I would be called in to give advice.

Sunday morning after church, the phone rang. It was Joel Klein. I remembered him from my Covad days. I had sued one of the Bells in an antitrust case and I was asked to come to the Justice Department in Washington, where Klein was the assistant attorney general in charge of the antitrust division. Now he was chancellor of the New York City school system, the nation's biggest, and the most challenging by a large measure.

"Bob, we've got a tiger by the tail here and we've got to change the outcome for these kids in New York City," he said. He talked to me about the children and what he and Mayor Bloomberg had committed to do. He asked me to come to spend a day with him and visit with the mayor to talk about what needed to happen. He said they had a bundle of ideas but that they needed a revolution.

I called Patti and asked her what she thought of school systems and whether they could be transformed the way we had transformed Amer-itech, US West, and Covad. She wanted to know what I had up my sleeve. I gave her no specifics.

In New York, Ron Beller explained to me that they had brought a wave of businesspeople into the school system, and they already had a strong lineup of former employees from McKinsey, Goldman, and others from the private sector.

I immediately liked Ron a lot. He was extremely focused, passionate, and his level of commitment was inspiring. Maureen Hayes was an example of the type of talent Ron was bringing to the table. Klein's chief of staff, she came from the banking industry and was a very accomplished executive who brought a lot of operational experience to the department.

Klein wanted to talk to me about setting up a leadership academy for school principals, but they weren't sure how to go about it. Education universities certified school principals, but that clearly was not working very well. Preparing principals to be just like other principals wasn't going to fix the problems that were wrecking public education in New York.

Beller said that Klein wanted something like General Electric's Crotonville, where Jack Welch had institutionalized succession planning and leadership development. I had constructed our own Crotonville at Ameritech and had used many of the parts of that process, with help from Patti and Tichy, at US West and Covad. I knew what it could do in a business.

What would happen if you took principals, the linchpins in the public education system, and got them all on the same page in the sense that they knew how to identify and solve problems, how to infuse their schools with creativity and accountability and a lot of other innovative ideas and concepts that New York City so desperately needed in its schools?

No one knew, because no one had tried it. That kind of situation is magnetically appealing to me, but I still had no idea I was going to be asked to take a job. I thought they wanted only solid advice based on experience.

The Bloomberg Meeting

Michael Bloomberg is one of the most impressive people I have ever met. The first thing I noticed was that he was warm, self-deprecating, and incredibly comfortable in his own skin. He was also expert at making everyone else feel comfortable. We talked about being mayor of New York, how big that job is.

Mike's vision for New York City was very clear. Education was at the top of the list of things he was committed to fixing. "Do you think you could change the outcome for principals with the kind of stuff you have done at Ameritech, US West, and Covad?" he asked me.

I told him I thought that what I had done at those places was applicable whether you were running the city dump or an ice cream stand. It didn't matter. The transformation process is transferable.

Bloomberg said, "But we've got a tough union."

I said, "No tougher than the union at the phone company."

After a couple of hours, the mayor said, "Will you come and help us?" When he said it, that old clarity settled on me again and I knew. Still, I said, "I don't know. I thought I was here just to give you opinions."

"Who told you that?" Bloomberg said. "We need you to join us."

At that point, I told Joel Klein I didn't need to meet with any more of his deputies. I had seen and heard enough. He told me the former GE chairman and legendary business leader Jack Welch had agreed to be the chairman of the board. Richard Parsons, the Time Warner chairman at that point, would serve as co-chairman with Jack.

"You know, if you come, most of these kids that you and me need to help? They look like you," Klein said.

The last stop of the day was a school. I will never forget it. I went into this classroom and visited with the kids. There was a little Asian child who couldn't take his eyes off me, and every time I looked his way, he gave me this big smile. When it was time to leave, he came over and grabbed my pinkie and looked up at me and said, "Mr. Knowling, are you coming back?"

Inside, I'm thinking, whoa! I am not ready for this. I had been thinking about my next corporate job. But this kind of experience, those lovely little angelic children looking up and practically begging for help, that's not easy to resist.

I called Patti and told her all about it. I told her I was going to say yes, but only if she said yes, too. She said to hold on, that she didn't know if ALA had the capacity to take on the New York City school system. I told her I thought it would be a lot of fun.

Finally, she said yes. Then I said yes. It's interesting that Tichy is the genius behind action learning and has a long list of successful organizational transformations that he has been involved with. He is my long-time mentor and friend, yet, since my Ameritech days, it's always been Patti whom I reach out to first, and I know it's because of the coaching and contribution to my life that she has made. I always want to get her on the team first. Tichy and I don't have to ask each other anything. We are very similar and love working together, so I always know he's up for the journey.

My three years working with the New York City schools were the highlight of my career. I had signed up with Bloomberg and Klein for only one year, but the level of excitement and the energy were just too much to walk away from.

Before I started, I got a call from Jack Welch. I'd been in a meeting with Jack once, but I figured he probably didn't remember me, so there was some anxiety on my part.

"How exciting is this?" he said. "Bob, look at how much we are going to learn."

We did learn a lot, and Jack was a great leader/teacher in the academy and personally for me as my boss.

I called my mother to inform her that I was on a new journey in my career as CEO of the NYC Leadership Academy. It's true what they say about boys and their mothers. Every time anything good happens to me, the first person I typically call is my mother. All I can say is that I seek her approval in everything I do. My number one priority in life, after ensuring that my wife and kids are taken care of, has been to make my mother's life comfortable and carefree. With a lot of excitement in my voice, I explained to her what I would be doing as CEO of the academy.

"Well, it's about time you did something meaningful," she said. "I'm proud of you."

Building from Nothing

With this new job, I had a blank sheet of paper. I did not work for Joel (even though I had a cubicle near his office) or the school system. I had a board to report to, with Welch and Parsons as co-chairmen. I had no money. I had no employees. The school year was already under way; it was January. I was starting out behind. There were only a couple of concerns. Everything else was euphoria.

Even as I was saying yes, Klein was selecting an "academic dean" for the Leadership Academy. (He asked me if I wanted to interview the candidate and I declined; they were very far down the road, so why slow the process?) He told me he recognized that this would be a shotgun wedding, but we had to have an educator on board or I would have no credibility. The person he ended up selecting was Dr. Sandra Stein. I met her about a week later. I had no filters up. She seemed fine to me. I liked the fact that she was an educator at Baruch College. I also liked that she had many ties to the poor community. She had worked for several years in Latin America, and was fluent in Spanish. She had a clear disdain for the affluent who had no social consciousness. She didn't like hierarchy and she didn't actually have any warmth for Fortune 500 companies. She didn't fawn over me. She was perfect!

For this to work, I knew I would have to treat her as my equal rather than as a subordinate. I had no problem with that. We were able to communicate, and she proved to be a great teammate.

If I had to rate my job satisfaction helping transform the New York City school system—other than the fact that I had real issues with much of New York's media—I would give it a ten. Every day I went to work I was turned on.

It was a great job.

A Passion for Helping Kids

The passion I had for those children and changing outcomes for them was there every day. The wild card in the deck was whether I could actually change the principals. It didn't take long to find out.

In addition to running the Leadership Academy, Joel Klein asked me to serve as his coach. He had run a division of Bertelsmann, but running the New York City schools was like running a Fortune 500 company. It was a $14 billion operation with more than 100,000 employees and 1.2 million children.

One of the first things we did was identify the top one hundred people in the Department of Education and take them away to Crotonville for a weekend event. That was a cathartic experience for everyone. We took them through mission, goals, roles, and visioning. We took them through where the school system was going and how it was going to get there. We worked with them on defining their leadership agenda and helped them address their strengths and weaknesses as leaders.

There was some fallout. Some retirements occurred the Monday morning after the event, but that was to be expected in a large-scale transformation. And it was a good thing. We went back to Crotonville with the top team every two months. These were high-octane, high-energy, high-impact meetings.

Tichy and Patti and I would design each weekend and then go in and facilitate the event. Michael Brimm even worked with us the first year. Each evening, we would meet with Joel and talk to him about the process, the outcomes for the day, and his team members.

Joel is one of the most courageous leaders I have ever been around. He will speak at my memorial service; that's how much I love him. His commitment to the cause of public education was unrelenting. During my time with the Leadership Academy, I watched him stand in the face of the media that preyed on the school district every day. Sometimes you would see dozens of stories appear in one day in the various newspapers, most of them negative. The media took a shot at everything he did, but he just got back up on that horse every day and rode again.

In three years, I never got used to the media hits. My feeling was that many of the reporters in New York were so vile that I would not give them access. But that didn't stop them. I would be less than fair to say that every New York City publication preyed on the Department of Education and the Leadership Academy. In reality, there were only a handful of reporters who made it their business to rain on the parade. And of course, there were favorable stories, too, but the ones you remember are usually the unfair stories: stories about my salary, about Covad's bankruptcy long after I left, about the cost of the academy's programs, about the businesspeople working in the system, about the salaries Klein was paying his leaders. (Coming from the private sector, I didn't understand the fuss people were making over $100,000 a year in compensation, and that wasn't just my naïveté.)

This was disheartening, because we were working in a school system where in numerous schools only 30 percent of the children could read at grade level. That was a 70 percent failure rate! When you walked into a classroom, one of the things that really grabbed you, if you were looking at twenty-five kindergartners, was the knowledge that not even half of them were going to make it through the system. Maybe ten to twelve of them would see their way through to high school graduation.

Into the Field

The Leadership Academy was not formally a part of the New York City Department of Education. It was a 501(c) (3) separate entity that funded itself. But everything we did had an impact on Joel Klein and what he had to deal with every day.

At every point, Joel supported me, my team, and the academy, and I grew more and more impressed with how he did his job. Over time, he asked me to attend public meetings with him, even though that wasn't part of the Leadership Academy job.

At the town hall meetings he held, Joel would run into some very angry crowds, because the parents were so upset about the schools. Early in the game, he had picked up on how easy it was for me, while walking through the schools, to identify with the kids and the staff. So I would go to the meetings with him, and together we would disarm the crowd. I would give those in attendance some of my own history. By the time I had done that, it was easier for us to explain to them what Joel was up to, that we knew things weren't perfect, that we understood that parents had every right to complain.

Joel would get up and give his speech, and then I would run a question-and-answer session. Those town hall meetings were wonderful. Several of Joel's direct reports, who accompanied him to the meetings, would chime in during the question-and-answer period. Joel was very good about telling parents when he didn't have an answer that he would look into the matter and come back to the parent. We were getting standing ovations some nights. But not all nights. There were confrontations. I was separated from the security detail during one of the events and was attacked by a woman with a shoulder bag. Fortunately, that was not a defining moment. The kids were the defining moments.

After all, Joel's vision was compelling, because it was always about the kids. The decisions he made, the people he hired, the changes he was driving—they were all being done to improve the situation for the kids.

The Bureaucracy

The Department of Education in the city of New York was its own world, a structure of ten regional superintendents responsible for some 125 schools each, geographically dispersed. The superintendents reported to the deputy chancellor of teaching and learning, one of three deputies who reported directly to Joel. This was the new structure Joel and the mayor implemented well before my arrival. This structure replaced forty-six independent school districts, each with its own local board of directors and handpicked superintendent. There have been many stories and books written about the New York City public school system and its history of corruption and mismanagement, and the lack of control by the chancellor. By taking direct control of the system and dismantling the local school boards, the mayor had enabled Joel to control the destiny of the school system.

The Leadership Academy operated outside of that structure. Even though we had a physical space within the department's building, we had our own organization. We started with three employees: me, Sandra Stein, and Suluh Lukoskie, one of my PIGs from a previous company and our chief of staff. Suluh was responsible for everything we did until we got big enough to need more structure.

Because the system had gone from forty-six superintendents to ten, this meant that some of the displaced superintendents might be good choices for the Leadership Academy. Typically, you don't consider hiring the people who don't make the cut for key jobs in a new organization, but two things were at work here. One, this was a massive reorganization where superintendents and deputy superintendents were being displaced, so the people who were not selected were not necessarily all C- and D-grade players. Because there were only ten regional superintendent slots available, and Joel had filled a few of those jobs with dark-horse candidates, the law of averages suggested that some A- and B-grade superintendents had not made the cut.

My taking some of those who were displaced when Joel shrank the structure meant getting good talent, not merely leftovers. Second, the mix of private-sector personnel working in concert with pedagogical personnel would create a very interesting culture that would mirror what Joel was doing at the Department of Education.

I decided to organize the academy according to program tracks. (Sandra deserves a lot of the credit for this organizational design.) One track would be the Aspiring Principals Program, which Sandra would own. That would be the flagship program open to the best ninety candidates we could find anywhere in the world. The only requirement to apply to become an "aspiring principal" was that you had to have five years of teaching experience. Sandra designed a very vigorous application process for this program, one that required a bulletproof résumé, sparkling references, and a broad sampling of the candidate's writing. If a candidate made it through the application process, then members of the academy staff would conduct face-to-face interviews with that person.

The program didn't require doctorates. In fact, you didn't even have to have a master's degree. Based on the partnerships we'd arranged with Columbia University and Baruch College, we could ensure that a master's degree would be earned by anyone who successfully passed through the academy's Aspiring Principals Program. You might have been a teacher, a guidance counselor, an assistant principal, or someone from the private sector—as long as you had five years of teaching experience in your background, you could be an aspiring principal.

The first group we interviewed included applicants from many of the fifty states and a couple of international candidates, even an assistant district attorney and an investment banker. The first cohort of ninety candidates came from a pool of more than five hundred applicants, and each year the number of applicants grew larger. If you made the cut and were selected for the Aspiring Principals Program, you came onto the Leadership Academy payroll at a principal's salary.

Candidates accepted for the program started in what Sandra called the summer intensive program. She developed three fictitious schools: an elementary, a middle school, and a high school. When our aspiring new colleagues came in, Sandra would give them a simulated model of a school that included a staff, the demographics of the community, the number of students, the profile of the students, the challenges in the school, and the school's performance record.

She designed the program so that there were thirty elementary school candidates, thirty middle school candidates, and thirty high school candidates. The process was rigorous. The candidates had to develop budgets, program their school, create a school calendar, put an academic program into place, provide for professional development for staff, set up talented-and-gifted tracks, create a parent coordinator strategy, and develop student-parent involvement. In short, they were required to perform every task a real principal would perform to get ready for the next academic semester.

Everything you had to do to run a school was there.

The program was designed so Sandra could detect fallout early. Assessments were done frequently. We could ill afford to burn resources on candidates who were only at the margins, especially with the requirement that those who successfully finished the program would be placed in our most challenging schools as new principals. If there were truly any doubts about a candidate, Sandra would focus on that person and let him or her go if improvement did not occur immediately.

When the actual school year started, the candidates would be assigned to schools in pairs. They were placed in the schools not as assistant principals but rather as aspiring principals, whose task was to assist the "mentor principal" in their schools. We prepared these mentor principals, too, bringing them into the academy to discuss their expectations, to have them experience many of the same tools the aspiring principals were armed with, and to work with them on how to establish relevant roles for the pair of aspiring principals in their school and manage and monitor their performance. Forty-five principals/schools were selected for that element of the program.

Every Friday, the aspiring principals would come back to the academy for more training. They would share their various experiences at their schools. The APP program leaders would facilitate the sessions.

Sandra and the academy staff also went into the schools to see how the aspiring principals were doing. She never wanted to have any surprises. There was just too much at stake in the investment we were making for us merely to hope that these newly trained principals got by. These on-site evaluations happened throughout the semester. Sandra would also collect status reports from the mentor principals on how the aspiring principals were doing. After the Christmas break, the aspiring principals would be sent to a different school to experience another environment. They would do that for a month, and then return to the school they started in.

Much of my job in the first year involved working with the ten superintendents to make certain they supported the different program tracks and were comfortable with me and the academy. I also facilitated their leadership development workshops. I actually got very close to six of the ten and spent a lot of time working with them on succession planning and paving the way for our APP candidates to get placed in the right school. Remember, the commitment on our end was that if a candidate got through the program successfully, he or she would become a school principal. I took the superintendents away for a weekend at Crotonville to lead them through succession planning well in advance of graduation. It was a great session, and it allowed me the opportunity to really show them how succession planning worked. It also gave me the time to fully explain the process we would be using to place these aspiring principals.

Not all of the superintendents bought into the process, though, and I knew this coming into the meeting. Some of them were highly skeptical about taking unproven principals into their system, especially into poorly performing schools, as I had been advocating for the placement of our candidates into the tougher schools from day one of the program. A few of the superintendents didn't care that the potential candidates had had a unique training experience with us. Their thought was that no one could pick principals better than they could.

Around 77 candidates remained in the APP cohort when we all went to Crotonville for the draft/placement weekend. I got 55 of them into targeted schools whose superintendents were willing to accept them for the fall semester once they'd graduated as principals. We knew there were going to be more than 150 job openings; in fact, it was more like 250.

The academy still owned all the APP candidates for the summer, including the ones selected during the Crotonville weekend. The theory was that even though we had placed them via the April draft, they remained with us so we could oversee their continued development and help them prepare to open the school they would be assigned to in the fall.

Sandra provided the academic context for all program tracks. Noel's company, ALA, and I provided all of the process and leadership development components.

Think of the levels of preparation involved in the process and the integration required to give principals a unique development experience. Before we opened our program, the pathway of a newly assigned principal was that he showed up in September and jumped into the deep end of the pool. There was no preparation for that job at all, other than what training a superintendent could provide. This meant that, under the old structure, you could have forty-plus variations across the school system on how to develop a school leader.

By comparison, look at what these aspiring principals were getting from us. We were treating them like corporate assets. We also paid no attention to where they wanted to work. We told them that although we knew they might want to work in Queens or Brooklyn, they might well end up on Staten Island. They knew all of that coming in. Yes, we allowed them to tell us their first and second preferences in terms of New York City boroughs, but at the end of the day, we placed them where the system needed them most.

All of my experiences had taught me that corporate resources (the top-tier talent in a corporation) were owned by the CEO and you simply were loaned these resources in your business unit. I applauded the superintendents for supporting this corporate asset concept. We had to teach everyone that the needs of the system outweighed the needs of the individual. We prepared the aspiring principals uniformly for what they were about to do. In that sense, they were interchangeable.

So, back to my challenge of finding a spot for those remaining twenty-two principals.

That is where my own growth came.

Resistance

I am not used to having to persuade people to do things.

It was difficult for me to see that a few of the superintendents did not want the principals from the Aspiring Principals Program. This was especially true if the candidate didn't come from their region. That told me two unpleasant things: one, I didn't have total buy-in from those few superintendents, and two, I had not told our story well enough and given them enough exposure to see how good these new principals were.

I knew that in the next iteration of the program we would need to have a lot more engagement, input, and exposure for the ten superintendents to make the job of placement a little easier. In the meantime, how could I get these resistant superintendents to want these principals Sandra had just developed?

I knew I could slam-dunk it by going to Joel and making the case for why we had to be very controlling in how we delivered these incredible new principals into the system, and that he must take a hard line with the resistant superintendents. I also knew this would not work. Doing so would have placed the newly minted principals into a situation where they were being forced on their superiors. Instead, I needed to work on the superintendents to try to get them to *want* the principals we had created. I was really disappointed in myself that I had not done the proper framing with this important group of constituents.

It was quite a selling process, but I got it done. I had to work my butt off to get those twenty-two jobs. When Sandra or I learned about an opening, we would sit down with the individual superintendent to explain why a certain candidate was ideal for that position. We took a look at the fifty-five aspiring principals who had been gobbled up so quickly, and what we found was disappointing but understandable.

Those who were selected were former teachers, assistant principals, and guidance counselors—prospects the superintendents knew and who came from their regions. This taught me that I had not created the right level of excitement and anticipation that feasting at the clambake should produce. If this is the right program, I concluded, I needed to have these people fighting over these candidates. That was the biggest lesson for me about the first-year APP cohort.

One of the things that Sandra did to help the superintendents get to know the candidates better with the next cohort was a Wednesday night development session for APP principals utilizing Microsoft's Manhattan office. She invited the superintendents into those sessions to make presentations and then to observe and interact with the candidates. This went over very well. We also got Microsoft to lead sessions helping our principals understand how to use the Microsoft suite of applications for every program track we had. We knew we were creating stars with our training; we just had to get the superintendents to see this and to want those stars as principals.

We looked for "sparklers," so we would know the strong candidates long before we sat down to talk with the superintendents about them. Sandra had her team create biography books for the superintendents in which every candidate was profiled.

But that was just one of the tracks we created. The second track was for every new principal who had been promoted. In that first year, we had 240 new principals. The program track for a new principal started with week-long training at the academy in the summer.

And just as those new principals were preparing to head into school for their first year on the job, we were getting ready to welcome a new class. Every year we did it we kept getting better.

Just-in-Time Training

When the school year opened, we instituted "just-in-time" training. This involved the newly promoted principals coming to the academy for two to three days every other month. A major portion of those development sessions focused on things that the principals would be facing for the first time in a school.

When we knew the principals were just about to go into their first parent-teacher conference, we used just-in-time training to prepare them for that. By the time they were ready to make some decisions about their teachers, we gave them just-in-time performance management training. In January we knew they were going to be facing the demands of creating a comprehensive education plan. These new principals had never faced that kind of challenge before, so we prepared them for that strategic work.

But it did not stop there. We went out to visit all 240 of our new principals. We also provided every new principal with a Leadership Academy–trained mentor principal (the majority were retired principals). This meant we had to teach the mentor principals how we wanted them to mentor. We used the regional superintendents to help us pick the mentors. They knew who the good principals were, and this reinforced our working relationship with the superintendents.

The Leadership Academy was the repository of best practices, even with the mentors; it gave us a chance to spread best practices in mentoring all across the new principal group. With each new program and commitment to developing principals, we got more buy-in from the superintendents. We shared what we were doing, asked for guidance, and kept the superintendents involved every step of the journey.

It worked so well that these first-year principals went to the mayor and chancellor and asked them to support a second year of leadership development for them from the Leadership Academy. It cost about $2 million to do that, but we found the money.

More Dog Food, Please!

Then there was a third track: training incumbent principals.

All I could think of as we developed the program for the system's incumbent principals was, "Will they eat the dog food?"

Brian Dunn, an entrepreneur and bright young African American with a training background, had joined our team. I had him paired with a former superintendent, Claire McIntee, one of the most highly decorated superintendents in New York City. Her district had been one of the top two performing districts in the system. Claire was the heart and soul of the Leadership Academy, respected by everyone as a great instructional leader. Her warmth and genuine care for people stood out and endeared her to everyone on the team.

I didn't fret the age difference, gender difference, or race difference between Claire and Brian. Brian was capable of replacing me to run the academy, and Claire could have done the regional superintendent job in her sleep, so I thought there might be some magic there if I put the two of them together.

To my great surprise, the group of incumbent principals was the most fun to work with. There was a lot of buzz among them about how the new principals were treated in the new principal program (summer workshops at Citigroup, American Express, and IBM; new laptops and training from Microsoft for every new principal; a mentor), and all of these veterans, these incumbents, were asking, "What about us?"

Initially I was worried about the potential cynicism in this veteran group. I should not have worried. They became my inspiration.

There is a big difference between training novices to become principals for the first time and retraining people who have been principals for many years. No one could afford to assume these veterans knew nothing. Identifying and embracing their best practices became a key part of the content of the program.

I was a firm believer in the fact that somewhere in New York City, because of its sheer size, someone had cracked the code for unleashing the power of teachers to help children excel in the classroom. But the current system had no operating mechanisms to capture that, so those bright spots sat out there on islands. Part of the mission of the academy was to become the repository of best practices. And part of getting these veteran principals on board was recognizing that they were doing some very good work and if we just understood how that happened, it could be replicable in other parts of the city.

That became very cool: to hear a principal describe how her math students had managed to get to 93 percent and explain the methods she used to get them there.

Imagine the power of the information exchanged by six principals at one table sharing best practices.

I also wanted to redefine what a business partnership was. I brought in executives from Tommy Hilfiger, Estee Lauder, and Best Buy. I brought in Bette Midler's friend Norma Kamali, the famous designer. She told the veteran principals that the worst thing any one of them could do was ask for a check. She told principals she wanted to know what they were working through, what challenges they were facing. She wanted to be a thought partner.

The message was clear: If you can engage me intellectually, you will never have to ask for a donation, because that will come like a river flowing through. Getting those principals to see that, to understand that, and to see some real cases where principals had forged some great partnerships changed how they viewed business partnerships.

We had some remarkable interventions.

I recall one principal, however, who was about as sour as he could be. He was a talented, young, and aggressive guy, but he had a huge log on his shoulder. The day Jeanette Wagner, the former vice chairperson from Estée Lauder, came to teach, he sat there stone-faced.

Here she was, retired from Estée but full of energy like a teenager, wearing red-framed glasses and looking very stately, hip, and inspiring. One of her teaching messages? "I don't care how bad business is doing, never come out of your office without a smile on your face. It is contagious. It is infectious." She then talked about the powerful influence a leader has on the mood of an organization. Profound stuff.

At one point she looked over and saw my scowling principal and said to him, "I'll bet when you do smile you have got to be the handsomest man in the world." Well, you could have heard the ice break. He started smiling.

"Ladies, check him out. Why don't you do that every day? You are such a handsome man. Who wouldn't want to follow you?"

That guy will tell you to this day he is a different person because of that small intervention. That's the kind of thing that was happening in the workshops. Multiply that by a thousand. Jack Welch, Dick Parsons, Walter Shipley—they all came to teach.

It didn't take long for word to start filtering back to us that this was working, that principals of every style and experience were carrying academy lessons out into the field and using them. I would walk into a principal's office and see all the stuff needed to complete the egg drop team building exercise (where you design a container that can keep an egg from breaking when the container is dropped from a certain height). They were proud to show us they were using the tools and getting the benefit and lift from them.

We worked hard to incorporate the valuable practices we learned from the incumbent principals. That had to happen. It validated them and it let them know we appreciated their work and their thoughts about how to run a school. But there were some practices we had to fix.

You might have two schools on one block, an elementary school and a middle school, with no real connection between them. They never talked about their common purpose. They never interacted. In fact, they never even talked to one another. We found instances where there were several schools in the same building with principals who didn't even know one another's names.

During a visit to one school, a principal told me that her middle school students weren't eating lunch until 1:00 PM, and school was let out at 3:15. "My kids are going six hours without any food," she said. I asked why she didn't just negotiate different times, and she told me the high school kids had the early lunch hour.

"Let's go talk," I said.

We trudged up several flights of stairs to meet with the high school principal. I explained that the high school students had all the early lunch hours. The middle school principal had told me that some of the high school students didn't even start class until 9:00 AM. "They would probably like that 1:00 PM lunch spot," I said. "We can work something out."

Before you knew it, those two principals who had had no relationship to point to were talking about how to solve the problem. They got on it and fixed it right away. It was that simple. There were examples like that all over the place.

Our own jobs developed, too. Teachers and principals began to rely on us for day-to-day problem solving. We became consultants to them. People used us to eliminate barriers, to fix problems.

One superintendent from the Bronx would have very little to do with us, so I made it my job to get her to warm up. Eventually we became the best of friends. Irma Zardoya and I are still friends today. She is one of the most talented school leaders I've ever worked with. She benefited tremendously from the Leadership Academy programs, and I learned a lot from her about the superintendent job. She and I and her assistant superintendent, Ray Rosemberg, would meet often, plan together, dine together, and we were always aligned. They were two very special leaders who made my job so much fun.

Unintended Consequences

One of the most interesting developments came when individual principals came to us to ask if we could work with them and their entire teaching staff. I gave the request some thought and then sat down with my team and asked who would be willing to give up a weekend or two to go off to Crotonville with a principal and all of their teachers to help them launch their school transformation. Every program leader on the staff said yes.

So we started to take entire school faculties up to GE Crotonville starting on Friday evening and working with them until midday Sunday. These weekends were magical for the schools and important reinforcement for my team.

When the word spread, we hit the wall: we just could not service all the demand. We got creative and started putting two to three schools together in the same workshop room, so we could get the multiplier effect. It worked so well that we had the schools help and coach one another. These weekends were emotional for everyone. Part of that was probably because we had a chance to treat these educators—principals and teachers—to a great career experience and a great personal development experience, too. For most of them, particularly the teachers, the Crotonville experience was a first. They were exposed to great dining, good wine, and recreation in the evening. The place was first class all the way. Usually they had to pay for their own training, but what we did at Crotonville cost them nothing, thanks to GE CEO Jeff Immelt's incredible contribution of allowing us access to this world-class and legendary learning institution.

These schools were feeling as though they were the most valuable people in the city, state, nation, the world—and to me they were.

Measuring Success

In the private sector, if you reported that you had a 3 percent improvement over a year, you would be out of a job. But in the New York City schools, if you created a 3 percent improvement over a year, you would have improved the lives of 30,000 students. The signs of success were that direct. Ten percent meant that more than 120,000 students were going to have a better chance.

I think I would have kept re-upping and stayed at the academy forever. But I could not. By being away, I was really compromising my relationship with my family. I was not there for my kids. Jenni was starting a new job in Washington, D.C.; Aimi was living in Hartford, cutting her teeth at ESPN; Audrey was in college at the University of Colorado; and Jason was in high school. For a dad to come home only four times in a year just wasn't right.

Then I got a call from Jacques Nasser, a good friend and the former CEO of Ford Motor Company, asking me to have lunch. Over lunch I learned that he was a partner with JPMorgan's private equity arm, One Equity Partners. Jac told me about one of their portfolio companies, Vercuity (later renamed Telwares), which was created when OEP bought five telecom expense management companies to create the largest company in the space. The company headquarters was located literally in my backyard, in Denver less than two miles from my home. It was a good alignment of the stars for me. I was excited about the company and the prospect of reconnecting with my two younger children.

I was proud of what we did in the New York City schools. It added up to a three-year commitment for me. We had been asked to respond to a crisis, and what we did worked. It helped us create a critical mass of new leaders in the New York City schools.

The Leadership Academy model has been shared with numerous cities and countries. We shared it with Oprah's people, who were working on the formation of her school in Africa. We shared it with Tony Blair's staff, who visited us from England. A large number of school systems made their way to New York City to benchmark what we were doing. On day one, Sandra and I had agreed that whatever we created we would share freely with the world, and that's just what we did.

The model is strong, but it requires a strong buy-in from the business community if it is to thrive. Maybe the best description of why this is so important came from Sy Sternberg, the CEO at New York Life and one of my board members: "I have no choice but to invest in you," he said. "That's my labor force!"

When I think of the three years I spent working with those teachers, with those principals, I think of what might have been the most significant part of my career bridge—which, by the time I sat down with Mike Bloomberg to talk about the schools, stretched over some very long distances.

I will always carry the memory of that child who looked up at me during that school visit and asked me if I would be coming back. I didn't know then what we would build, but I know now it was an effort that will be measured forever in the lives of children who were able to thrive in schools that were as good as their newly dedicated principals could make them.

It is easy to get caught up in a job assignment where the work-life balance gets out of whack. That was clearly the case with me in this assignment. I simply could not stay in New York forever, though. My family needed me back in Denver, as I was missing important time with Audrey and Jason. As much as I loved my work at the Leadership Academy, I had to get that balance back. You get only one chance to celebrate a child's sixteenth birthday, to witness a first date, or to see the smile on the face of a teenager when she gets her driver's license. When you miss those moments, they are lost forever. No job is important enough to sacrifice those joys.

Home Again

Vercuity got me back to Denver, but it also got me into a company that had just developed a severely impaired operating system to provide a platform for the expense management services it offered.

One of the first things I did when I arrived at Telwares was call Steve

Ballmer at Microsoft for assistance with this impaired application. He introduced me to Avanade, a joint venture between Microsoft and Accenture. Avanade was an impressive organization with more than four thousand engineers/developers who solved large, complex problems like the one I'd just inherited.

It didn't take Avanade long to diagnose that the application would require a lot of intensive surgery and that I would be better off taking an application from one of the five companies that had been purchased to form Telwares and upgrading that.

My team and I worked hard to compete in the market without a robust application, and we ended up licensing another firm's software. I recognized that we could not make the company work to perform to the endgame that the investors and I wanted for the company, so we agreed that I would stay on to help with a transition, which took well over a year.

Months after I left the Telwares CEO job, I got a call from Rick Smith, one of my board members and a senior guy at One Equity Partners. He asked me if I could let him know when I would be in New York again, as he'd like to spend a few minutes with me. Within a few weeks we got together. Rick told me that he wanted to apologize for the condition of Telwares and to thank me for my hard work, diligence, and help with the business right up to the end. He said that he, David Walsh, Chuck Auster, and Alex Russo all realized that I had given the job my very best shot and that sometimes investments don't pan out. They all thought very highly of me as a leader and executive. I was moved that he'd thought enough to express these sentiments.

Then again, that is the class and caliber of the partners at that firm. Even though I know you can't win every time, I don't like losing, so this meeting with Rick meant a lot to me. I would work with the OEP guys again without hesitation. David Walsh, who was my chairman, was a guy I had admired from afar, as he was a stellar telecom executive at Global Crossing, and it was a sheer delight to work with him.

Management and Boards

The management-board relationship has evolved over time. After some of the most catastrophic business failures in our lifetime (Enron, MCI, Arthur Andersen, Lehman Brothers, Bear Stearns), today's requirements for board oversight, coupled with new regulations, have put tremendous pressure on the CEO job, creating unpredictable behaviors and a new definition for the once cozy relationship between a board and a CEO.

It's no wonder that CEO tenure is less than three years today, and CEO wreckage litters every highway in every industry.

After I took Covad public in 1999, I asked Ram Charan, the renowned management consultant and expert on board development and governance, to help me build my board. I needed to move away from angel investors and venture capitalists and toward a more conventional public company board. Even with that agreed-upon plan, the dynamics with my board changed overnight with my first ever quarterly miss, and I was shocked at how quickly the board's memory of all the great things I had done faded.

I learned a lifetime of lessons working through the change in my relationship with the Covad board, and while I made some mistakes and missed several cues that were right in front of me, the unfairness of the abrupt change in the level of support really didn't matter, because at the end of the day I owned the business results. Those results were my responsibility, regardless of what was happening around me and the company. This is a hard lesson, but if you want to occupy the corner office, you have to understand that when it comes to business performance, you are a constituency of one.

I've been serving on boards for more than twenty years and I recall with fondness my first board assignment, back in Indianapolis. It came via a unique leadership program opportunity that Judy Myers had nominated me for. More than five hundred people (under the age of forty) had been nominated for the Stanley K. Lacy Executive Leadership Series, which was an annual program run by the Indianapolis Chamber of Commerce. The Chamber of Commerce would select twenty-five up-and-coming leaders to participate in the program. SKL met every month for one full day, exposing the participants to CEOs, the mayor, the governor, and other city leaders in a series of conversations on various issues confronting the city and state.

On one particular day, when we were meeting with Ben Lytle, the CEO of Blue Cross and Blue Shield of Indiana, I established a genuine connection. After the session, Ben told me about one of his new guys, an African American, whom he wanted me to meet. Weeks later I finally got the chance to meet Mike Wright, the executive vice president and chief information officer at BCBS. What an impressive guy. Tall, handsome, bright, and very articulate, Mike was the strongest person of color I had ever encountered in my professional career. We became friends, and I had a new benchmark! Angela fell in love with Mike's wife, Gloria, and the four of us enjoyed many dinners together. When Angela and I moved away, we kept in contact with the Wrights. In 1997 they came out to Denver and spent New Year's Eve with us.

Soon after meeting me, Mike called me one day and asked me if I had ever served on a board. I told him no, and he said it was time for me to gain that experience. Ben Lytle had recently transformed the Blue Cross company, creating more than a dozen small insurance companies under the brand name Acordia. Mike introduced me to Sherry Nord, the CEO of the Acordia Company, serving colleges and universities. I joined Sherry's board, and after serving as a director for one year, I was named chairman of the board. Mike's mentoring and confidence in me had opened the door for the first of numerous board assignments for me. That first assignment gave me a tremendous boost of confidence. I also learned very quickly how serving on a board outside of my industry could broaden my knowledge.

After I served on the Acordia board, the Shell Oil Exploration board came along shortly thereafter, and then Heidrick & Struggles, and Ariba. Then, in 2000, one of my good friends, Carly Fiorina, called to ask me to join the HP board. Carly is one of the most intelligent executives I have ever known. What happened to her could add another chapter to the unwritten *Annals of Boards Gone Wrong* (maybe just after the chapter on Covad). Carly had been a magnificent connection for me, as I was a significant customer for her first at Ameritech and then at US West and Covad, and we'd stayed in close touch. It was only natural that we'd reconnect when the Reverend Jesse Jackson invited us both to attend a town hall meeting during President Clinton's administration.

I had become a magnet for attention at Covad, with lots of offers to serve on boards, publicity (which I was not comfortable with), and public acclaim. But the invitation to join the board at HP was very attractive. As a charge agent in a large corporation, I knew how important and how difficult the changes at HP would be. Based on the board's makeup at the time, I would be bringing a rare combination of experience and skills that would provide a unique perspective. So when I was asked to join HP's board, of course I said yes.

The company had some serious challenges when she was hired to lead it. High-tech businesses have to move at the speed of light, and resting on an old reputation for building reliable personal computers and printers wasn't going to cut it in the Internet era. There were lots of aggressive competitors in that market. HP needed fresh thinking, fresh life, and a breakthrough leader to force it at least back into, if not to the head of, the pack.

For six years in a row beginning in 1997, *Fortune* magazine called Carly "one of the most powerful women in business." She faced high expectations and big challenges. HP had lost its way and was looking at the wrong end of the curve in the Internet economy, even as its competitors tapped emerging technology and invented some of their own. As a member of the board, I believed Carly was doing a great job. Under her leadership, Carly set the foundation for the success that followed. She changed the culture, she created a consumer powerhouse, and she turned HP into a diversified global technology leader. Still, it was natural that she would have detractors, with the changes she'd brought to the company. She was a bold player in a field full of bold players, but I was surprised, and a bit put off, at how often she was asked to make personnel moves that seemed inappropriate or consider strategies that didn't make sense to me. I believe that at the end of the day a board should focus on three things: financial oversight (fiduciary responsibility), CEO succession planning, and risk mitigation. Things got really heated years into my tenure on the board, and there were leaks aimed at the corner office. Meanwhile, there was plenty of media coverage of HP's problems, which only reinforced the members of the board who saw Carly as a problem.

Just as I had seen at Covad, as the company's position eroded, some of HP's directors became aggressive. They tried to inject themselves into the kind of decision making that, to my mind, is the province of the CEO. When Carly pushed right back (which she could do very effectively), they complained (and loudly) that she would not take advice or counsel from board members. Carly missed her numbers for a couple of quarters, and that didn't make things any easier in the boardroom. Of course I was among a core of Carly supporters on the board, but we were outnumbered.

By 2004, five years into her tenure, the situation had become toxic. In early February of 2005 the board called an emergency meeting in Chicago, near the airport. It had been clear to me since Thanksgiving that something was up, that some directors had been meeting privately. Minutes of sessions that were supposed to have been private were making their way to the *Wall Street Journal*, a clear violation of the board's privacy agreements. Board members were gathering in little pods even during our off-site sessions. When you walked up to them, they would be pleasant but they'd stop talking. I had seen this before. It started to feel like my experience at Covad, when I walked in one day thinking we had a board-backed plan to turn the company around and ended up being asked to leave.

I thought Carly had done a great job at HP, but we were a divided board and I was on the weak side of the proposition. When she was fired, I resigned in protest. I thought the decision to remove her was an arbitrary one. The frequency with which that board stepped over the management-board line of responsibility got lost in all the noise and the headlines.

It was a sad experience for me to see a friend put through that kind of turmoil.

I can report that Carly most certainly is a great survivor and has lost none of her drive or passion. After she left HP, she fought a valiant battle against cancer (a much bigger threat than an unsupportive board) and then waged a determined, but unsuccessful, close campaign for the U.S. Senate. We haven't heard the last of her, and that is good.

By 2009 I had closed the door on my Telwares experience and was ready to launch my own consulting business. I was now free to write my book, free to spend more time with my family, free to spread the message of transformation around the world, free to tell the people who looked up to me that hard work, honesty, and treating people well was more than just a slogan. It was a way of life.

CHAPTER TWELVE

Knees, Karma, and the Most Important People in My World

I faced my mortality in 2004.

After what most people would view as a lifetime of challenge in sports and business and a sense of drive that could push a freight train over a mountain, my knees wore out.

My longtime orthopedic doctor in Indianapolis, Jeff Van Meter, said the problem was that my joint had basically worn down to bone on bone, with all the basketball, football, baseball, and golf that had consumed my life. Climbing up telephone poles, hiking up mountains with coworkers, and rushing for an endless collection of airplanes hadn't helped.

I don't regret a single minute of my life in sports, of course. I found my mentors, my role models, and my competitive spirit there. But nothing in life comes without a price. Sometimes you have to manage your body the way you manage your business, calling in specialists to deal with the problems that won't heal on their own. I knew it was time to get help.

Over the years my legs had bowed to the extent that Patti started calling me "Tex," because I looked like I'd been riding a horse my entire life. The condition of one knee had regressed to the point where I could not run on that knee, and whenever I jarred my leg, the pain was unbearable.

One night in New York City, while dining with friends, my knee locked up when I rose to leave the restaurant. I limped out of that place fully committed to calling Jeff in the morning to get on a knee replacement schedule.

Jeff laughed when I reached him the next day. I told him what had happened, and he said he knew I would know when to mail it in. He told me that he wanted me to get the surgery in New York City, because some of the best orthopedic surgeons in the country worked at the Hospital for Special Surgery.

I didn't like that. I have had only one knee doctor my entire life, and for this very serious surgery, he was handing me off to another doctor. But Jeff explained that unlike my other knee surgeries, this one wouldn't let me get up on my feet in a few days, resuming my hectic travel schedule. I needed to be in one place for about thirty days. At the time, my work was in New York City, and with all the great doctors there, I accepted his decision. He sent me to see Dr. Thomas Wickiewicz. Dr. Wick, as I called him, and I clicked immediately. He and his colleagues had repaired a lot of the broken, dented, and strained New York City professional and college sports athletes.

After performing all of his exams and looking at all the X rays, Dr. Wick told me that we should replace both knees. I had to do a crash course to understand everything about this surgery. I learned how complicated it was, what the procedures were, how long it would take to heal. I also learned that people had died from blood clots or infections after the surgery. The number of fatalities was small, but that spooked me, knowing I might not make it through knee replacements. Still, the pain was such that I didn't care what the risks were; I needed relief. So I decided to go "all in" and have both knees replaced. What I could not anticipate was the impact that being so close to death would have on me. It was as though a whole army of invisible accountants and assessors had moved in to help me review what I had done with my life.

We scheduled the surgery out several weeks, because I had to have my own blood drawn every week to use in the operation. This would cut the risk of my being exposed to infected blood.

Angie flew into New York to be with me for the surgery. When we left for the hospital at 3:00 AM, I silently wondered if I would return home. I was in the prep area for what seemed like hours, but I know it was only twenty or thirty minutes, and all I could think of was not making it through the surgery. I needed to get my karma back in order.

There are many opportunities in life when it's easy to slip into negative thoughts about your circumstances or those of the people around you. There is simply no benefit to that. The mental part of that formula is most important. You can't always believe your way to success. Life is not a fairy tale. But you can certainly wreck your chances by being negative.

During that waiting period in the hospital, I began to think about some experiences that had delighted me: playing hoops, walking thirty-six holes in Scotland, or playing softball with the boys. That seemed to work. When I got into the operating room, a wave of emotion flooded through my mind. When it was time to go "under," I thought about my family and whether this was my final moment of consciousness in this life.

Had I been the man I wanted to be? Had I been the leader? The father? The husband? What if I had taken a different turn back at Wabash and headed off to Yale, for divinity school? One of the merciful aspects of anesthesia is that eventually you do go "under," along with your thoughts.

I heard a lot of banging. I heard people talking. Slowly, my eyes opened to whiteness and a bright room. Was I in heaven? Why were the voices all so muffled? I was awake, but not aware. I had no sense of time. Eventually, I recognized Dr. Wick's voice.

I had woken up in the middle of surgery!

I called out to Dr. Wick and got his attention. He said something to somebody and answered me by telling me that they were very busy and that I was going back to sleep.

I woke up in intensive care. I was so glad to be there.

I learned shortly after my one-night stay in intensive care that I had had some blood clots. There were other developments that reawakened my concerns about death. For example, my first day in the rehab hospital, my roommate died just hours after I arrived. I'd been in the bed next to him for only an hour and they brought dinner. I didn't eat but he did. An hour or so later when they brought in our medicines, he was gone. The frantic effort of about six hospital personnel to revive him played out five feet away from me. They thought I might be traumatized and moved me to a large suite that was unlike any hospital room I had ever seen and sent numerous hospital personnel to talk with me for several days. I was fine and didn't mind talking to everyone who came to see me, because this was a very cool hospital room and I didn't mind staying there.

What had I done with my life? What had I done with the talents that God had given me? Had I made the world better or had I merely occupied space and been a taker? What kind of job had I done in helping to raise Jenni, Aimi, Audrey, and Jason? Thinking about my legacy was humbling, and at the end of that assessment, I did not feel good.

I had spent way too much time building my bridge and helping people at work build theirs and not enough time helping the members of my family. There was so much more that I should have done with and for my siblings. Why had I made more contributions to strangers than to my own flesh and blood? I had spent so much time coaching, mentoring, motivating other people, yet other than occasionally providing them with some money, I hadn't done enough to help my brothers and sisters.

I felt ashamed and embarrassed.

There were many days to think about this guilt during my rehabilitation. The successful surgery gave me new knees and a second chance at an active life. The time spent in that facility gave me time to renew my spirit and commit myself to doing better for my family.

Does that sound like a common regret in business success stories? Probably not, but it should be. We rarely get the chance to stand far enough away from our experiences to see what they actually meant, whom they helped or harmed. There is a great irony at work in my knee replacement experience. I went into the hospital fearing death, and I came out with a different slant on what my life had been. It was an amazingly cathartic experience. It led me to reassess, to set new values for my life, and to see where my bridge had taken me.

Digging Deeper in the Well

There are those events that never leave us. Negative or positive, they are carved into our memory and are normally not far from the surface. I've drawn on those experiences often to motivate myself. It's funny how a painfully negative experience can become such a positive motivator for success, but such experiences have done just that for me. I tell some of those stories early in this book, and I want to revisit some of them before I leave you, perhaps to help you look at your own life and the lessons it has taught you.

Former Intel chairman Andy Grove captured what I'm referring to here in his 1996 book, *Only the Paranoid Survive*. The fear of failure, the fear of being trapped, and the fear of losing control of your destiny can be abated when you draw on experiences that provide the fuel for great execution. These experiences force you to work harder, become more aggressive, take more risk, stay focused, and grind your way to victory.

When faced with having to birdie the hole to win the golf tournament, Tiger Woods visualizes only the perfect swing from past experience. I'm certain that when Michael Jordan is faced with having to make the basket to win the game, he thinks about being cut from his high school team and about all the people who didn't believe in his ability and about how he has put in the work to be in that moment. Or Derek Jeter, who wants the bat in his hands with the game on the line: he is one of the best at drawing on the hours of practice and preparation to execute in the moment.

I am drawing from a much different pool of experiences. I believe that the measure of maturity is when you can transform something overwhelmingly bad into a positive force.

When Mr. Stewart beat me with that paddle back in the sixth grade for something I hadn't done, the immediate fear was how many licks would be administered to my backside. At the time, the situation felt like a bad nightmare that didn't have an ending. It got scarier by the minute. Even when the whacks no longer hurt, the feeling of being trapped and of not having an out had me so frightened that I couldn't think rationally. I longed for my grandmother or grandfather to walk through the door and make Mr. Stewart stop. I thought of my mother. But then the blanket of shame consumed me. I didn't want my grandparents or my mother to walk in and see their child being beaten, cursed, and treated so harshly. That is when the tears started to flow. They were tears of despair. They were tears of helplessness. How could I take care of my mother, my family, when I couldn't even take care of myself?

That feeling of sheer panic and of not knowing how to change the situation was not foreign to me. The early days of changing homes, of living with various relatives, of being picked on and laughed at in new schools, of the family having no resources to allow us even to have our basic needs met, and of witnessing dysfunction all the time—made living through every day a struggle and a challenge.

Obviously as a kid you are not prepared for these things, and when there are no role models to look to anywhere, you end up just existing, with no direction, no purpose, and no hope.

The rest of the day of that beating was a fog for me.

Mr. Stewart was a racist who resented the fact that black kids had access to his school. My teacher looked at me as if I had leprosy. Going home on the bus, I thought about my grandfather's stories about lynch mobs and fire bombings, and somehow I understood those stories better. At eleven years old you don't have a lot of higher-order thinking skills. In my mind, I felt that lynching and harming innocent people was still the order of the day, and this dreadful experience with Mr. Stewart was even more of a reason for me to say nothing and to comply with everything that was asked of me.

My grandmother noticed right away that there was something wrong with me as I came down the lane from the bus. Typically, my brothers and I ran to the house, but I came up the two steps that led to the front porch very slowly. She asked what was wrong. I thought about telling her that I'd hurt myself on the playground, but I quickly abandoned that story and lowered my head and told her that I'd gotten paddled by the principal.

She lifted my shirt to inspect my back. She must have looked for two or three minutes and never said a word. All she did was gently rub her hand over the area. She rose from her seat and took my hand and led me to her bedroom. She told me to take my clothes off. She laid a towel across her bed and had me lie down face-first on the towel. I fell asleep. She left the room and returned with a washtub. Some moments later I could feel her hands on my shoulders. She told me to get in the washtub.

I was hardly able to move, so she lifted me off the bed and lowered me into the water. She sat in a chair next to me and while she softly rubbed me, she hummed old spirituals. We didn't talk. She just hummed. I could not bear to look up at her because I feared what I would see on her face, so I just sat in the hot water and enjoyed her sweet caress on my back and shoulders. Later she would take me to the hospital, where the doctor gave her ointment to rub on my back, thighs, and butt when I went to bed. My grandmother told the doctor that I had been paddled at school.

Today, this type of incident would have been treated very differently. People would have been arrested. But back then, nothing was ever done to punish my teacher or Mr. Stewart. My grandparents never went to school to confront the principal. The episode deepened my relationship with my grandmother. She didn't let this incident change her view of my potential. Her reinforcement of my destiny to do something great and significant became constant encouragement.

And Mr. Stewart became a positive inflection point for me as I aged. When faced with difficult challenges, I draw inspiration from the Mr. Stewart incident and all the times people told me I wasn't good enough, smart enough, or capable enough to get it done.

Let's be clear, the catalyst in my life has never been hate. Everything that I have faced in business is child's play when weighed against the difficulties I've had to overcome on my personal journey. And I thank God for every one of those experiences. I've been asked from time to time if I believe I could have achieved what I've done in my life without those experiences, and the answer is yes, but maybe not with the same passion for the task at hand or compassion for the people who have been with me on the journey.

When You Know You Are Different

No one ever asked me what I wanted to be.

I heard teachers ask the white children that question all the time in elementary school. I even heard the white kids casually mention what they were going to grow up to be when they were out on the playground. I came to understand that black kids didn't participate in conversations like that.

Why was I never asked what I wanted to be? Was I so different from the others that my teachers figured I would have no chance to be anything?

I hated history class. That was the only time that the word *Negro* came up. When that word was read aloud, white kids would look at me and the other black kids. There was always this silent awkwardness in the room.

I never made the "honor roll" until very late in my school career, and I knew only two other black kids who did, John and Bonita Coleman. Were we not as smart as the white kids? Why were the Coleman kids so smart? Obviously I didn't understand any of the socioeconomic conditions that influenced a child's readiness for school, but when you see the reality of the white kids excelling and the black kids just getting by, you start to believe that you are not as capable. I was no exception.

Birth determines only the starting point for one's life. You can be born with the inherent advantage of a good family structure, economic resources, and the proper preparation and a good support system at home, or you can be born into utter despair, where just making it to adulthood is the ultimate test of survival.

The Importance of Caring

I wanted something better for my mother, my brothers and sisters, and for me. I wanted my mother to experience a "good" life with no stress or want for anything material. My love for this woman was profound. Whenever we were in a car driving across a bridge, I would plan my lifesaving routine in the event that the bridge collapsed. I knew I could save my mother, and then I would think through the one or two other people I could rescue in the three or four minutes I would have to save them, and those choices changed depending on which sibling I was fighting with at the time.

I believe we have to care. Leaders cannot be afraid to be kind, giving, and vulnerable. Kindness starts with being approachable and willing to listen. For a long time I thought that toughness was a leadership prerequisite, that people could respect you only if they feared you. The military has perfected the art of command and control, and on the surface we cringe at that management system today. I would contend that the military needs strong discipline and a clear understanding of rank and order. But what gets lost when you take a casual look at the military system is that they also teach their leaders the soft skills. Countless soldiers will tell heartwarming stories about how their leaders influenced their lives, cared for their growth and development, and turned them into outstanding men and women. At the root of great military leaders is their ability to genuinely care for people.

You also have to care for the feeding of your soul. What is to be gained if success is all about what you can attain and earn? I understood the key to success early in life through sports. I never single-handedly won any sporting contest, regardless of how many points I scored. I owe a great debt of gratitude to Coach Dick Haslam for instilling in me the fact that great players make and enable other great players. The joy should be in that rather than in individual fame.

But caring goes deeper. You have to want it for others as much as you want it for yourself. The scriptures say that of those to whom much is given much is required. I believe that investing in someone's career and life supersedes any monetary contribution you can make.

Colleagues, Friends, and Mentors

That is why I hold Judy Myers, Dick Notebaert, Sol Trujillo, and Jack Welch up as the greatest role models in my life: because I experienced their care and nurturing. They taught me how to trust people and how to coach when the moment presented itself.

I still marvel at the fact that in three years of being my chairman while working in the New York City schools, Jack Welch never told me what to do. He always asked me what I thought I should do about a certain situation, and he was skilled at getting me to think about a plan B and a plan C, but he didn't give me answers. He knew I had the ability, so he could trust and have confidence that I would come through with good decisions. I always felt strong and confident every time I left his office, because of the confidence he was building in me.

Dick Notebaert and Sol Trujillo took a chance on me as the leader of some of the most important work in the former Bell Operating Companies of Ameritech and US West. These great leaders didn't boss; they enabled and nurtured me. These exceptional men provided the perfect environment for my talents to blossom.

Coaches such as Patti Stacey and Dick Stonesifer made it even easier for me to excel. I was blessed that my leaders had only one requirement of me at the end of the day, and that was to perform. I put the same processes in play with my direct reports and with those I mentored.

There are no words to describe Noel Tichy's contribution to my career and my life.

Knowing About "Ruth"

I recall a Sunday school lesson from my childhood when I learned the term *ruth*. When the Pharisees and Sadducees had finished all of their bickering, they finally understood that they had to come together in their community to care for the feeding and nurturing of their people. *Ruth* is the term they used to refer to caring for others. *Ruth* is the opposite of *ruthlessness*. So when you have progressed to the level where you are focused on others, you are practicing ruth.

We are reminded in Matthew 25 that we cannot receive the Kingdom of Heaven if we don't practice ruth. "Assuredly, I say to you, inasmuch as you did not do it to one of the least of these, you did not do it to Me."

Early on in my professional journey I told my family that we would never be rich, as I planned to give most of our wealth away once our basic needs were met. I gave away more than I should have from the moment I got my first professional paycheck. Angie and I have a good debate about whether our basic needs had been met yet, but it just seemed right to me to be a giver from the start of my professional journey. There are so many people who establish personal milestones for wealth before focusing on giving back. I sincerely believe that perspective is flawed.

There is no perfect time to find your heart and to care. Besides, financial giving is the easiest form of giving. Giving your time and energy is the most gratifying contribution you can make and the one that busy executives have the hardest time committing to.

In the Gospel of Matthew, we get the clearest message of all on how we should conduct our lives. We are told to feed the hungry, give drink to the thirsty, provide shelter to the homeless, clothe those who are naked, tend to the sick, and visit those in prison. Matthew 25:34: "Then the King will say to those on His right hand, 'Come, you blessed of My Father, inherit the kingdom prepared for you from the foundation of the world.'"

Some will do these things because it is a requirement. I do them because they just seem right.

A Company Needs a Soul, Too

I created the Wind Walker Award in 1997 as the ultimate form of recognition within my business. You create your culture from what you practice and model for others, what you pay and reward people for, and I use the same criteria to make hiring choices and obviously, the same is used when you have to terminate someone. The Wind Walker was my way of pointing out stellar behavior and performance in individuals and teams in the company.

I thought a long time about the symbol I would use. Back in my Ameritech days, I recalled my obsession with winning one of the Navigator awards (which I didn't win). I knew that I exemplified the behavior and performance that the leader of the business wanted. I wanted to create an honor that would overwhelm anyone who received it. I wanted that to work on two levels. The criteria would be tough, and the symbolism would be stunning.

In the acting profession, nothing compares with winning an Oscar. I wanted my Wind Walker to be like an Oscar. Everything about the eagle is grand to me, and many of its behaviors relate to the kind of behaviors I wanted to see in my company.

My first President's Club ceremony was held in Maui. More than one thousand people and their guests were selected to attend. When Linda Fuentes, my administrative assistant, and Jimmy LaValley sat down with me to go over the final list of names selected to attend the President's Club, Jimmy pointed out that we had overlooked administrative personnel. He was right, and we fixed that. He also made a point of highlighting one employee who epitomized what we wanted to recognize: Ruth Ann.

Ruth Ann worked in our supply/logistics organization. Her job was to help technicians with equipment and supplies. She never let anyone rain on the parade or take her smile away. Anybody who had an encounter with her was blessed. Despite having congenitally deformed arms, she performed her job with care, passion, and excellence.

Seeing the look on Ruth's face and the tears in her eyes when she arrived in Maui was one of the most moving experiences for me. As she held my hands and thanked me, I had to hug her so she wouldn't see my own tears. Her mother, who came as her guest, looked on with pride. Their reaction to the President's Club experience told me that I was doing the right thing, building a culture where people were taking pride in their work.

Legacy

Tichy sometimes asks executives to write their obituaries. That takes you to a place that most people give little thought to.

What is my legacy? Well, first, I'm not finished with my life yet. But I've had a wonderful professional career. You've traveled with me so far on every mile of that long bridge I've built. What mark have I left?

I hope I will be viewed as a firm, tough leader who had passion for people. I hope that I made more positive contributions to the lives of people and had few negative impacts.

I won't be the judge of how I performed, but I will go to my final resting place knowing that I cared more about the success, accomplishments, and victories of those I mentored and developed than about my own personal accomplishments.

I hope that creates a legacy in the people whose lives and careers I have touched. I hope they will do the same for others.

The highlight is seeing people soar—even like birds of prey—and reach their potential.

My minister used to close Sunday service with the following phrase: "You never know where someone has had to come from to get to where they are right now." When I look back over the years and end up back at the starting line in Kokomo, Indiana, I recall one powerful image that has stayed with me to this day. There was a man in my community whom I cannot name. I saw him frequently when I was a child as he went to work. He wore a white shirt and a tie to work every day. I had no idea where he worked and there was no one else in the neighborhood like him. Why someone from our poor neighborhood was going to work in a shirt and tie was a mystery to me. He was a beacon, a promise of what others could do with their lives. Seeing him day in and day out planted the thought in my head that I wanted to wear a white shirt and tie like that to go to work someday. You *can* get there from here.

Acknowledgments

Just as Adam was not self-made, neither am I.

I am surrounded by my friends and colleagues who helped me construct the long span of the bridge of my life. I must start very close to home, thanking those who were there at the beginning of my life, my career, even my book. Angela has been at the center of my heart and head since before the day I married her, and our children are the beneficiaries of her decision to forgo a medical career so that she could provide the nurturing, support, guidance, and love of having a parent at home. Her sacrifices have given Jenni, Aimi, Audrey, and Jason the foundation and preparation for success. So much attention has been pointed my way, but the real success behind Bob Knowling and these great children has always been Angela.

I must tell Jenni, Aimi, Audrey, and Jason that they are my greatest accomplishment and there is nothing else close to it. While they are each different and unique, the one thing common to all of them is the inspiration that they give me every day of my life to soar like an eagle. At the University of Notre Dame, there is a sign on the doorway as you leave the locker room that says PLAY LIKE CHAMPIONS TODAY, and I've always admired that statement. I'm blessed to have a reminder of playing like a champion every day when I leave home just by looking at these great kids, because they deserve a father who is willing to put it out there every single day. Jenni is the de facto "mother" of the group, and she sees the world and situations so rationally. She understands me better than any of the others, and whenever Angela has a question about how

I would handle something in my absence, she will consult Jenni. I just find that marvelous.

Then there is Aimi. She honestly believes that her birth was special and that it must have been a day of recognition all over the world. She lives life each day to its fullest. Full of life, confident, and a natural-born leader, Aimi has unbelievable potential.

Audrey will always be my baby girl. I was pressed into duty to deliver her at home because repeated trips to the hospital and misdiagnosis by a doctor put us at home when the moment of truth was upon us. Having to resuscitate her and experiencing her first waking moment in life, as she saw me and I saw her, put me closer to God and, of course, her. Everything she does in life is well planned; she's the one child who has a road map of where she's going, and nothing seems to deter her. A beautiful child who has grown into a beautiful young lady, but she's still my baby girl to me.

Jason is the spitting image of me. Painfully shy and an ultra introvert, he will have to find a way to shed that skin, but I'm so proud of him. Respectful of others, he's got the kind of heart that people mistake for weakness, when in reality he just puts others' needs before his own. He's found his passion recently, and I'm excited about his pursuit of a profession that he loves so much (video game programming). He is so funny that I think he would be one heck of a stand-up comedian, but only those of us in the family get to see that side of him. His grandmother calls him "Hero," and that's exactly what he is. Stricken with juvenile diabetes at four years old, he has lived with that insidious disease most of his life, but not once have I ever heard him complain or whine about his condition.

I'm so excited for all four of them as I watch them build their life bridges, and I want them to know that I'm the luckiest guy on the planet to be their dad.

Charles Madigan had me in tears twenty minutes into this project when he asked me to start telling him my story, and I began with injuring my brother with a baseball bat when I was five years old. I had not thought about that incident for a very long time and was surprised at how raw the emotion was for me. After pausing to compose myself, I told him that I didn't like what had just happened. He told me that if he did his job right, my story would come out and that it would be a very cathartic process for me. He was right on both counts. This project would not have been possible without Charles's expert coaching and guidance. He helped me tell my story and work through the flood of emotions that comes with the process. I'm proud of the book that he helped me produce, and I'm equally glad to now call him a friend for life. Thank you, Charles, for helping me tell my story.

The joy in my life is defined through people. Helping Kim Sharp launch her career and hit her stride has been one of my rewards. After successful runs with me at US West and Covad, she has gone on to senior positions at Neustar and is now head of human resources at Grid-Point, working for Mike Lach, another leader I worked with at Ameritech and Covad and whom I adore. Kim cast her lot with me right out of graduate school and has been in a front-row seat at every company I've been with since then.

Kristin Von Fischer took a leap of faith and called me on my first day at US West. There is something special about the first person to join forces with you, and there can be only one first follower. Kris and I had a good cry when she came out to "interview" with me in Denver. The tears were simply signs of the mutual admiration we had for each other and the desire to do great things together. She was the first PIG at US West.

Carra Wallace joined me at Ameritech as head of the PIGs and made the journey with me to US West, Covad, the NYC Leadership Academy, and Telwares. I always knew that I could count on her to make the journey with me, and she never disappointed. What a remarkable soldier she is. It didn't matter what job I gave her. Her capabilities were so wide ranging that I merely had to pick a problem area, tell her what I needed her to deliver, and get out of her way. A master at building teams, she provided the glue on my senior team and really defined our soul. Carra is the most admired executive I have ever had on my team. She contributed to my personal growth in many ways. From her, I learned to forgive and to bury grudges. She also taught me with her born-again Christianity.

Tanya Van Court went on to successful tours at ESPN and is now a senior vice president at Nickelodeon. She's come a long way from the mailroom at Ameritech. She came to US West as the general manager of Nebraska, and from there she was a vital member of the Covad management team, helping us to build all the processes for our new and growing business. Tanya is one of the smartest people on the planet, and I've been fortunate enough to see her have a family. It's such a joy to be around them. Her daughter calls me Uncle Bob. Tanya has not yet reached her pinnacle. I know that. There is something great coming for her. It may not be climbing into the CEO office, though. She has a passion for children, education, and helping those who can't help themselves.

How do I even capture what Cathy Hemmer has meant to me? Cathy was already very accomplished when she made the decision to join me at Ameritech. She did a great job for me, so I wasn't surprised to hear from her after I joined US West. She played a key role for me there, amazingly replacing three departing executives. At Covad she created our national operating centers and reengineered our operations organization so that we could scale the business. Eventually I appointed her chief operating officer of the company. Cathy later went on to become the COO at Time Warner Telecom and is currently a partner at Brimstone Consulting. Our last stint together was really special, as I was finally able to persuade her husband, John Hemmer, to join us. I had been a longtime admirer of John, who has a remarkable track record of building data networks. He joined me at Covad with the assignment to build our broadband network. He built the largest network in the industry in record time, and that was one of our greatest competitive advantages in the fight for market share in the new broadband industry. I took Cathy with me to meet Carly Fiorina, then the president of Lucent Technologies, on one of our trips to the New York City area, to expand Cathy's network. The very next week Carly was appointed CEO of Hewlett-Packard, which delighted both Cathy and me.

Yemane Gebre-Michael had a childhood and upbringing very similar to mine. You would never guess that he could not speak English when he came to America, yet now this young man is fluent in six languages, has an MBA, and has come through my PIGs team ready to lead an organization. His knack for business development is uncanny, and he has handled some very meaty assignments for me over the years. Of all the people I have coached and mentored over the years, Yemane is the fastest study I've encountered. His ability to learn and pick up things is amazing.

The best blossoming-flower story I have is about Sue Nokes, who was stuck in middle management at Ameritech. When I first ran into her in the early Ameritech Breakthrough Leadership days, she was just finishing a stint in the quality organization under Hank Carabelli. She was an exceptional athlete, but few people knew that. I saw raw potential in her during our first encounter. She was on the short list of people I wanted to bring onto my team. Smart, quick, motivating, she did everything with passion. When she walked into a room, the room got bigger and brighter. She made you want to run to get it done! When I called her from Denver to see if I could persuade her to leave Michigan, I ran into the most stubborn mule I had ever encountered. I had never been turned down by anyone, but Sue didn't want any part of moving to Denver. She told me she was a simple Michigan girl and couldn't see herself moving. Bummer. I filed the rejection away. Still, every six months or so I'd call her to check in and see how she was doing. I'm sure she thought I would give up. Four years later, when I was at Covad, I picked up the phone and called her again. I said, "Noksie, what the hell is your problem? The world is moving ahead, the industry is booming, and there is a greater calling for you out here somewhere. When are you going to go forward and make your contribution to the world?" Her response was "What you got for me, Knowling?" BINGO . . . stop the presses, Nokes is on the way! Sue joined us at Covad and went on to an executive position at Walmart.com and eventually to T-Mobile, where she ascended to the COO job. I'm so proud of Sue. I read *Fortune* magazine's profile of her with utter joy.

Mike Lach grew up at Ameritech with me. We were friends and fellow basketball junkies. The first time I encountered Mike on the hardwood, he came downcourt and did a spin move on me that was straight out of the hood. I was shocked. He had a little French pastry in his game, and I could tell that he had learned it in the inner city. Mike and I would talk about things we would do and change in the business if we were ever in charge. Our opportunity came when Dick Notebaert appointed me to run Network. Mike was one of my first picks. He was such a thrill to work with. He had very little operational experience to be in that job, but I've always felt that if you have smart people who work hard and have courage, they will not fail. Mike quickly became the leader on my team.

My CFO, Diana Moshivitus, was a real spark plug on the team, and Mike and Diana eventually got married. They are now one baby short of a starting-five basketball team. Mike and Diana joined me at Covad, and I was thrilled to assist Warburg Pincus in recruiting Mike to become president at Neustar, which was the highest-performing IPO in 2005. To this day, I get excited when Mike calls to catch up or needs some advice.

Martha Sessums, my head of corporate communications, called me one morning to ask if she could bring one of her interns down to meet me. That was my introduction to Suluh Lukoskie. Suluh seemed charming and eager, but I couldn't help noticing the blue jeans she was wearing. Yes, it was dress-down Friday, but this was an intern being introduced to the CEO of the company. Once all the pleasantries were over with, I told Suluh never to let me see her in jeans in my company again. Talk about a first impression! Suluh has moved with me to every company I have run since Covad, and, like Carra Wallace, she is a fantastic utility player. Suluh has never required instruction on how to do anything. She has worked for Carra a couple of times, and I always enjoyed watching the senior team fight over her. Her bandwidth is incredible, and I have yet to see how much capacity she really has, because she just consumes anything you give her to do, and her work is always first rate. At the NYC Leadership Academy, she wore four hats. She was the head of human resources. She was the first CFO. She was the chief of staff, handling numerous tasks, including attending to all matters for the board of directors. And she was the head of marketing and communications.

Michael Fritzlo came late in my career. Michael is the best sales leader I've ever worked with. He was in a senior position when I went in as CEO of Telwares in 2005. The company had a lot of issues and a lot of gaps in terms of talent, and I didn't know whether the team in place would be up to par. Michael simply showed up one day early in my tenure and said, "Okay, boss, how are we gonna fix this place?" He made this very tough assignment worth the journey, as I relied on him and his group. He and I made a wonderful team, and I learned a lot by working with him. He was a street fighter in the market but a great boss for his people. He was clearly my leader at Telwares, someone whom I sought out to discuss my ideas. Michael always made my thinking better.

Jane Marvin came into my life in 1993. I was looking to bring some external talent onto my Ameritech Leadership Institute team, and Noel Tichy had given me the names of several candidates, from GE, Shell, PepsiCo, and Digital Equipment. I hired Jane, who was at Pepsi. Jane and her husband, Scott, moved to Chicago and became a part of the Knowling family. The chemistry on my team changed immediately when Jane joined us. She was very familiar with the Tichy methodology, her association with Noel going back to the University of Michigan, where she had been one of his MBA students. Jane was an awesome change agent. One could easily be fooled by her warm demeanor, adorable English accent, and radiant smile, but Jane Marvin had an edge. She could cut to the heart of an issue and confront matters head on better than anyone else on our team, including me. Because of her experiences in other companies and with other cultures, she was able to take our team's performance to another level. Her courage was infectious and her style nonthreatening, which was very effective with the clients she worked with. A few years after my departure, Jane left Covad to go to AT&T Wireless as head of human resources, until the sale of the company to SBC, and she now works at Ross as the senior vice president of human resources.

I could go on and on about the wonderful people I've been blessed to work with and for: Jeanne Hoagland, my district manager at Indiana Bell; John McDevitt, the Northwestern University classmate who ran sales for me at Covad; Terry Moya, my CFO at the NYC Leadership Academy and at Telwares; Cheryl Deveran and Linda Fuentes, my administrative assistants at Ameritech and US West. The list is far too long for me to capture everyone who has participated in my life journey. I owe so much to so many people.

I also owe deep appreciation to my coaches in junior high school and high school, men who saw talent in me and had the wisdom, and the time, to help it grow beyond my own expectations. I might well have been a competitor without them, but I would not have been a winner. Joe Goodman, Nello Williams, Dick Haslam, and Ben Bowles are my Mount Rushmore of tribute. Their voices are with me almost every day, quiet inspiration when I need them the most. I hold continuing affection for my friends and mentors at Wabash College, and Coach Mac Petty, Coach Rob Johnson, and Professor Raymond Williams deserve my sincere gratitude for their guidance, care, and tough love that ushered me into adulthood. Even when I felt isolated and out of place, they nurtured me and taught me how to tap my own intellectual and moral strength. Had I pursued my early plan to become a preacher, the ethical compass, sense of humanity, and determination they fostered would have prepared me well to carry the reverend's challenge into the material, sometimes uncaring world.

At any point in my career at Indiana Bell, and later at Ameritech, I might have been turned away by my veteran colleagues. Instead, they filled me with knowledge and experience the way strong rains fill a reservoir, and I am forever indebted to them for that. Joe Hall, Ivan Jahns, Dick Murdock, and of course Judy Myers gave so much of themselves in making me a success. I also still know how to skin a pole or install phone service in a house, and there aren't many executives who can say that. Thank you for helping me learn that business from the ground up.

Across my long career, I built milestones in tribute to the people who reached out to help when I needed it, and who accepted my own offers of help when they were in need. I cherish the counsel of Dick Notebaert at Ameritech and Sol Trujillo at US West, as well as the wisdom of master consultant Noel Tichy and his partner Patti Stacey, a woman who came to mean so much to me as an adviser and friend.

I will hold close to my heart forever the three years I spent working with Joel Klein and Michael Bloomberg on developing principals for New York City's schools. It may well have been the most important work of my life, a contribution of lasting and transformative value, for the school system and for me, too.

There have been so many people who responded to my calls for help, or who bonded deeply with me across their own careers, that I am reluctant to try to name them all, fearing I might miss one and cause offense. Mentioned or not, they are a part of what I have become, and I thank them for that. I cannot let the moment pass without offering my deepest thanks to Diane Jones, my longtime administrative assistant, who moved all over the country with me in a show of commitment that is unprecedented. Diane is the silent contributor who made my work so much easier because she was invested in me. I struggle to find the words that describe what she has meant to my life and my career. I love you, Diane, and I thank you.

Then there is the most important person, Geneva, my mother, she who toiled without complaint in the harsh vineyard of life, raising me and my brothers and sisters. She remains a compelling inspiration and an influence on my life. My mother deserves the ultimate credit for whatever I've done with my life. She is the only person on the planet whom I still look to for approval. The Bible says that the greatest of all gifts is *agape*. When it comes to my mother I've wondered if there is something greater than love, because I am not capable of describing this overwhelming feeling I have for her. She means everything to me.

People think I have accomplished a lot in my life and have been a role model. I pale in comparison with Geneva. They say that Jack Welch is the greatest CEO of our lifetimes, and it's hard to argue with that point, but then, hardly anyone has heard about the incredible CEO who gave me life, coached me to adulthood, inspired me to greatness, and instilled love in my heart to care more about others than I care about myself. No, Jack is the *second*-greatest CEO of my lifetime. He has to take a backseat to my mom.

I hope that the legacy I leave this world will reflect my mother's influence not to except limits on my life, and I hope and pray that my kids will follow the same road as they build their life bridges.

Index